SOHO

Dan Cruickshank is a renowned television presenter and author of numerous books on historical architecture, including *Spitalfields* (2016). He was a founding member of Save Britain's Heritage in 1975. He is a member of the Executive Committee of the Georgian Group, and sits on the Architectural Panel of the National Trust. He is also an Honorary Fellow of RIBA. He lives in east London.

SOHO

A Street Guide to Soho's History, Architecture and People

DAN CRUICKSHANK

WEIDENFELD & NICOLSON

First published in Great Britain in 2020
by Weidenfeld & Nicolson
This paperback edition published in 2022
by Weidenfeld & Nicolson
an imprint of The Orion Publishing Group Ltd
Carmelite House, 50 Victoria Embankment
London EC4Y 0DZ

An Hachette UK Company

1 3 5 7 9 10 8 6 4 2

A CIP catalogue record for this book is
available from the British Library.

ISBN (Mass Market Paperback) 978 1 7802 2495 4
ISBN (eBook) 978 0 2978 6933 7
ISBN (Audio) 978 0 2978 6933 7

Printed in Great Britain by Clays Ltd, Elcograf, S.p.A.

www.weidenfeldandnicolson.co.uk
www.orionbooks.co.uk

Contents

Illustrations

Introduction

Soho is the heart every city ought to have. In fact, most great cities do have their own versions of Soho, for example Saint-Germain-des-Prés on Paris's Left Bank, Kreuzberg in Berlin and the Lower East Side in New York. What do these areas have in common? Not much perhaps – certainly very little architecturally – but what they do share defines their essence.

They all exist within the centre of the city, yet are outside the conventional orbit of city-centre life. They are enclaves that evolved for communities of 'outsiders' of various sorts where, historically, rents have been low for sustained periods of time – often for a wide range of complex reasons. This has meant that old buildings tend to survive, creating a rich architectural setting. Notably, all are places where immigrant communities have established themselves, along with exiles and artists, to create vibrant, cosmopolitan areas that have sometimes shocked, but more often culturally enriched, the cities in which they have flourished. Soho is most certainly no exception. Berwick Street, with its exotic and long-established street market, Italian then Jewish in its essence, regularly enthralled more adventurous Londoners. Virginia Woolf remembered it in the early twentieth century as a place 'fierce with light' that pleased 'me to the depths of my heart' (see p. 112).

Within such enclaves, when at their best, a feeling of

companionship evolved, no doubt engendered by shared difficulties, along with a sense of independence and of liberty. By tradition they have become places where coexistence has bred tolerance, and where grass-roots democracy – and equality – have flourished. These qualities have given most of them – certainly Soho in much of the nineteenth and twentieth centuries – the atmosphere of a village within the city, in which residents know each other and are enriched by their differences. They become distinct communities, thriving against the backdrop of historic but still-living buildings and streets.

But they are incredibly fragile. Traditionally they are protected by the presence of noisome or potentially noxious trades or industries, by poverty, by neglect, by all those things that make them unattractive to the average city dweller or business. But when the balance shifts – when the threat of change becomes certainty and stability is established – the vulnerability of such areas is only too apparent. As the mix of uses and character ceases to be odd, different and exotic and becomes mainstream in its appeal, then doom looms.

Most wayward urban areas fall victim, these days, not to slum clearance or mass demolition for roads and office-building – as was the threat in London in the 1960s and 1970s, which almost obliterated Soho's neighbour, Covent Garden – but to their own success. Their sense of community, their vivid life, their central locations are inherently attractive, and when noisy trades or troubling industries move away and legislation is enacted to reduce their perceived problems (in Soho's case, the overt sex industry), then those who make their living through property investment – attracted by the new sense of stability – take a keen and greedy interest. Rents rise, independent enterprises are forced out, communities are dispersed, family homes are lost, historic but commercially inconvenient building fabric is cleared away (often with façades retained in an attempt to screen the scale of change), and what was once real, true and alive is suddenly false, fake and dead.

This complex process is now usually summed up – by disgruntled observers or by those who have suffered – as 'gentrification'. An odd word, the meaning of which is somewhat subjective, which is generally used to describe the displacement of an indigenous urban community (usually artisan or trade- and craft-based) located within a decaying inner-city area, by a more affluent but essentially alien and transient community that covets the location or the buildings it colonises and has the wealth and influence to get what it wants. The result can be the repair of long-neglected historic buildings and even the reinstatement of their original grandeur, lost through decades of multi-occupation or the mix of inappropriate uses. This is sometimes seen as a good thing, which no doubt it is. But this is to take only a superficial view. By tradition, the old residents more often than not lived and worked in their area. The new occupants tend not to live in their 'occupied' area full time, and do not work there. It becomes a dormitory, a second home, and their transience means that a new sense of community does not evolve. The authentic life, lived among the architecture of the past, within the theatre of historic streets and courts that gave the area distinction, is dead. This is the process happening within Soho now. Most contemporary debate about Soho focuses not just on its 'gentrification' but also on its 'sanitisation', as the remnants of the sex industry are fenced in or cleared away to allow new buildings and attract new businesses and residents who, we are led to believe, are not interested in the old 'sleazy' side of Soho. So its image is to be remade and its history doctored to make it more marketable to those who, paradoxically, want to be there but who are actually not too keen on the traditional character of the area they proclaim to like.

It can be argued that Soho is now on the cusp of irreversible change. That those things which have made it special and given it its distinctive character for the last 200 years or so are in the process of being snuffed out. This state of affairs makes a book like this, about the evolution of Soho's character and about its architecture, urgent and necessary. It can help to ensure that the debate about its future – about what makes it special – is informed and focused.

A history of Soho can also offer some solace. There is no doubt that the current threat to its long-established character, which still exists and is still distinct, is real and alarming. But it is important to put this threat into historic context and remember that change has heralded the supposed death of Soho several times in the past – so the current claim that Soho as we know it is dying would have been familiar to past generations of Londoners. Indeed, dramatic change has, arguably, been crucial to the formation of Soho's special character. As early as 1921 Sophie Cole observed that Soho was 'a question of "change ... in all around I see". Old landmarks gone, and brand-new buildings, mostly offices in their place.'[1] I know this from my own direct observation. I have been photographing

Soho's streets, buildings and people since 1971, and in 1975, when writing a chapter on Soho for a book entitled the *Rape of Britain*, I observed that Soho's survival was a 'miracle' since it was 'under ever-increasing pressure' that threatened to make it 'the all-too-familiar dead city centre'. I also mentioned its 'fragile nature' and argued that 'every time a community shop like a butcher's or a button maker's is replaced by an office block ... Soho's pulse weakens'. This was to prove correct, and during the last forty-five years most such shops have closed, and the area's pulse has indeed weakened.[2]

My compulsion to document Soho made me witness the deaths of many buildings: I remember 36–44 Brewer Street, a group of eighteenth- and nineteenth-century houses and shops typical of Soho. In the early 1970s I photographed their tragic end. They were empty, in the process of demolition but with the names of the lately ejected tenants still emblazoned on shop fronts and windows. They were a microcosm of Soho's then vibrant and diverse life and trades. At number 40 was the Margaret Café, a most homely place that I had used in the past, and on the corner with Great Pulteney Street was the erstwhile London base of Bob Fletcher, 'international shirt designer' – a well-known purveyor of handmade shirts when a handmade shirt was a potent symbol of stylish youth and something to which most young men of the time aspired. Fletcher, along with the tailor John Stephen, were creatures of 1960s 'Swinging London', when nearby Carnaby Street was an unlikely epicentre of world fashion. Fortunes could – and were – made in this industry. Photographs of the Glasgow-born Stephen, credited with being the 'founder' of

the Carnaby Street phenomenon, outside his shop at
52–55 Carnaby Street, one with his foot set cockily on
the fender of his Rolls-Royce, say it all. Making a vast
income by selling fashion to the young is commonplace
now, but it all started in Soho in about 1960, mostly
in modest Georgian houses like this one in Brewer
Street. But, of course, the establishment of the fashion
industry in Soho proved a two-edged sword. It brought
prosperity and fame, but also had baleful consequences
as independent operatives like Bob Fletcher were soon
ousted to make way for the impersonal shops of fashion
chains that have raised rents and done much to expunge
life in large tracts of Soho.

A similar fate soon befell the block of late-eighteenth-
century and nineteenth-century buildings on Brewer
Street, running between Great Pulteney Street and
Bridle Lane. In 1975 I illustrated this terrace in *The Rape
of Britain*, noting that it was 'to be replaced by a new
office building' and appealing for its preservation. But it
did no good. I particularly remember the late-Georgian
house on the corner with Bridle Lane. It housed 'woollen
merchants' on the upper floors and, in the ground-floor
shop, 'House Bros.', cutlers and tool makers. The window
display was a lively affair, exhibiting knives, axes, saws and
all manner of implements, their cutting edges displayed
with gay abandon. I caught its last moments on camera.
It was soon destroyed (plates 1 and 2).

But such serial killings of historic buildings and businesses in the 1970s did not, in fact, lead to the death of Soho.
It has proved surprisingly resilient and retains a distinct
character still worth fighting for. And this ability to survive
frightful, seemingly terminal onslaughts tells another story.

Characterful shop on corner of Brewer Street and Bridle Lane in early 1970s, now demolished.

As is usually the case in great and vibrant cities and urban quarters, from the debris of death and destruction has sprung new life, often strange and exotic – and in many ways different to what went before.

Soho's first death took place sometime in the early 1720s, when the original aristocratic Soho of the late seventeenth century, with its large terrace houses and mansions, was transformed into a merchants', craft and manufacturing quarter. In a sense this merely extended the influence of the Huguenots, who had settled, largely in south Soho, from the late seventeenth century and introduced the valuable and exquisite precious-metal trade. Part of this process was the replacement of larger buildings, often less than fifty years old, with smaller houses, workshops and courtyards.

But this wave of change made the fabric and life of Soho more complex and rich than bland. This was partly through the introduction of courts of smaller buildings, but also because Soho's social spectrum remained broad and its mix of uses increased. The new merchant and manufacturing areas were set cheek by jowl with streets and groups of houses that remained firmly aristocratic in their aspirations, such as the early-eighteenth-century houses in Great Marlborough Street and Poland Street; while from the 1750s London's highly valuable sex industry took significant – and initially discreet – root in the area.

Around 1795 Soho again started to be transformed by change, with light industry, commerce and manufacturing rapidly increasing in scale – partly because of a local economic boom due to the Napoleonic Wars, and partly because of the technology and wealth that resulted from the Industrial Revolution. The evidence lies in the history of numerous buildings. Numbers 12–13 Greek Street, in origin a late-seventeenth-century mansion, until 1795 housed the London showroom of the master potter Josiah Wedgwood, who in brilliant manner had combined the technological advances of the Industrial Revolution with fashionable neoclassical taste to mass-produce high-quality consumer goods for an eager public. Number 163 Wardour Street became the base, in the mid 1790s, of Thomas Sheraton, one of Britain's most influential and successful furniture designers, and numbers 4, 5 and 6 Soho Square – a group of late-seventeenth-century houses – were replaced in 1801 by a warehouse built by

John Trotter, an army contractor who had profiteered with great personal financial success during the war with France. In 1816 Trotter converted his then redundant military warehouse into the Soho Bazaar, a fascinating, pioneering example of West End retailing.

These rebuildings and changes of use heralded Soho's next great transformation, which, from the 1840s, made it home to succeeding waves of generally impoverished economic and political foreign immigrants, starting with Italians and followed by Jews fleeing 1880s pogroms in Russia and Russian-occupied Poland. These immigrants included, in the 1850s, Karl Marx and his family, who settled in sordid and cramped rooms on Dean Street.

And so Soho descended into a poverty that was spiced with extraordinary flashes of creative genius and idiosyncratic and sometimes dangerous charm. This made it a place of inspiration and of potentially fatal attraction for successive generations of artists.

In 1907 Joseph Conrad used Soho as part of the setting for *The Secret Agent*, a tale of anarchy, espionage, terror and human frailty; and a few years later Virginia Woolf was enthralled with the bustle and trade of Berwick Street market (see p. 112). It is the memory of this odd and bohemian manifestation of Soho, as a different and even perilous place, that lingers today and continues to attract and fuel our imagination. And it is this vision of Soho that we now see as under remorseless attack by developers, social sanitisers, gentrifiers, by characterless chains of shops, restaurants and consumerism generally, and by roving crowds of well-meaning but hapless tourists who can make lifeless the very things they tour to see. But even this latter threat is not new.

By the late nineteenth century Soho's Continental charms, lurking below the surface of decay and squalor, were well recognised and savoured by more observant Londoners. Most were aware that the life and the death, the charm and the decay, of Soho were intrinsically linked, and it was obvious that the more common it became as a place for ordinary Londoners to frequent, the more 'common' Soho would become. As early as 1915 Thomas Burke, something of a London *flâneur*, delighted in Soho's cosmopolitan character, 'where every street is a song', and Old Compton Street in particular. As he told readers of his *Nights in Town*, 'step aside from the jostle and clamour of Oxford Street into Soho Square ... cut through Greek Street or Dean Street, and you are in – Paris, amid the clang, the gesture, and the alert nonchalance of metropolitan France'. But for Burke the combination of qualities that made Soho special were already under attack. Today we might feel that the waves of tourists and suburban Londoners having a boisterous night out in London's 'Latin Quarter' are swamping the place and diluting its character. Over 100 years ago Burke felt much the same: 'Now, I love my cockneys, heart and soul [but] I wish to goodness they would keep out of Soho cafes ... and leave [it] for people like myself who feed there because it is cheap.' Cockneys, surmised Burke – along with 'the girl-clerk and the book-keeper' – invaded Soho in a futile 'quest' for 'Bohemianism'. If this did not stop, fretted Burke, Soho would be ruined.[3]

So change – and anxiety about change and the dilution of Soho's character – are part of Soho's history. But this must not make us complacent about the current threat to the area. Perhaps Soho can weather the storm – even thrive on it – and once again remake itself in creative manner. But, arguably, the change now looming – and actually taking place – is far greater in scale and nature, and perhaps in speed, and more absolute than ever before. Admittedly, the swathes of demolition proposed in the 1960s and 1970s were more fundamental than anything happening now and turned out to be no more than a wicked fantasy. What we are seeing today is change actually taking place, insidiously and on an almost daily basis. Even as I write, the rebuilding of the modest, late-Georgian number 21 Great Windmill Street is being completed, its demolition agreed by the local authority – Westminster City Council (WCC) – because the building's owner argued that repair was uneconomic (plate 3). Despite its age and charm the building was not on the government's list of buildings of architectural or historic interest and so had limited statutory protection. However, it was – as is all Soho – within a Conservation Area, designated and in theory monitored by WCC. Historic buildings, listed or not, within Conservation Areas should be protected as part of the general policy to safeguard and enhance the designated area's established architectural and social character. Every time an historic building is lost, Soho as a whole is diminished.

More significant is the large hole created in recent years at the north end of Dean Street for works to Crossrail. This involved the loss of a considerable amount of old fabric, but just as alarming is the way the new railway will open up to Soho yet more people: it has been estimated that 1.5 million will have easy access to the area, leading to yet more droves of tourists, more business, more rent increases and more 'boutique' hotels – something of a recent Soho phenomenon. Of course, this can be viewed as an economic blessing for some, but it also represents yet one more thrust at the vitals of the old, authentic Soho.

Bahar Durmaz-Drinkwater and Stephen Platt, academics conducting research on Soho, have made statistical discoveries that help explain what is happening in the area. But their research also suggests the future – and it's alarming. Based on an analysis of Berwick Street, Old Compton Street and Wardour Street – Soho's main locations for shopping, leisure and the media – they found that between 2008 and 2016 21 per cent of the independent businesses had closed or moved away. There has also been great transience, with, during the same eight years, an average of 60 per cent of the business premises on these streets changing in occupation.[4] This transience is at least partly explained, point out the academics, by an estimate, published in 2017 in the *Financial Times*, that between 2012 and 2017 land values in Soho increased by 52 per cent, which makes it a very expensive and exclusive place in which to live or do business. These high land values, leading directly to high rents and increased transience, explain the speed with which modest independent businesses have been replaced by corporate initiatives, such as chain shops and restaurants. These are not only willing and able to pay high rents, but they establish rents at levels that price most independents out of the market. Their analysis makes it clear that, while these conditions continue, this trend – which sucks the authentic life out of Soho – will inevitably continue.

At the moment, with the forces for change and those resisting it locked in unresolved conflict, it is hard to see where it will all end. The Soho Society, the community organisation that has battled for Soho's body and soul for over forty years, is far from sanguine and remains in a state of alarm and high alert. This is what Tim Lord, the Society's chairman, told me in late 2018:

> Soho survived cholera epidemics, German bombing raids and criminal gangs but it may not survive the current greed of property developers and rapacious landlords. The Soho Society increased social housing and established the Conservation Area, but property developers and many landlords just see Soho as a place to make money with no thought or feelings for the place itself – and often unfortunately backed by the Council. The Soho Society sees this precious square mile for what it is – the jewel in London's crown.

This is a call to battle. London's 'jewel' is under attack and anyone who doubts the seriousness of the assault, or thinks it exaggerated, need only walk to the north end of Dean Street, where it joins Oxford Street, to see what Crossrail has done, or to the east of Soho Square, at the junction of Sutton Row and Charing Cross Road. Vast swathes of demolition have taken place, deep holes have been dug in the ground and historic grain and buildings obliterated.

Losses in these areas include the good late-Victorian Bath House public house and the Black Gardenia bar, both in Dean Street and both demolished in 2011, and the Astoria Theatre in Charing Cross Road, which was a most commanding building. It had been constructed as a warehouse, turned into an Art Deco cinema in 1927, into a theatre in 1977 and in 1985 into a nightclub and live-music venue. The building's story of creative change and adaptation is the epitome of Soho's life as a centre for trade and entertainment – indeed the Astoria was, in its way, Soho in miniature and with its demolition in 2009 it seemed as if part of Soho's twentieth-century history was being murdered. And more of the same is planned. The Curzon cinema on Shaftesbury Avenue, a significant cultural institution and the only independent cinema in the West End, is under threat of demolition for the construction of Crossrail 2. This government project currently – and incredibly – envisages the destruction of all or most of the buildings in a block defined on the west by Dean Street, on the east by Greek Street, on the south by Shaftesbury Avenue and on the north by Romilly Street. A number of significant eighteenth-, nineteenth- and twentieth-century buildings would be destroyed, including the Golden Lion public house in Dean Street, and the south end of historic Frith Street eradicated. No timescale has been agreed for this work – which requires an Act of Parliament and involves the creation of a new station entrance on Dean Street – although Crossrail 2 hopes to start construction around 2025. At present the block is merely 'safeguarded' by Crossrail 2. But already the buildings on the site and immediately bordering it are beginning to suffer from 'planning blight'.

In place of the streets, alleys and buildings already lost around Dean Street and Greek Street, large commercial developments of startlingly contemporary, and arguably most alien, design are being completed. True, this transformation is not occurring in Soho's heart, but it is happening within its boundaries. Such losses and additions greatly affect the feel and the appearance of this 'precious square mile' and the nature of the activities that take place within it. Similar large-scale opportunities may not often present themselves within the heart of Soho, but these peripheral developments, often heavy handed, have set a precedent and represent an alarming intent that is perhaps already justifying some extensive rebuilding projects in central Soho – for example, at the junction of Broadwick Street and Berwick Street, where a large hotel is (in early 2021) under construction.

The Coronavirus epidemic that hit London hard in early 2020 might yet prove a game-changer for Soho. It is too early to tell what the long-term implications might be and perhaps they will prove relatively insignificant when faced by the pressure of the market forces that have in recent years shaped Soho's character. But, in the shorter term, it is likely that a number of businesses – especially cafes and bars – will not reopen having been obliged to close in haste due to the Government-imposed 'lockdowns', and the regulations about 'social distancing' might echo through Soho for years if it proves impossible to eradicate the virus or to find a workable vaccine. At the moment it's predicted that Soho will achieve only 20 per cent of its pre- Covid-19 trade for several years. One strategy to support Soho's 'hospitality' industry is to pedestrianize streets south of Soho Square to make the area more attractive and to offer leeway for social distancing. This means that Soho will become a quieter place, less polluted, and with a return to its introspective village-like atmosphere. If this is the case then Soho – and the life lived in it – might, utterly unexpectedly, have just undergone yet one more most radical change.

Dan Cruickshank, July 2020.

Using this book

This book offers – primarily – an architectural history of Soho, with its focus being a gazetteer organised not alphabetically but geographically, as a walk through the area. So it is a street-by-street, building-by-building appreciation of Soho that tells histories of buildings and their occupants, that outlines the aspirations of the landlords, leaseholders and speculating builders who made Soho and that identifies the former monastic lands, fields, closes and footpaths that still echo through the streets and fabric of modern Soho. Because much of the story is told through the walk – through the physical evidence that survives – the emphasis is on buildings that can still be seen.

Soho is exceptionally rich in architectural history, with most of its interest and quality dating from the eighteenth century. Traversing the eastern portion is fairly straight-forward: the route follows the right-angular grid of its main streets, organised south and west of Soho Square, only brief 'excursions' being necessary into a number of the smaller streets and courts that generally join the main streets at right angles.

The exploration of west Soho, between Wardour Street and Regent Street, is an altogether different affair. Here the development pattern is fragmented, more dependent on ancient field boundaries and once-rural paths, far less co-ordinated and consequently more complicated and meandering.

Soho: An Overview

Boundaries

Before exploring Soho, its boundaries must be set and some general facts established. First, the physical extent of Soho. This, quite naturally, has varied over the centuries, with boundaries only gradually being established. At the time of the Reformation and the Dissolution of the Monasteries in the 1530s a large part of the area that became Soho was seized by Henry VIII from various religious houses and ancient institutions such as the Mercers' Company which had benefited from donations of property, usually for religious reasons. Some of these newly acquired parcels of land were soon leased off, but much was retained by the king for his own use, notably for a northern extension to his royal hunting preserve – the core of which is now St James's Park – to serve his recently founded or enlarged palaces of Westminster, Whitehall and St James's.

As far as we know, Soho's name evolved from its role as part of the king's preserve, 'Soho' apparently being a hunting cry, much in the manner of 'Tally-ho'. It is fanciful but possible, with the first recorded use of the name occurring in 1636, in a list of ratepayers in the parish of St Martin-in-the-Fields.[1]

During Henry VIII's reign the royal park and hunting preserve covered what is now Trafalgar Square and extended at least as far north as the east–west road that was to become Oxford Street, or the road to Uxbridge. This road was linked to the royal mews on what is now the north side of Trafalgar Square, and to the royal quarter of Whitehall and St James's by Colman Hedge Lane, which eventually became Wardour Street, and which in its various guises and under different names – Old Soho, Wardour Street, Princes Street – was the virtual spine around which Soho grew from the 1660s onwards.

Soho in early maps

The so-called 'Agas' London map of *c*.1562 – a bird's-eye view over London looking north – shows the terrain very well. Oxford Street is named 'The Waye to Uxbridge', and on each side of it cattle graze in fields. Running southwest is 'The Waye to Redinge', which is now Piccadilly. Two roads run parallel to each other and south from what is essentially now Piccadilly Circus; the road to the west is Haymarket with, to the east, Colman Hedge Lane connecting with Whitcomb Street that leads south to Charing Cross and the site of Trafalgar Square. On each side of these roads cattle wander, people stroll and clothes are laid out to dry. The east boundary of what became Soho is marked by the church and village of 'St Gyles in the Fyeldes', from which a lane runs north – the future Tottenham Court Road.

Running south from the west end of St Giles is St Martin's Lane, leading to St Martin's Church. The south-east boundary of the fields that became Soho is marked by the Charing Cross. Deer can be seen in what was to become St James's Park, while the rest of the hunting preserve appears to be grazing land. Whitehall Palace is shown as a large, sprawling affair of courts, gardens, towering gatehouses and Thames-side ranges of lodgings.

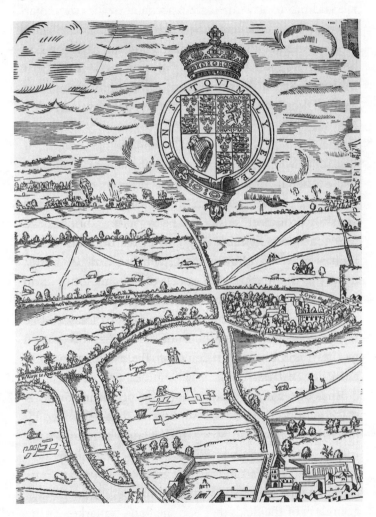

Northern portion of the 'Agas' map of c.1562. The 'Waye to Uxbridge' is Oxford Street. Charing Cross just off the bottom edge.

Braun and Hogenberg's London map of 1572 shows much the same condition, but the fields of Soho are less populated, with no grazing cattle – although some clothes are laid out to dry. An early land ownership/estate map of 1585[2] shows little had changed. But Wenceslaus Hollar's map, created in about 1675, makes it clear that Soho had been caught up in the general flurry of construction that took place in post-Restoration London. Buildings are shown along Piccadilly – notably the palatial Clarendon House, built between 1664 and 1667 to the designs of Roger Pratt for the Earl of Clarendon – and south of Piccadilly, where the Earl of St Albans had developed his 'little town' from 1662, focused on St James's Square and Jermyn Street. To the north of Piccadilly, a few buildings are shown on both sides of the very east end of Oxford Street, around Colman Hedge Lane/Wardour Street and Leicester Fields. Here Leicester House had been built in 1635 by the Earl of Leicester, who enclosed common land in front of the house to create a private garden. The parishioners appealed successfully to Charles I to reverse this selfish act and most of the garden was opened to them and known as Leicester Fields, subsequently Leicester Square.

But, on Hollar's map, the heart of future Soho is still shown as open fields. All, however, had changed by the time Ogilby and Morgan's London map appeared in 1681/2. This captures Soho almost immediately after its transition from fields to the piece of city that, in its essential plan-form, still remains.

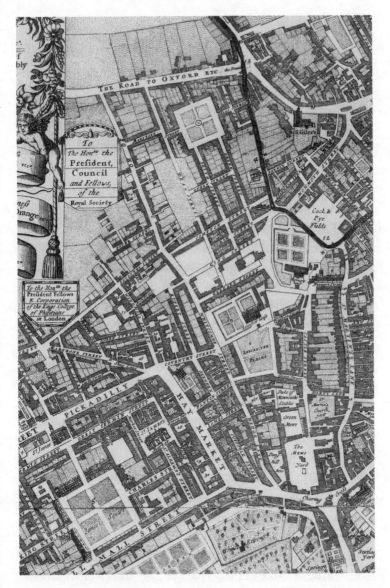

Soho from Ogilby & Morgan's map of 1681–2. The road marked So Ho is Wardour Street.

Soho Square

Soho Square – in 1681/2 called King's Square – had by then been laid out and all four sides fully built. Greek Street and Frith Street ran south from the square and were lined with houses as far south as King Street, now lost, which stood roughly on the line of the wider, late-nineteenth-century Shaftesbury Avenue. To the south of King Street, the south side of Gerrard Street was also fully lined with buildings, as were the streets running east and west off Soho Square, and as was much of Dean Street, Compton Street (now Old Compton Street) and Church (now Romilly) Street. There were also buildings along the north–south-running Colman Hedge Lane/Wardour Street, which on the Ogilby and Morgan map is merely called 'Soho'. This is not surprising given that it is an ancient thoroughfare and far older than Soho's coherent development. Indeed, as early as 1643–58 Faithorne and Newcourt's map shows a significant scattering of buildings on or near Colman Hedge Lane.

The right-angular grid of fairly wide streets forming the heart of Soho to the south of the square gave way, further south and to the west of Colman Hedge Lane/Wardour Street, to generally narrower and less regular streets and courts. In the west these led to Swallow Street (see p. 26).

In the late seventeenth century a western boundary of Soho emerges but it does not last long. When St Anne's Church, probably designed by Sir Christopher Wren and William Talman, was completed on the southern end of Wardour Street in 1686 (see p. 275), and a new parish carved out of the larger parish of St Martin-in-the-Fields, the western boundary of that parish was Wardour Street.

Consequently, Wardour Street was viewed as the western edge of Soho. The land to the west was in the parish of St James, Westminster. But during the eighteenth century the Wardour Street boundary – although a legal reality relating to the administration of the parish – became less relevant. The nature of the development that took place west of Wardour Street in the first decades of the eighteenth century – its architectural character, its type and mix of residents and uses – united it with Soho rather than with grander and more aristocratic developments in the south-western portion of St James's parish or in Hanover Square and the adjoining streets of the Burlington estate. During the eighteenth century the de facto western boundary of Soho became Swallow Street – far to the west of Wardour Street – and so it remains, because Swallow Street was widened and slightly realigned in the early nineteenth century to form Regent Street, which now gives Soho a very tangible and precise western edge.

Blome's map of the parish of St Anne, dating from about 1690, reveals that considerably more development had taken place in the few years since Ogilby and Morgan's map. 'St Anns' (sic) church had just been completed, as had the development of the central portion of Dean Street, including, running west off Dean Street, St Anne's Court and two cul-de-sac courts that would soon become Richmond Buildings and Meard Street. To the south, Gerrard Street had buildings along its north side as well as its south, and to the east more construction had taken place east of Greek Street to connect Soho more firmly to Hog Lane, which formed the area's eastern boundary with St Giles until the lane was replaced in the nineteenth century by the wider and straighter Charing Cross Road.

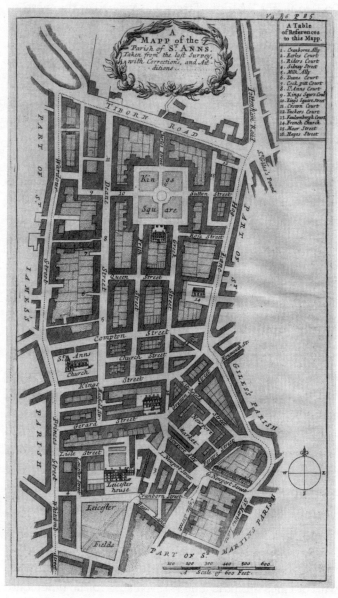

Blome's map of the parish of St Anne's, *c.*1690.

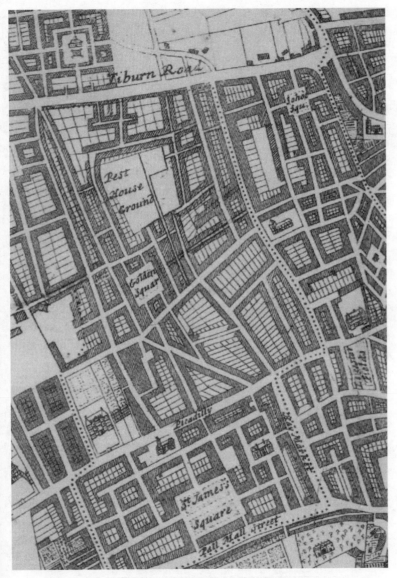

Detail of John Strype's London map of 1720. The 'Pest House Ground' lies to the east of Carnaby Street.

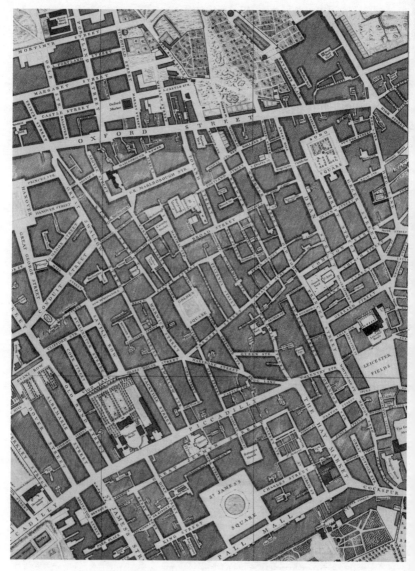

Detail of John Rocque's London map of 1746.

The Soho area shown on John Rocque's London map of 1746 is much as depicted on the maps of the 1680s and 1690s, although it records a little more development and the completion of significant urban spaces to the west of Wardour Street – notably the wide and straight Great Marlborough Street, started in 1704 and named after the military hero of the moment, the Duke of Marlborough – and Broad Street, now Broadwick Street.

Daniel Defoe, in his *Tour Thro' the Whole Island of Great Britain*, published between 1724 and 1727, wonders at the speedy growth of Soho, but puts it within the context of the phenomenal growth of London's West End that had taken place from the 1660s: 'let us view the two great parishes of St Giles's and St Martin's in the Fields, the last so increased, as to be above thirty years ago, formed into three parishes [where] the increase of the buildings ... is really a kind of prodigy'. Defoe, who would have been more accurate if he had put the growth within the last sixty rather than thirty years, noted that between Piccadilly and 'the south side of Tyburn Road [as Oxford Street was then known], including Soho-Square, Golden-Square, and now Hanover-Square, and that new City on the north side of Tyburn Road, called Cavendish-Square, and all the streets about it' (the east portion of Marylebone), there 'is by calculation, more in bulk than the cities of Bristol, Exeter and York if they were all put together; all which places were, within the time mentioned, meer fields of grass ... emply'd only to feed cattle'.[3]

As Defoe wrote this account one of the more significant changes in Soho's built history was just starting to take place – and it was a change that makes the apparent similarity between the late-seventeenth-century maps and

Rocque's 1746 map deceptive. During the fifty-five to sixty-
five years that separate these maps, much of the urban
fabric of Soho had been rebuilt. The streets, courts and
spaces defined by buildings on the late-seventeenth-
century maps generally survived in the mid 1740s, but
many of the buildings themselves had gone. Most rebuilding had taken place from around 1718 to 1738, with, for
example, much of Dean Street being reconstructed during
the decade after 1720, usually with a greater number of
smaller buildings and fewer larger houses. The reasons for
this rebuilding were numerous. The original houses had
mostly not been built well – certainly not to last beyond
the length of the leases granted by the landlords to the
speculative builders and occupiers – and many of these
leases were for no more than forty-one or sixty-one years.

The Huguenots

By the 1720s the physical nature of Soho had changed,
as had its social make-up and the aspirations of its
landowners and major leaseholders. When development
hopes were high in the 1680s, it was assumed that Soho
would become a genteel, perhaps aristocratic area to
rival St James's. But this had not happened. The houses
around Soho Square were well occupied, and remained
so for most of the eighteenth century. But the high
social ambitions for Soho were quickly compromised.
This started as early as 1681, when, instead of being an
aristocratic retreat, much of Soho started to become a
refuge for French Huguenot émigrés who, being Calvinist
Protestants, fled persecution in their Catholic homeland
to gain religious freedom in Britain. When, with the

Revocation of the Edict of Nantes in 1685, practising
the Protestant faith in France became illegal, yet more
Huguenots fled to Britain – often in very dangerous and
difficult circumstances. The majority settled in London,
mostly in Spitalfields and Soho. The seizure of the British throne in 1688 by the firmly Protestant William and
Mary, who replaced the Catholic and pro-French James II,
encouraged yet greater numbers of Huguenots to escape
to Britain and settle in Soho.

A large, highly intelligent and hard-working portion
of the Huguenot refugees to London soon developed
a valuable silk industry in Spitalfields and a precious-
metals industry in Soho. This community of
Huguenot craftsmen and entrepreneurs gave much of late-
seventeenth- and early-eighteenth-century Soho an
affluent mercantile but also a somewhat manufacturing
character, which was reinforced by the growth in the
area, from the late seventeenth century, of a tapestry
industry. This was centred around the northern ends of
Greek Street, Frith Street and Dean Street, in Bateman
Street and in Soho Square, where many designers and
makers had their homes and places of business. For
example, during most of the 1720s Joshua Morris, 'one
of the best of the Soho tapestry makers',[4] occupied a
house and workshop on the corner of Frith Street and
Bateman Street. After Morris left this building in 1728 it
was taken over by the tapestry maker William Bradshaw
and the designer Tobias Stranover. After four years they
separated, Bradshaw moving to 27 and Stranover to 8
Frith Street. Work by Bradshaw survives in Ham House,
Richmond, and in Holkham Hall, Norfolk; his pieces,
based on paintings by Watteau, have been described as

'the most beautiful tapestries ever produced, a master-piece of English craft'.[5]

When, after 1717, the Cavendish-Harley estate and then, a few years later, the Grosvenor estate started to develop their land to the north of Oxford Street and to the west, it captured aristocratic interest, and Soho was left somewhat marooned, its fate all but sealed as a merchants', manufacturers' and immigrants' quarter. Added to these communities were an increasing number of marginal if often apparently respectable inhabitants, such as professional and literary men, doctors, artists, superior actresses and reasonably higher-class – or at least generally discreet – prostitutes.

The silver and gold industry soon became the most significant of Soho's trades. From the late seventeenth century Huguenots established themselves, mostly around Gerrard Street, Great Windmill Street and the Newport market area, where they fashioned and dealt in expensive and beautiful objects wrought in silver and gold. The French silversmiths and goldsmiths who settled in Soho brought their skills with them and quickly – and most astutely – exploited the fact that in England there was a demand for high-quality wares with a French sense of style and elegance. This was, they realised, a tremen-dous opportunity.

The leading members of the Soho trade included Peter Archambo, Paul de Lamerie and Paul Crespin. Archambo became an apprentice in 1710 to a fellow Huguenot sil-versmith named Jacob Margas who had a workshop in St Martin's Lane, which was then the south-eastern bound-ary of Soho. The problems that Archambo faced were typical of those that beset Huguenot silversmiths and goldsmiths in late-seventeenth-century London and were among the key reasons for the establishment of their silver trade in Soho. Initially most Huguenots working with precious metals settled near Goldsmiths' Hall, in the City of London, the capital's traditional centre for the silver and gold trade and – most conveniently – near a French Protestant church in Threadneedle Street. But problems soon arose. Silversmiths and goldsmiths needed to be granted the freedom of the City of London through a livery company in order to trade in the City. The obvious one to join was the Goldsmiths', but this was controlled by London-born tradesmen who were suspicious of the talented Huguenot arrivals, jealous of their skills and feared that they would win many commissions. So the London tradesmen closed ranks and kept the Huguenots out of the Goldsmiths' Company. But the Huguenots were nothing if not canny and determined, and would not be stopped. Their solution was to make jealousy their friend. They played on traditional City rivalries and found that other livery companies were happy to accept them, even if only to upset the arrogant Goldsmiths. So in 1720 Archambo became free of the Butchers' Company and Paul Crespin free of the Longe Bowe String makers, and through these companies gained the freedom of the City. Establishing themselves among their London rivals near Goldsmiths' Hall presented other problems, so the Huguenots founded their own centre of trade in south Soho, which was near the other French Protestant church in London, located in the Savoy, just south of the Strand. Typically, John Strype, when describing south Soho in his 1720 edition of the *Survey of the Cities of London and Westminster*, observed of Newport Court that it was 'for

the Generality inhabited by the French, as indeed are
most of these Streets and Alleys, which are ordinarily
built, and the Rents cheap'.[6]

One Huguenot who did manage to join the Goldsmiths'
Company was Paul de Lamerie. He became one of the
most able and successful tradesmen and has been called
by the Victoria and Albert Museum 'the greatest silversmith working in England in the eighteenth century'.[7] De
Lamerie was born in April 1688 in 's-Hertogenbosch in
the United Provinces (now the Netherlands) and came to
London with his immigrant family – of minor aristocratic
ancestry – when just one year old.

At the age of fourteen de Lamerie was apprenticed to
a Huguenot goldsmith named Pierre Platel and in 1713
opened his own workshop, probably in Great Windmill
Street, where he established his own mark. But not, it
seems, until after some difficulties with the Goldsmiths'
Company. In 1714 he was called before the court of the
company for failing to have his work hallmarked. This
was a serious charge. By the early eighteenth century
silverware was meant to possess various hallmarks to
establish the date and location of its manufacture and
the quality of the silver from which it was made. These
marks could also include an emblem or initials to indicate
the manufacturer of the piece – and only makers who
traded under their own names and whose association
with a piece could enhance its value were in the habit of
signing their work. But hallmarks that included a maker's
identifying mark could prove a problem. If a maker put
his mark on a piece it was difficult for him to dodge
paying duty, as he was obliged to do by law. It would
seem that the avoidance of duty was the main reason de

Lamerie sought anonymity. Certainly, the company took a stern view of his actions and fined him a hefty £20. (To give an idea of money values, a London craftsman earned about £50 a year.) De Lamerie's response seems to have been to mock the company and attempt to undermine its authority. He purchased a stock of second-rate unmarked silver objects made by anonymous London smiths and had it hallmarked as his own. The company got wind of what was going on and accused him of having bought 'Foreigners work and got ye same toucht at ye Hall'. The contest between de Lamerie and the Goldsmiths' Company was prolonged, and in 1717 he was again charged with selling large quantities of plate which he had not brought to the company to be marked 'according to law'. The eventual solution to the long-running dispute was for the company to admit de Lamerie as a liveryman and to control him by making him part of the precious-metal establishment.[8] From around this time he seems to have regularly marked his products, his initial mark being a capital LA with a crown and small star above and a fleur-de-lis below.

In 1716 de Lamerie was appointed gold- and silversmith to George I and by the 1730s was dominant in his field, supplying the rich, powerful and titled in Britain and abroad with artefacts of consummate beauty – characteristically reflecting the favoured Rococo manner of the time – and of extraordinary expense.

In 1738 he moved his home and probably his workshop to 40 Gerrard Street, then the best address in the heart of south Soho's silver and gold district. When he died in 1751 he was buried in St Anne's Church, Soho. This was typical Huguenot practice. Although de Lamerie probably

did not worship at St Anne's but in a Huguenot 'temple',
he was happy to be buried in an Anglican church. This
was partly because Huguenot temples – always built as
cheaply as possible – tended not to have extensive burial
grounds or vaults, but also because in Calvinist belief the
final resting place of the mortal remains was of relatively
little importance in comparison with the fate and value
of the immortal soul, which, as far as Huguenots were
concerned, was enhanced by the pursuit of a vigorous
work ethic. Honest trade and toil were seen as godly, and
success and the massing of legitimate wealth and worldly
goods as admirable.

It is difficult – or at least complex – to determine
how exactly this hardworking, extremely useful and
increasingly prosperous French Protestant community
was viewed by late-seventeenth- and early-eighteenth-
century Londoners. What is certain is that the French
soon represented a significant proportion of the population of the capital. It has been estimated that between
1670 and 1710 around 50,000 to 80,000 Huguenots fled
France, with more than half of them coming to England
and, of those, more settling in London than in all other
British locations combined. Of the capital population of
575,000 in 1700 at least 5 per cent were Huguenots.[9]

It is also pretty certain from contemporary documents
that while the authorities and the elite of the land wel-
comed the arrival of Huguenots, thus demonstrating the
spiritual and mercantile superiority of British parliamentary and Protestant monarchy over the absolute Catholic
rule of Louis XIV, London's working people were more
suspicious. They feared that the French might undercut
their wages or, worse still, with their intelligence and

Calvinist work ethic supplant the native workforce, particularly in the weaving trade. There were fears of riots in
Spitalfields in 1683 and actual riots in Norwich.[10] But as it
became clear that the Huguenots were not stealing jobs or
reducing wages, but – with their silk and precious-metal
trades – actually creating new and valuable industries, dis-
turbances settled down and workers in London, especially
those involved with silk-weaving, set themselves the task
of learning, and profiting, from the French. The prevailing
attitude is probably reflected accurately by John Strype,
who in 1720 wrote in his *Survey of the Cities of London and
Westminster* about the 'Poor Protestant Strangers, Waloons
and French' who had been forced to become exiles from
their own country and 'settled themselves in their several
Trades and Occupations', bringing great 'advantage ... to
the whole Nation'. Strype also noted that the 'Benefit' to
the 'Neighbourhood' in which the 'Strangers' settled is
that they served 'for Patterns of Thrift, Honesty, Industry,
and Sobriety'.[11]

This is a most positive analysis, but some ambiguity
remains. A few years after Strype a slightly more nuanced
view of the French Protestant community, specifically
that in Soho, was offered by William Hogarth. In 1736 he
painted his series of four canvases entitled *Four Times of
the Day*. As was usual with Hogarth, these works carried
subtle and generally coded moral messages. The canvas
representing 'Noon' shows the French Church in a court
between Greek Street and Hog Lane (see p. 54), and its
departing and smartly dressed Huguenot congregation.
The French, seemingly wealthy and well mannered, are
in stark contrast with an opposing group – presumably
non-French Londoners – that looks chaotic and uncouth.

In this group a lascivious black man fondles and distracts a servant girl, and an errand boy cries over a spilled pie while a street urchin gobbles up the remains. So at one level it seems that Hogarth is honouring the Huguenots. But Hogarth is Hogarth, and other readings are possible. For example, although uncouth, the people on the Londoners' side appear healthy and food abounds (indeed, a street sign proclaims 'good eating', and a joint of meat is even being thrown from a window), while the well-dressed French appear more pinched, more artificial – perhaps more artful – and as the cherubic little errand boy howls over his lost pie his counterpart, a French boy of similar age, is dressed grotesquely as an adult, with wig, coat and long waist-coat, and hobbles around on a crutch. Exactly what points Hogarth was making are, of course, open to debate. But there seems to be a lingering suspicion of the French, who, despite the wealth and fashion of their appearance and their courtly manners, harbour dark and even unhealthy secrets; perhaps the crippled child suggests inbreeding or the presence of a congenital disease such as syphilis.

If so – as appears to be the case with depictions of sickly children in others of Hogarth's works, such as painting three of the *Marriage A-la-Mode* series of 1743–5 – then he might be making reference to prostitution, another of Soho's eighteenth-century industries, and implying a French connection. Perhaps significantly, the surgeon depicted in the *Marriage A-la-Mode* painting, being consulted about the sickly child-prostitute's syphilis, was intended by Hogarth to be French, a certain 'M. de la Pillule'. So, for Francophobe Hogarth, was syphilis the French disease and were all Frenchmen therefore syph-ilitic and French quarters like Soho hopelessly tainted?

Congregation leaving a French church in Soho, depicted by William Hogarth in 1736 in his series *Four Times of the Day*.

The Georgian sex industry and Soho

The sex industry – which by the late eighteenth century had become one of London's most valuable enterprises[12] – seems to have taken significant root in Soho by about the time Hogarth was painting *Four Times of the Day*. Initially its practitioners – as well as its clients – favoured discretion, unlike the manifestations of the trade in Covent Garden, with its disorderly bawdy houses, bagnios and taverns, along Fleet Street and the Strand and latterly along Oxford Street, where audacious street prostitutes abounded. Prostitution was not illegal in Georgian Britain, but street prostitutes could be harassed and arrested as vagrants, and bawdy houses – if noisy and too public – could from the mid eighteenth century be closed as 'disorderly houses'. And certain sexual acts and activities were severely punished by law. For example, penetrative sex between men was a capital crime and if proven in court to the satisfaction of the jury could (and very occasionally did) result in execution. Indeed, certain sex acts undertaken by women could be classed as 'buggery' or 'sodomy' and severely punished, as could 'unnatural' acts between men and women. So there were lots of good reasons for keeping Soho's sex industry below the radar of inquisitive or patrolling parish officers, moralistic magistrates and societies for reforming public morals. Consequently, the area did not become a high-profile hunting ground of street prostitutes and a place of uproarious misbehaviour; instead it housed kept women, actresses of dubious morals and prostitutes who operated from their lodgings or from fashionable and well-ordered bordellos or brothels.

The mid-eighteenth-century pioneer of this discreet aspect of the city's sex industry was the Soho-based Mrs Goadby. She opened an establishment that reflected the growing fashion among men of wealth and taste – inspired by examples in France and Italy – to make the practice and enjoyment of prostitution more elegant, safe and private. A peculiar book entitled *Nocturnal Revels*, published in London in 1779 and purporting to be written by a 'Monk of the Order of St Francis' – in other words, a member of Sir Francis Dashwood's famed 'Hellfire Club' – records the moment of change. In 1750 Mrs Goadby, fired with a determination 'to refine our amorous amusements and regulate them according to the Parisian system',[13] opened her first premises in Berwick Street, which she immediately 'fitted up ... in an elegant stile'[14] distinguished by its discretion and outwardly sober appearance.

Ivan Bloch, in *Sexual Life in England Past and Present*, builds upon the text of *Nocturnal Revels* and explains that Mrs Goadby chose to term her superior brothel a seraglio, after the French *sérails* that were in turn inspired by the well-ordered harems or sarays of the Ottomans. Mrs Goadby had, records Bloch, 'made several journeys to France, and had been initiated into the secrets of the famous Parisian sérails ... the principles of which ... Mrs Goadby to a great extent made her own'. These principles included accepting

> only the most beautiful girls, and preferably those from different countries and of different faiths. All, however, were equally subject to the rules of the brothel and had to submit unconditionally to the orders of the brothel keeper, whose authority was supreme. It was also the duty of the girls to show 'le zèle le plus sincère pour les rites et les cérémonies de la décesse de cypros' and to satisfy all fantasies, caprices and extravagances of the male visitors, carrying out their wishes in every particular.[15]

In the Parisian *sérail* the women were to 'avoid all gastronomic and alcoholic excess in order that their behaviour should be modest and decent even in the pursuit of pleasure', but Mrs Goadby – clearly a realist well aware of the London harlot's love for restorative alcoholic beverages – abandoned any prohibition against strong liquor. The women of the seraglio either promenaded during the day or spent their time relaxing indoors until clients arrived in the evening, 'when their custom was to offer a handkerchief to the lady of ... choice. If this was accepted, she belonged to the man for the night.'[16]

Mrs Goadby soon 'engaged some of the first-rate *filles de joye* in London' and equipped 'her ladies in the highest gusto', thanks to the great quantity of silks and lace she'd brought from France.[17] Evidently the secret of her success was to give her brothel the grace of an exclusive aristocratic mansion where 'only people of rank and men of fortune' were welcome.[18] Another of Mrs Goadby's successful innovations was to display a concern for the health of both her employees and her clients. She went to great trouble to demonstrate that the prostitutes in her elegant brothel were healthy and that all possible attempts were made to prevent the spread of venereal disease. She employed a resident surgeon to ensure that they were 'sound in wind and limb' and supplied her women with 'Mrs Phillip's famed New Engines',[19] which were condoms made of sheep's gut or bladder and secured to the male member by means of a playful ribbon. Condoms, available since the late seventeenth century, were used more as a preventative against disease than pregnancy, as Daniel Turner pointed out in his book

Syphilis of 1717, where he wrote that 'the cundum' was 'the best if not only preservative our libertines have found at present'.[20]

The success of Mrs Goadby's establishment was noted and soon emulated by other entrepreneurs of London's sex industry – notably Charlotte Hayes, who in 1767 took the model to a new level of sophistication. She opened a smart and exclusive brothel in the very heart of fashionable St James's, in King's Place, which was only a few yards from St James's Palace. Her methods and manners are recounted in great detail in *Nocturnal Revels*, which is no surprise since the subtitle of the book is the *History of King's-place and other Modern Nunneries* – which reflects the fact that Charlotte termed her high-class brothel a 'Nunnery or Cloister', with herself as the 'Mother Abbess' and her prostitutes its 'Nuns'.

Perhaps stimulated by the competition offered by Charlotte Hayes, Mrs Goadby relocated to larger premises in Soho, in Great Marlborough Street, and soon emulated the playfully erotic and mildly blasphemous terminology of her rival, as an advertisement in a 1773 edition of *The Covent Garden Magazine* makes clear:

> Mrs Goadby, that celebrated Lady Abbess, having fitted up an elegant nunnery in Marlborough Street, is now laying in a stock of Virgins for the ensuing season [and] has disposed of her Nunnery in such an uncommon taste, and prepared such extraordinary accommodations for gentlemen of all ages, sizes, tastes and caprices, as, it is judged, will surpass every seminary of the kind yet known in Europe.[21]

This was indeed a step up in the world. Great Marlborough Street was handsome and in the very early
eighteenth century had been a place of aristocratic fashion (see p. 366). But even in the 1770s it was one of Soho's
better streets, although places of dubious entertainment,
offering sexually titillating masquerades that presented
tempting opportunities for predatory prostitutes, had
started to appear in the street: for example, the 'Cassino'
at number 48 in 1774 (see p. 374).

Mrs Goadby's Soho establishment, her prostitutes and
other Soho-based courtesans had a greater influence on
the development of British culture than many may suppose. In the Royal Academy there resides the collection
of pocketbooks that belonged to Sir Joshua Reynolds,
one of Britain's most famed and successful eighteenth-
century painters and long-serving president of the RA.
The pocketbooks – essentially diaries recording appoint-
ments – date from 1755 to 1790 and, as about 20 per cent
of the volumes are missing, admittedly offer only a partial
picture of Reynolds's activities. But what becomes clear,
even from this incomplete record, is that Reynolds spent a
lot of time with prostitutes – particularly those associated
with discreet West End establishments such as the ones
in Soho. In his pocketbooks Reynolds does not reveal that
any of the females he met were prostitutes. Much of the
evidence is circumstantial, and many of the girls mentioned are only known to have been prostitutes because
they are named as such in other sources, or because he
met them at locations known to have been brothels. For
example, in his pocketbook for 1773, opposite the page
for 5 April, Reynolds notes the address of the well-known
brothel run by Mrs Goadby at the 'Green Lawn' in Great

Marlborough Street. Was the 'Cassino' at 48 Great Marlborough Street associated with Mrs Goadby? Perhaps.
'Green Lawn' is an odd name, and the colour green plays
an important role in roulette, a favourite casino game,
invented in late-eighteenth-century France; and both the
'Cassino' and Mrs Goadby started business in the street
in 1773 or 1774. 'Lawn' might also be a reference to a type
of linen or cotton cloth used, by tradition, for dresses,
nightwear and lingerie and for liturgical vestments. It
was common in the late eighteenth century to refer to
superior prostitutes as 'nuns'. It makes one think.

The references to young ladies that litter the pages of
Reynolds's pocketbooks suggest that he fancied many of
them for very particular reasons – notably for exemplary
parts of their bodies which he simply and solely wanted
to study and draw. In his pocketbook for 1772, opposite
the page for 27 July, Reynolds referred to a 'Miss Boothby
at Mrs Fields, Church Street, next door to the Cheese
House', possibly Church Street (now Romilly Street) in
Soho. Miss Boothby was, records Reynolds, a 'Model for
neck'. And in the back of the pocketbook for 1779 he
noted a 'Mrs Ruth, Childs Rents, Tuthill Street, Westminster' to whom he reminded himself to 'send a penny
post letter, when I want her for a nek'. It's possible these
references have an obscure double meaning, but there
really is no reason not to take them at face value. For
Reynolds, a good neck to draw was his lifeblood as an
artist whose portraiture, to succeed, had to be based on
a thorough understanding of the human body. No doubt
when he had these girls at his disposal he would ponder
their forms and the artistic possibilities offered by their
bodies, sketch them and, ultimately, apply his insights

when executing a commissioned portrait.

In the pocketbook for 1773 another telling location is mentioned, this time associated with the name of a harlot who was to become a famous and powerful courtesan. On the page of the week starting 8 June, Reynolds wrote: 'Mrs. Armistead, at Mrs. Mitchell's, Upper John Street, Golden Square', Soho. Elizabeth Mitchell ran an exclusive seraglio, or brothel, in Golden Square, and also from 1770 in King's Place, St James's, and Mrs Armistead was evidently one of her young ladies. Mrs Armistead became the long-term mistress and from 1795 the wife of Reynolds's friend, the politician Charles James Fox – a rare example of the harlot who successfully made the move from brothel to security and respectability.[22]

The names that appear in Reynolds's pocketbooks reveal much about the sexual geography of mid- to late-eighteenth-century Soho. On the back leaf of the pocketbook for 1769 Reynolds wrote: 'Model Miss Wilson at Mrs. Stoobs in Bentick Srt, Barwick Srt, Soho'. What Mrs Stoobs was we do not now know, but the Berwick Street area was a likely location for a brothel, so she was probably a bawd. And in the pocketbook for 1773 (opposite the week beginning Monday, 7 June) a Miss Metz is noted as living at 'Mr. Richters in Newport Street' and described enigmatically as 'Novblin Eleve de Msr. Casanova'.

One location where Reynolds probably met some of these young ladies survives in Soho. In the centre of the north side of Gerrard Street stands a fine but decaying 1750s building that now houses a Cantonese food shop and storerooms which was originally constructed as a tavern, named the Turk's Head (plate 4). Beneath shelves and displays of exotic foods survives fine panelling, and, at the heart of the four-window-wide building that is now number 9 Gerrard Street, is a large and spectacular staircase that once carried customers to the tavern's elegant upper floors. The tavern was popular with artists and actors and was frequented by the fashionable swordsman Henry Angelo, and from 1764 was home to 'The Club', founded by Reynolds and Dr Samuel Johnson, whose original membership of nine gradually expanded to thirty-five by the time Johnson died in 1784. During its heyday the membership of The Club included Edmund Burke, Oliver Goldsmith, David Garrick and James Boswell.[23] The Club met for dining, drinking and literary debate and, judging by its membership, conversation would have been as free-ranging and inclusive as humanly possible.

The Turk's Head would also have been a most convenient place for Reynolds, who lived in nearby Leicester Square, to meet the girls who lived and worked in the surrounding streets. Two females whom Reynolds might well have arranged to meet at the Turk's Head are named in the pocketbook for 1768, on the week beginning 7 March. They are 'Mrs Clive' and 'Miss Hart'. One must have been the actress Kitty Clive, who, once married to a relative of Lord Clive, was a good friend of Handel, David Garrick and Horace Walpole and aged fifty-seven at the time, was almost certainly not being courted by Reynolds as a life model. Indeed, Kitty Clive, despite impecunious origins and youthful entry into the acting profession, was one of the few actresses of the eighteenth century who seems to have led a morally exemplary life. The other name mentioned – 'Miss Hart' – is more tantalising. Lady Hamilton, when a teenage prostitute, had at one time used the name Emma Hart; but, despite there being some debate about her date of birth (all that's known for certain is that she was baptised in May 1765), Emma must have been well under ten years of age in 1768. This surely would have been too young, even for the precocious Emma, to be out on the streets and meeting men in taverns (plate 0).

Additional insights about Georgian Soho's sex life can be gathered from other contemporary sources – notably *Harris's List of Covent Garden Ladies*. This directory of London prostitutes seems to have been started in the late 1740s by Jack Harris, a pimp and 'head-waiter' at the Shakespeare's Head tavern in the Covent Garden Piazza, and the hack writer Sam Derrick, who was later to replace 'Beau' Nash as Master of Ceremonies at the ultimate Georgian pleasure ground of Bath. The first editions were no more than handwritten manuscripts kept by Harris for his own use and that of his immediate friends and clients. But by the late 1750s the list was printed, circulated and regularly revised. Harris's book not only lists the names of the 'ladies', but also gives their addresses and their charges, and describes – in satirical and often wittily erotic manner – their sexual specialities, preferences and charms. It seems the 'ladies' paid Harris and Nash 'poundage' to be included in the book, for a 'listing' in such a popular publication was good for business and made their whereabouts known – a most important consideration since the ladies listed most probably worked, at least part of the time, as freelance whores operating from their lodgings or from bagnios, rather than from brothels run by bawds, and certainly not on the streets.

Addresses listed in the 1788 edition of Harris's List suggest the locations in which superior West End pros-

titutes preferred to live and work – and many of these
were in Soho. It seems that Lisle Street, Wardour Street,
Berwick Street and Poland Street played an important
role in Soho's late-eighteenth-century sex industry. There
was, for example, a Miss Dunford, at a Sadler's, Charles
Street, Soho. The entry, a masterpiece of innuendo, is
typical. She was 'fond of music, plays with the greatest
dexterity, [is] full skilled in pricking, altho' the principal
part of her music is played in duets ... she has not the
smallest objection to two flats ... she generally chooses
the lowest part [and] sometimes plays the same tune
twice'. The reference to 'flats' meant that Miss Dunford
was available for lesbian intrigues.

One of the most poignant tales of Soho's sex industry
is told by Thomas de Quincey in his *Confessions of an
English Opium-Eater*.[24] Writing in 1821, de Quincey recalls
how, twenty years earlier when a school runaway, he
was obliged, having perhaps lodged in desolate circumstances at 58 or 61 Greek Street (opinions vary), to live
as a famished vagrant upon the streets of London. For
various reasons he haunted Soho, where he 'fell in ...
with those female peripatetics who are technically called
street-walkers'. These women took de Quincey's part
'against watchmen who wished to drive me off the steps
of houses where I was sitting', and numbered among
them was the 'noble-minded Ann' – a street prostitute
fifteen years of age. De Quincey called her 'Ann of Oxford
Street', presumably because, like many streetwalkers at
the time, she plied her trade along this busy shopping
street on the edge of Soho, illuminated in fairyland
fashion late into the evening by the flickering oil lamps
outside shops or atop parish posts.

For many weeks de Quincey 'walked at nights with this poor friendless girl up and down Oxford Street, or ... rested with her on steps and under the shelter of porticoes'. It was during one of these meanderings that the event occurred for which de Quincey would be ever grateful to the girl: 'One night ... after a day when I felt more than usually ill and faint, I requested her to turn off with me into Soho Square.' There they sat on the steps of a house, de Quincey leaning his 'head against her bosom', when 'all at once I sank from her arms and fell backwards on the steps'. This, to de Quincey, was the crisis moment of his life on the streets of London. Looking back, he believed he was, at this point, near death. Ann rushed to Oxford Street and bought him a glass of port wine and spices, which had an 'instant power of restoration'. Ann 'without a murmur paid out of her humble purse ... when she had scarcely wherewithal to purchase the bare necessaries of life'. De Quincey was convinced 'the generous girl' had saved his life. Soon afterwards he started to resolve his deeply disordered life. He borrowed money, improved his appearance, 'gave one quarter to Ann' of the money he obtained, and 'soon after six o'clock on a dark winter evening ... set off, accompanied by Ann, towards Piccadilly ... through a part of the town which has now all disappeared, so that I can no longer retrace its ancient boundaries – Swallow Street, I think it was called'. He was referring to the destructive creation of Regent Street and Regent Circus (now Piccadilly Circus) that had taken place since he wrote. The pair 'bore away ... into Golden Square ... near the corner of Sherrard Street' (he of course means Sherrird, now Sherwood, Street), where they sat down in intimate circumstances,

'not wishing to part in the tumult and blaze of Piccadilly'. De Quincey was going away to get more money
and told Ann he would never desert her when he 'had
power to protect her', for he 'loved her as affectionately
as if she had been my sister'. When they kissed 'at our
final farewell, she put her arms about my neck and wept
without speaking a word'. De Quincey told Ann – 'the
saviour of my life' – that he hoped to return in a week
at the latest, and 'agreed with her that on the fifth night
from that, and every night afterwards', she would wait
for him at six o'clock near the bottom of Great Titchfield Street'. This had been their 'customary haven ...
of rendezvous, to prevent our missing each other in the
great Mediterranean of Oxford Street'. He left to secure
loans from friends at Eton, but, circumstances becoming
complicated, it was many months before he could return
to London.

And 'what had become of poor Ann?' De Quincey
claims he 'sought her daily, and waited for her every night
... at the corner of Titchfield Street'. Naturally, after such
a long time Ann did not appear. De Quincey claims he
looked for her as best he could and assumed that they
were 'in search of each other, at the very same moment,
through the mighty labyrinths of London; perhaps even
within a few feet of each other', and in the end concluded
that 'a barrier no wider than a London street' amounted
'in the end to a separation for eternity!' After that tearful
but hopeful kiss near Golden Square, de Quincey never
saw Ann again. He blamed Oxford Street, that 'stony
hearted step-mother', and London's voracious sex industry. This, I suppose, was easier than blaming himself. He
accepted that Ann was dead – and this was probably the

case – but de Quincey never forgot her, or the debt he owed and the love – brotherly, he claimed – that he'd felt for her.

The presence of the sex industry in Soho stimulated the foundation of a number of peculiar institutions, notably the White House Hotel, located at 21 Soho Square, which was a brothel that flourished from 1778 to 1801 and in which sex and horror were mixed in a most individual manner (see p. 164), and Mrs Cornelys's assembly rooms at Carlisle House – also in Soho Square – which was dedicated to pleasure, promenades and the masquerade. Carlisle House was famed, among other things, as a place where the highest and lowest in the land could rub shoulders with relative discretion and (when masked) anonymity, and where young harlots – in fashionable and frivolous attire – could snare customers well endowed with riches. Both these establishments are described below in more detail.

Life in Georgian Soho

It is worth reflecting for a moment on the quality of life in eighteenth-century Soho. Much changed dramatically, of course, in the 100 years between 1700 and 1800, notably by the gradual replacement of fashionable and aristocratic households with commerce, trade and light industry, often accommodated in the smaller houses and courts that started, in parts of Soho from the late 1720s, to replace larger, earlier houses. But despite these changes there were features in common through the age.

Sewerage arrangements tended to be made when streets were first laid out. Brick culverts were constructed under the auspices of the Commissioners of Sewers, but these sewers were intended to carry away street water and only a very limited amount of domestic liquid waste. Domestic human waste was deposited in cesspits, generally in rear yards or occasionally in street vaults, which had to be cleared, from time to time, by night-soil men. This remained the standard arrangement well into the nineteenth century.

Water was supplied by private water companies, but in limited and inefficient manner and at too low a pressure to reach the upper storeys of houses. Only from the 1820s was there a significant replacement of leaky, sleeve-jointed, hand-wrought elm pipes with cast-iron pipes. So water often had to be fetched from public pumps, such as the one in Broad Street. Street lighting was generally organised by the parishes, some residents paying a parish rate as their contribution or agreeing to put lamps – burning whale oil – outside their homes to the standard required by the parish. In affluent, well-organised parishes this could be successful. A German visitor, Johann Wilhelm von Archenholz, observed in 1780 of London's street lighting that 'nothing ... can be more superb. The lamps ... are enclosed in crystal balls and fixed on posts at a little distance from each other [and stretch along] the great roads within seven or eight miles of town ... the effect is charming.'[25] In July 1790 the parish of St Anne's, Soho, contained 744 lamps, of which 496 were 'parochial' and the rest run by various occupiers. It cost fifteen shillings to operate each lamp per annum, according to one Jos. Hayling, the lamplighter contracted by the parish to light and maintain the lamps.[26]

As well as organising street lighting, the parish – essentially the basic unit of local government in Georgian and early Victorian London, run by the vestry – took responsibility for paving, cleaning and watching – or policing – the territory within its boundaries. Money came from a rate charged on eligible parish residents and the results were more or less effective, depending on particular circumstances. Naturally, parishes with numerous affluent occupants did better than those with large numbers of poor who would not or could not pay rates. Cleaning was usually organised under a parish-appointed 'scavenger' working closely with the beadle, the head parish officer answerable to the vestrymen. The beadle had many duties. He took charge of the poor of the parish (generally only those born in the parish were eligible for parish relief under the Poor Laws), who might be consigned to the workhouse as the most economic solution to their predicament. The eighteenth-century workhouse for the parish of St Anne's survives in Manette Street (see p. 174). Other duties included stopping people setting up stalls in the street, dumping filth or making a nuisance of themselves. The beadle was also responsible for security, including the supervision of parish constables and nightwatchmen or 'Charlies' and the apprehension of miscreants, who would be brought before the local justice of the peace.

The Estates

East of Wardour Street

The main cause of the physical change that overtook Soho from the 1720s was its shifting social and economic character. But the agencies that realised the change were Soho's highly varied freeholders and leaseholders who controlled the ground. As with much of Georgian London, Soho consisted of a large number of relatively small private estates, held freehold or leasehold, each with its own aims, aspirations and financial means. There were nine main estates holding land in Soho east of Colman Hedge Lane / Wardour Street, and significantly more west of Wardour Street, with the pattern of landownership complicated by an overlying pattern of ancient field boundaries or closes that might – or might not – be under the same ownership, or indeed with their ownership passing, from time to time, from one estate to another. From the late seventeenth century these estates powered the development of the area.

The fields, closes and estates of Soho on the following page are overlaid on John Rocque's map of 1746. They are numbered west and east of Wardour Street, because the land to the west was divided by numerous ancient boundaries into fields and closes – each sometimes controlled by different estates, while the land east of Wardour Street was largely Soho Fields with a smaller number of estates.[*]

---

[*] Information from *Survey of London*, vol. XXXI, p. 27, and vol. XXXIII, p. 21.

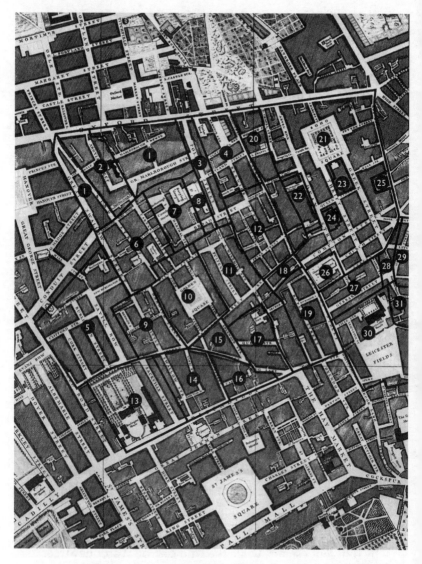

The mosaic of estates, closes and fields on which Soho was built during the 17th and 18th centuries. The boundaries are overlaid on John Rocque's map of 1746.

1. Millfield
2. Portion of Millfield developed in the early 18th century under the control of the Duke of Argyll
3. Little Gelding's Close
4. Doghouse Close
5. Ten Acre Close
6. Six Acre Close
7. Pesthouse Close, developed by Lord Craven
8. Part of Little Gelding's Close known as Pawlett's Garden
9. Mulghay Close or Dog Field, principally developed by the Pulteney estate
10. Gelding Close
11. Windmill Field – portion principally developed by Pulteney estate
12. Colman Hedge Close
13. Stone Conduit Close
14. Swallow Close, under control of the Earl of St Albans
15. Round Rundles, under Sherard control
16. Round Rundles, under the Earl of St Albans' control
17. Windmill Field, portion principally developed by Colonel Thomas Panton
18. Laystall Piece or Knaves' Acre, developed by Pulteney estate
19. Laystall or Vesey's Garden and Watt's Close
20. Pulteney estate
21. Portland estate
22. Pitt estate
23. Monmouth House estate
24. Pitt estate
25. Greek Church and almshouses
26. St Anne's Church
27. Military Ground
28. Waste Ground
29. Newport estate
30. Leicester estate
31. Salisbury estate

To the east of Wardour Street the largest parcel of land was Soho Fields, which was to have Soho Square at its heart and which in 1698 became the Portland estate. This estate stretched south from Oxford Street to King Street, which was roughly on the site of what is now Shaftesbury Avenue. The eastern boundary was Hog Lane, now approximately the line of Charing Cross Road. To the west the boundary of the estate was more complex. It reached to just beyond the west side of Dean Street, but not as far as Wardour Street except in one small area, near what was to become the west end of Old Compton Street.[1]

The land forming the east side of Wardour Street, and stretching east to, and abutting with, the Portland estate was the Pulteney estate. The west side of the middle portion of Dean Street, adjoining the Pulteney estate, was the Pitt estate, which also owned a small parcel of land on the east side of Dean Street. South from Soho Square, stretching to Bateman Street and sandwiched between Greek and Frith Streets, was the Monmouth estate, which commemorated the site of Monmouth House and its garden (see p. 60). To the north of the west end of King Street was the small area of freehold land on which the Parish Church of St Anne was constructed between 1677 and 1686. The west boundary of St Anne's parish was defined by Wardour Street, which also formed the west edge of the small Military Ground, set to the south of King Street. To the east of the Military Ground was the Newport estate. South of both of these was the larger Leicester estate, organised around Leicester Fields; to its east was the Salisbury estate.

THE EARL OF ST ALBANS AND SOHO SQUARE

Soho Fields was former monastic land forfeited to the Crown in 1536 at the time of the Reformation and the Dissolution of the Monasteries. In the late 1620s Charles I gave it to his wife, Queen Henrietta Maria, who in 1661 granted a lease on the land to Henry Jermyn, Earl of St Albans, her loyal stalwart and perhaps lover during the long years of exile and uncertainty after the execution of her husband in 1649. At the time St Albans received control of Soho Fields he was starting the development of St James's Square and Jermyn Street to the south. St Albans's aim was to attract the resurgent aristocracy and courtiers of nearby St James's Palace to this development. He was successful, and his speculative adventure was credited as the starting point of London's West End.

During the 1670s St Albans started to sublease parts of Soho Fields for development, notably to Joseph Girle, who in 1677 leased his interest to the bricklayer Richard Frith who, with associates William Pym and Benjamin Hinton, became the first of the area's speculating builders to launch the large-scale and architecturally ambitious transformation of Soho Fields into a city suburb. Frith's role was soon expanded when St Albans granted him control of virtually the whole of Soho Fields until the year 1733.[2] Frith sublet plots to other speculating builders and development was, as revealed by Ogilby and Morgan's map, largely complete by 1682.

Soho Square – at first called Frith's Square and then King's Square – was laid out in 1677, or very soon after, as were the streets leading into it on its four sides. The most important of these were the long avenues of Frith

Street and Greek Street. These terminated to the south at Compton Street, which was also laid out and developed at roughly the same time.

When first completed in the early 1680s Soho Square was one of the most fashionable places to live in London. Residential squares with uniform architecture – inspired by such Continental examples as the early-seventeenth-century Place Royale (now Place des Vosges) in Paris and the Plaza Mayor in Madrid – had become the vogue in London in the 1630s when Inigo Jones created the Piazza in Covent Garden for the Earl of Bedford. Existing open spaces, such as Lincoln's Inn Fields, Leicester Fields and Charterhouse Yard, were quickly lined with rows of houses to give them something of the quality of a formal square, and soon after the Restoration in 1660 a number of large aristocratic squares were initiated, notably Bloomsbury Square and St James's Square. From the late 1660s and into the 1690s a number of other squares were started in various parts of London and its environs – for example Red Lion Square, Bloomsbury; Wellclose Square near the Tower of London; New Square, Lincoln's Inn, and Hoxton Square (both begun in 1683); Kensington Square and, of course, Golden Square, Soho (see p. 341).

The creation of Soho Square was a key part of this ambitious and pioneering wave of urban transformation that gave London some of the residential grandeur and architectural quality of other great European cities. Formerly called King's Square, it had no doubt been named after Charles II to flatter him, to confirm the aspirations of the development and to attract grand occupants: from an early date it contained a statue of the king, and the street leading into it from the north was originally known as

Charles Street. The designer of the square and its related streets is uncertain, but it must be assumed that Richard Frith took responsibility for the layout of the square and its supporting streets. And, if so, Frith seems to have been well aware of the difficulties – and the various current London solutions – inherent in creating a square that was to be visually harmonious, even loosely uniform in appearance, yet formed of numerous individual terrace houses of various sizes and in the possession of different leaseholders. As well as the problem of achieving a degree of design unity, there was also the issue of the square's corners. Should they be closed, in which case a dramatic sense of enclosure would be achieved and privacy promised? But corner houses would abut at right angles with, potentially, a large and awkward rear space left between. Or should the corners be open with streets flowing in – a simple solution, but one that reduced the visual enclosure and intimacy of the square?

Varying solutions were applied to other London squares, but at Soho Square all four corners were kept firmly closed, with adjoining houses sharing the concealed corner spaces. Three of the four sides of the square were pierced by centrally placed streets, but on the south side Greek Street and Frith Street entered the square, offering generous vistas and framing the dominant site on that side, the palatial Monmouth House, virtually a free-standing country house for which the entire square could be perceived as the mere forecourt. This house was started in 1681 for the Duke of Monmouth, the illegitimate son of Charles II, with Frith himself included among its building team. The site of the house and its garden to the south were not part of the Soho Fields

estate and formed a small estate leased directly from the
Crown. All came to a premature and sticky end when,
in July 1685, Monmouth was executed for treason after
leading an unsuccessful Protestant rebellion against his
uncle, James II. Monmouth's estates were forfeited to the
Crown and his mansion, tainted by his disgrace, stood
unfinished and decaying until 1717, when it was purchased
and remodelled for Sir James Bateman, a City financier
and Lord Mayor of London, in a most startling Baroque
manner, perhaps the work of Thomas Archer.

North elevation of Monmouth House, Soho Square, as remodelled in around 1717.

Despite the setback of Monmouth's unfinished pile, the initial marketing ploy to associate the new square with the king seems to have worked. From its very early years it was the height of fashion. Its east side was dominated by the large mansions of Earl Fauconberg, Viscount Preston and the Earl of Carlisle. The south side was not only occupied by Monmouth House, but also by the homes of Baron Carew, the Earl of Bolingbroke and Viscount Granville.[3] So, for a few brief years at least, Soho Square lived up to the aspirations of its founders and became London's residential epicentre of aristocratic fashion. It is no doubt significant that the central area of the square was planted in a formal manner that, with imagination, could be seen as a modest evocation in miniature of the gardens of Versailles. This might reflect Monmouth's royal pretensions but was also, no doubt, an association that flattered the square's initial grand residents.

For nearly a hundred years Monmouth House was the dominant architectural feature of Soho Square, but after numerous vicissitudes it was demolished in 1773 to make way for a new court and terraces of small houses – a dramatic indication of Soho's fall from fashion by the late eighteenth century. Monmouth House and its demolition were described by the artist J.T. Smith in his autobiography *Nollekens and his Times*, published first in 1828.[4] Smith's evocative account of the last days of the house is an early expression in English writing of a romantic and deeply nostalgic feeling for a doomed building that was not of great antiquity but which conjured up generations and ways of life just passing, and reflected upon the atmosphere of decay, transience and abandonment.

Smith describes how he and Joseph Nollekens 'ventured' into the building, despite the fact that 'workmen were employed in pulling it down'. Smith noted in the dining room 'the carved and gilt panels' that had 'contained whole-length pictures', and in the corners of the ornamented ceiling and 'over the chimney-piece' the arms were still displayed of the ill-fated Duke of Monmouth. The pair ascended the main staircase 'of oak', with landings 'tesselated [*sic*] with woods of light and dark colours', and arrived at the 'principal room' on the first floor. This, which had as yet 'not been disturbed by the workmen', evidently had a haunted atmosphere of faded grandeur. The walls were 'lined with blue satin, superbly decorated with pheasants and other birds in gold', and 'from stains upon the silk' it was clear the piers between the windows had once been filled with ostentatious looking glasses. The chimney piece, 'richly ornamented with fruit and foliage', had above it 'a circular recess ... evidently designed for the reception of a bust'. But the bust – like the looking glasses and the once-grand residents of the house – was missing.

THE PORTLAND ESTATE

A decade after William III came to the throne, with James II's daughter Mary as queen, the ownership of Soho Fields changed. St Albans had died in 1684 and in 1698 the king – as owner of the ground – granted it as a freehold interest to his fellow Dutchman and favourite William Bentinck, by then the 1st Earl of Portland. In 1722 the earl's son, who had succeeded to his father's estates and titles in 1709 and in 1716 was created duke, set in motion a course of events that was to change the physical look and social nature of Soho's largest single estate and – in consequence – the nature of Soho itself. The duke granted his younger son, Lord George Bentinck, a 500-year term on the estate that was part of a financial strategy to raise him £30,000 by the time he came of age in 1735. The strategy – overseen by the young man's mother – involved a plan to increase the value of the estate by granting new leases to encourage rebuilding, with the new buildings tailored to the estate's – and Soho's – changing fortunes. In broad terms this meant the replacement of late-seventeenth-century aristocratic mansions with a greater number of smaller buildings and courts and workshops suitable for humbler occupants and for the use of the precious-metal trade and for tapestry manufacture. And so the creation of Georgian Soho, which constitutes much of the historic fabric that survives today, started to grow out of, and to replace, the faded grandeur of late-Stuart Soho.

THE PITT ESTATE

The Pitt estate was acquired on leasehold from the Crown in 1697 by Thomas Pitt, an MP who was the grandfather and great-grandfather of the two William Pitts who became Prime Ministers of Great Britain. Pitt had been Governor of Fort St George, Madras, and from 1701 owner of the fabulous 410-carat 'Pitt diamond'. He had bought the rough stone in Madras in mysterious circumstances, at a cost of £20,000. It was sent to London, where it was cut to make a 141-carat diamond with several secondary stones. These were sold to Peter the Great of Russia, the main gem being bought for £135,000 in 1717 by the

French regent, Philippe II, Duke of Orléans. It remains in the French Treasury and is on display in the Louvre. The possession of such tremendous wealth made the extraction of money from this small Soho estate a matter of no great concern or urgency for Pitt.

Soon after 1730 the Pitt family (Thomas had died in 1726) initiated a general rebuilding on its estate that was broadly in line with the policy being followed on the adjoining Portland estate. Meard Street is in its way a typical expression of the estate's desire for increased density. The west portion of it was started on the Pulteney estate in the early 1720s with the replacement of a court off the east side of Wardour Street with two facing terraces of handsome but modest houses. The east end of Meard Street, with a related development on Dean Street, was created about ten years later on the site of an existing late-seventeenth-century court on the Pitt estate. The two developments, although on different estates and years apart, are united by the fact that they were undertaken by the same speculating builder, John Meard the younger, a local carpenter. Both portions of the street have a remarkable uniformity, the earlier houses being smaller and simpler than the later ones, and the early 1730s pair of houses on Dean Street the grandest. The south side of Meard Street is intact and the portions on the two different estates are marked by a change of width and alignment that gives the street added visual charm. Sadly, all the early 1720s houses on the north side are long gone, but the early 1730s ones survive, although most have been severely altered (plate 5).

Not so typical was Thomas Richmond's work on the Pitt estate. In the 1730s Soho was socially complex. The prevailing trend, perhaps pioneered on the Portland estate, was, as we have noted, to build a greater number of smaller houses and workshops, but in certain minds the dream of at least parts of Soho as aristocratic in style – with grand, large houses commanding high rents – was not dead. During the first decade of the eighteenth century Great Marlborough Street and Poland Street had been created successfully as aristocratic enclaves. Some thought this approach could be extended. Among them were, it seems, members of the Pitt family and the carpenter and speculating builder Thomas Richmond, who developed a close working relationship with the estate. In 1732, on Pitt estate land, he started Richmond Buildings, a residential cul-de-sac of eleven good-quality houses, rising four storeys over basements, on the site of an obscure and generally uninhabited seventeenth-century court. Richmond's houses were very well detailed in the latest fashion. With their lofty interiors, they were aimed at the wealthy end of Soho's rapidly growing merchant and trade community. But in the middle of nearby Dean Street, on the Pitt estate land, Richmond was involved in the creation of a row of houses (75, 76 and 77) that were positively palatial and intended for the top of the West End housing market.

All but one of Richmond's palaces on Dean Street have gone, and the last six of his houses in Richmond Buildings were demolished in 1973 – a tragic loss. Despite years of multi-occupation, mixed use and poor maintenance they remained handsome, were well preserved internally with much good-quality panelling, and listed as buildings of historic or architectural interest. They were one of my favourite sites in Soho. The terrace was tucked away but packed with characterful Soho life: small trades of all sorts were practised in its various rooms, lodgers and visitors came and went, the historic detail, although abundant, was taken for granted and generally its charms and interest unappreciated. It was clear that most people who passed through the simple and solemn doorcases and along the panelled entrance halls, richly ornamented with dentilled (tooth-like projections) cornices and fluted pilasters, had no thought for their antiquity or beauty, shrouded as they were by mire and modern paraphernalia. This rich mix of residential and commercial uses rendered the houses accessible; their front doors were rarely closed or locked, which, of course, made the enjoyment of them not only easier but more thrilling, more personal as one penetrated their inner parts, dodging up the staircase past doors, each opening onto varied and exotic worlds.

Then, one day, I turned the corner from Dean Street and saw the terrace a heap of ruins. This type of thing could happen with ease in the early 1970s. Clearly, some absurd official had been fooled by the aura of pleasing decay that hung around the houses and really believed they were slums and had condoned the demolition proposed by a heartless developer or hapless planner. I remember staring in horror. Sticking up from the mounds of smashed brickwork were two of the large timber Doric fluted pilasters that had decorated an entrance hall and that I had long admired, and lengths of ornate timber cornice. I waded into the rubble, pulled out pilasters and cornices and – with assistance – took it all home on the Underground from Tottenham Court Road station. Goodness knows how I managed, but I was in my early twenties and driven by a passion of indignation that swept aside all ordinary obstacles. J.T. Smith had accepted such loss of Soho's history with sad resignation. I could not. Over the years I've kept the pilasters with me, stark if graceful reminders of the loss of Richmond Buildings, and they remain among my most prized possessions, the last physical remains of this once-splendid terrace.

The east end of the north side of Richmond Buildings, built in 1732 and demolished in the early 1970s.

THE PULTENEY ESTATE
(EAST OF WARDOUR STREET)

The small Pulteney estate – little more than a sliver of land
on the east side of Colman Hedge Lane / Wardour Street –
also played its role. The land forming the estate had been
surrendered by the Abbot and Convent of Abingdon in 1536
to Henry VIII, and was acquired leasehold in 1690 by the
Pulteney family, which finally obtained a freehold interest
in 1721.[5] During the first seventy or so years of the seventeenth century much of the land, lying next to the ancient
thoroughfare, was built upon, as is revealed byWenceslaus
Hollar's London map of *c*.1675. But most of these houses
were irregular, poorly built and vernacular in character.
In the 1680s ambition started to increase – and quality to
improve – as remaining vacant plots were developed and
small, old houses replaced by larger and grander new ones.
But still, in the mid 1690s, as the *Survey of London* observes,
there was 'no sign that Sir William Pulteney, who had
held the Crown lease, adopted any scheme of systematic
redevelopment ... Growth had been haphazard and no
attempt was made to integrate it with the new streets laid
out immediately to the east in Soho Fields in the 1680s.'[6]

This lack of foresight on the part of the Pulteney
family, and the failure of adjoining estates to collaborate
when laying out their land as streets, alleys and building
plots, is still apparent in the street pattern of east Soho
(see p. 54). The building fabric of the Pulteney estate
consisted largely of houses along the east side of Wardour
Street and along a series of narrow streets, alleys and
courts leading east off Wardour Street but with few of
them continuing directly to the adjoining Dean Street

on the Portland and Pitt estates. Indeed, many of these minor thoroughfares terminated abruptly at the estate boundary. The set-back halfway along Meard Street, now a piece of charming urban irregularity, marks the junction of the Pulteney and Pitt estates and confirms that the urban grain of these adjoining estates was not aligned. And the boundary between the two estates explains the fact that Richmond Buildings, although in 1732 lined with large houses, remained a court, with the long, narrow cul-de-sac Richmond Mews running south, servicing the largest and best houses on the west side of Dean Street.

The west end of Richmond Buildings stopped at the Pulteney estate boundary, and the estate did not bother to continue what could have been a fine street west to Wardour Street, the only connection being an exceedingly narrow alley. A similar story is told by St Anne's Court, immediately to the north of Richmond Buildings. The court is in fact formed by two alleys, one running eastwards from the Pulteney estate, which was in existence by 1681 according to Ogilby and Morgan's map, and the other (built by 1690, according to Blome's map) westwards from the Portland estate. The eastern alley marks the northern boundary of the Pitt estate; and the routes of neither align but meet with a set-back that, as in Meard Street, marks the meeting place of two estates.

THE MILITARY GROUND

The Military Ground, to the south of St Anne's Church and King Street, was so called because it was used as an exercise ground in the early seventeenth century. At the time there was a fashion for amateur soldiering –

encouraged by the Privy Council of James I – and citizens would swagger around on the periphery of London armed with pikes and practising drill with cumbersome firelocks. The Military Company of Westminster, founded in 1615, which exercised here was modelled on the Artillery Company based at Spitalfields and which exists now as the Honourable Artillery Company. By the mid 1650s the Westminster Company was in debt and by the early 1660s in negotiation with a former Royalist officer, Baron Gerard of Brandon, Suffolk, who wanted to acquire the two acres of ground for building. Gerard's dealings were long and complex: the freehold of the ground was owned by the Crown and at one point Charles II had an interest in it. By 1676 Gerard obtained not a lease but a grant of the freehold of the ground and the following year leased it to the ever-voracious speculative builder Dr Nicholas Barbon.[7]

Gerard (now Gerrard) Street was laid out in the mid 1670s, running roughly east–west across the centre of the ground with streets formed to connect with existing thoroughfares, notably King Street to the north. Between King Street and the newly laid out Gerrard Street was the free-standing Devonshire House, located to the north of the east end of Gerrard Street and fronting west. The major new north–south connecting street was aligned with Dean Street, and so of some importance, and was consequently named Macclesfield Street in honour of the fact that Gerard was created the Earl of Macclesfield in 1679. Barbon and John Rowley, his partner in this particular venture, soon let building plots to various tradesmen, and work proceeded with the usual amount of litigation that surrounded most of Barbon's cut-throat speculations. Things went relatively smoothly until late 1685, when

Macclesfield was outlawed for his involvement in the Duke of Monmouth's rebellion against James II.

Macclesfield fled the country and his property was forfeited to the Crown. However, it seems the Crown had no desire to stop Barbon's profitable activities on the Military Ground and, after some uncertainty, he was allowed to soldier on. Help should have been at hand in the person of Macclesfield's son, Lord Brandon, who was not accused of being involved in Monmouth's Rebellion. But Brandon had become embroiled in the Rye House Plot of 1683, which aimed at the assassination of Charles II and his brother the Duke of York – the future James II. Brandon was convicted of treason and attainted, and although not executed he was clearly in no position to help Barbon. However, the political landscape changed with incredible and dramatic speed in the turbulent years between Charles II's death in 1685 and William and Mary's Glorious Revolution of 1688. Fortune and power were obtained and reversed at almost the blink of an eye, so that those who had been suddenly thrust from position and possessions could as speedily recover both. In 1687 Brandon had been pardoned by James II and was able to claim his father's estates but – more dramatic still – Macclesfield returned to England in 1688 as a member of the bodyguard of the future William III.

With the accession of William and Mary, Macclesfield and his son rose rapidly in royal favour, but the wheel of fortune turned once again. Macclesfield died in 1694 and his son – heirless – in 1701. In 1728 John Jeffreys bought the freehold of the estate. By this time the houses of the Barbon development were mostly around forty years old and seemingly already showing their age. This appears to be confirmed by the fact that when Jeffreys sold the estate piecemeal between 1735 and 1738, many of its houses had been recently rebuilt or were in the process of reconstruction – typical are numbers 36–39 Gerrard Street, which were rebuilt in 1737. In common with the rest of Soho, the Military Ground had lost much of its late-seventeenth-century fabric by the end of the eighteenth.

THE NEWPORT ESTATE

The Newport estate, to the east of the Military Ground, has a complex and obscure history, entwined with that of the neighbouring Salisbury estate. It seems that much of it belonged until the Reformation to Vale Abbey in Cheshire and then passed through numerous owners until Lord Newport acquired a leasehold interest in the 1630s. He built himself a house on part of the site and obtained the freehold in 1654 from the Salisbury estate. The house remained in family ownership until the promise of profits generated by the speedy development of nearby Soho Fields proved too much. In 1681 Nicholas Barbon extended his operations and purchased Newport's house and gardens for £9,500 and – typical of his methods – instantly started to borrow money for building on the land, using the estate itself as security. He soon acquired over £30,000, accumulating interest, from half a dozen or so different investors. However, Barbon's financial method was only as solid as the individual investors and in this case one went bankrupt in sensational manner, with creditors including Charles II. In consequence the estate was seized by the Crown, all interested parties being obliged to plead their titles to the ground. A lawsuit followed, during which Barbon demolished Newport House, marked out streets and building plots, and let the ground to builders as part of a strategy to gain an income from ground rents. But in 1690 he was compelled by law to find a purchaser for the estate so that creditors could be paid, and it eventually became the property of Sir James Ward. By this time most of the estate had been built upon, in a pretty mean and utilitarian manner, with a series of alleys and courts and a pair of market squares. The best street was Litchfield Street, on the northern edge, which ran diagonally from the south-east corner of Greek Street. By the late nineteenth century the Newport market area had become shabby and in 1879 the Metropolitan Board of Works compulsorily purchased virtually the entire estate for slum clearance and the construction of a wide new road – Charing Cross Road – intended to link Trafalgar Square with Tottenham Court Road and Oxford Street and form part of a system of major new roads, including Shaftesbury Avenue and New Oxford Street, which had been cut through the St Giles Rookery. The system of boulevard-like roads, incorporating the Baroque-style Cambridge Circus as an intersection, was Parisian in manner, bold in concept if essentially mean in execution (see p. 208), and did much to change the character of Soho. This was particularly the case with Shaftesbury Avenue, which destroyed one of the area's principal streets – King Street – and cut off the southern third of Soho. But, despite all this destruction, a few revealing fragments of the Barbon-controlled development survive. In Newport Court, laid out by Barbon on the forecourt of Newport House, numbers 21–24a were built in 1688 on a sixty-year building lease granted by Barbon to a builder named Henry Webb. They are modest houses and the last buildings on the estate to preserve their original elevations (see p. 198). And in Litchfield Street, numbers 24–27 on the north side incorporate much late-seventeenth-century fabric and give an idea of the scale and design of the better Barbon houses, although all have been re-fronted in the eighteenth century and later.

The best place now to gain an idea of the exterior appearance of Barbon-era houses is Denmark Street, where a few remarkable examples survive, some with original elevations. These houses were not part of a Barbon development, but their elevations – with keystones and pronounced string courses above first-floor windows, one with a bold consoled doorcase – are much in the manner favoured by builders operating under his control. Interestingly, Barbon, although a businessman and not a hands-on builder, developed a house style. He clearly realised that the look of a building – simple, modern, classical and apparently well built – had great commercial value and made it easier to let to an ever more discerning public.

THE SALISBURY AND LEICESTER ESTATES

The Salisbury estate, consisting of three large closes that were once part of St Martin's Field, was purchased in 1609–10 by Robert Cecil, the Earl of Salisbury. Much of this land lies to the east of what is now Charing Cross Road and so is not part of modern Soho. But, before the construction of Charing Cross Road, Soho swelled gently to the east at its southern corner – as did the parish boundary of St Anne's, Soho – to reach as far as

St Martin's Lane and the western edge of Covent Garden. Much of the estate's old fabric was swept away by road construction and few pre-nineteenth-century buildings survive, most early buildings being concentrated in the portion of the estate that is now regarded as Soho proper – Little Newport Street leading to Lisle Street and towards Gerrard Street. Currently, the most characterful part lies to the east of Charing Cross Road, where a number of narrow courts – notably Cecil Court and St Martin's Court – connect with St Martin's Lane and contain a fine collection of nineteenth-century buildings housing shops, restaurants, pubs and theatres. Number 5 Great Newport Street, probably built in the 1670s, is the last surviving house on the north side of what in the early eighteenth century was one of the grandest streets in the area; in 1720 John Strype stated that its north side 'hath far the best Buildings, and is inhabited by Gentry'.[8] Sadly, the original character and importance of this house are almost impossible to recognise. In the 1930s it was faced in a jazzy Art Deco manner with glazed black tiles. But it does still contain the substantial remains of its original fine, large-scale staircase.

To the west of the Salisbury estate was the Leicester estate, stretching as far west as Wardour Street and Whitcomb Street, with Leicester Fields at its centre. The land had been in monastic and then royal ownership until it was acquired in 1630 by Robert Sidney, the 2nd Earl of Leicester, who built his mansion here between 1632 and 1636. In the late 1660s Leicester, perhaps inspired by the development in grand style of nearby St James's Square, conceived the idea of building along the sides of Leicester Fields to transform it into a somewhat informal, although generously scaled, high-class residential square. A building licence was acquired in 1670 and construction work soon started, through the usual mechanism of granting leases with covenants to a variety of speculative builders. In the manner of St James's Square, simplicity, uniformity and grandeur of scale were aimed at – along with sound construction. Each house was to be three storeys high (excluding cellars and 'cocklofts'), the main walls constructed of brick, their frontages (none less than eighteen feet wide) continuous and ranging in straight lines, windows and doors uniform and all the fronts ornamented with 'one strong and proporconable Balcony'. The piers between windows were to be 'broader than the half of window or doore next adjoining' and the windows in the top storeys square, and no shops could be set up fronting the square without the earl's licence.[9] To a degree these estate controls were inspired by the Building Act of 1667, which had been drawn up to guide the reconstruction of the City of London after the Great Fire. But such strictures – and the design formulae they enshrine for the construction of uniform and regular houses and urban places – are a reminder that eighteenth-century good building practice was rooted in the regulations that governed the more ambitious speculative developments in late-seventeenth-century London.

All obvious traces of these late-seventeenth-century houses around Leicester Square have long gone, with perhaps just a few house plots and elevations in Irving Street – running south-east off the square – surviving as a faint echo of the early development. The best early remaining fabric on the estate is in Lisle Street, named after one of the earl's subsidiary titles; the west part, originally a court off Wardour Street, was laid out in 1682, and the eastern part in 1792 on the site of the garden and outbuildings of the then recently demolished Leicester House. The seventeenth-century houses on the west portion of Lisle Street have all gone, but most of the 1790s houses on the north side of the east part of the street survive, along with a few at the east end of its south side. The houses are of good, simple and uniform design, many originally with shop fronts. The development was undertaken by a banker of Covent Garden named Thomas Wright, but exactly whose money Wright was investing has never been established. However, to judge from the location of his office, it could well have been profits made by London's booming sex industry, one of the city's most valuable trades in the late eighteenth century.[10] It is perhaps not a coincidence that the existing portion of Lisle Street was by the 1790s a popular working address for the area's prostitutes (plates 6 and 15).

Estates and closes west of Wardour Street

Wardour Street, formerly Colman Hedge Lane, is far older than Soho. As we have noted, anciently it was an important route connecting Tyburn Road, or the road to Uxbridge, as Oxford Street was known, to the royal quarter of Westminster and Whitehall. But perhaps most significantly for the growth of Soho, this ancient lane was also an important boundary between different parcels of land, of field closes and estates in different ownership.

To the west of Colman Hedge Lane were numerous small estates stretching as far as Swallow Street (Regent Street). Many of these estates related, in their boundaries, to fields or closes of sixteenth-century origin or earlier – although it is important to bear in mind that field and estate boundaries were not necessarily synonymous. Some of the larger closes were divided among several estates, while substantial estates acquired, wholly or partially, several smaller closes.

Some of these boundaries are still reflected, most vividly, in the street pattern of this part of Soho. For example, Bridle Lane, running north–south between Beak Street and Brewer Street, represents the boundary between Windmill Field and, to its west, Gelding Close, whose south edge is marked by the west end of Brewer Street. Similarly, the western part of what is now Beak Street – originally part of a pathway or bridle route that existed from at least the late sixteenth century – denotes the boundary between Mulghay Close on the south and Six Acre Close on the north. The cramped scale and sometimes tortuous pattern of these west Soho streets, alleys and courts are due, in part at least, to the irregularly shaped boundaries of the fields, closes and numerous small estates that echo in the existing urban layout.[11]

Each of these estates had its own ambitions, resources and chronology of development and many operated with scant regard to neighbours – which explains why both Rupert Street and Great Marlborough Street originally did not fully connect to neighbouring thoroughfares laid out on land under different control. Land ownership was the defining issue, and in Stuart and early Georgian London the authorities could – just about – control aspects of construction through Building Acts, or prevent building when it was deemed to be anti-social. But they could neither impose a uniformity of urban design in a bid to create visual harmony nor legislate to enforce a master plan in which beauty and utility were balanced; nor could they ensure that the activities of the individual estates were co-ordinated so that main thoroughfares connected and – aesthetically – that new areas like Soho were more than merely a sum of their parts.

The visionary plans for the City of London after the Great Fire of 1666 were all quickly abandoned because their execution was beyond the legal and financial authority of the royal court, to whom they had been submitted. This particular failure illustrates the general point. At least for the City there had been an aspiration for an overall master plans, but for Soho west of Wardour Street there had been none; and even its eventual set pieces – Golden Square and Great Marlborough Street – were not bold in their ambitions but largely the initiative of speculating builders or financiers whose concerns were only for the plots, or at the very most the estate, on which they worked.

To understand the nature of the growth of this part of Soho it's essential to know something about its ancient field pattern and land ownership in the crucial decades after the Restoration of 1660, when Soho started to take on its current form.

At the time of the Dissolution of the Monasteries Henry VIII coalesced the land he had acquired from religious houses west of Wardour Street into the vast Bailiwick or Manor of St James. Some of it, divided into numerous parcels reflecting ancient ownership or field boundaries – often defined by time-honoured footpaths or thoroughfares – was retained by the king for his own use, and that of his successors. But much was leased to a wide range of tenants, who tended to change, certainly in the early days, often in quite rapid succession.[12] The easiest way to appreciate these different parcels of land and estates within west Soho and discern their varied and distinct characteristics is to look at the most important ones individually.

DOGHOUSE CLOSE

A field of about five and a half acres, defined on the north by Tyburn Road, on the south by Colman Hedge Close, on the east by Colman Hedge Lane and on the west by Little Gelding's Close, the boundary of which was just to the east of Poland Street. The land had been part of the Hospital of Burton St Lazar until it was surrendered to the Crown in 1536. The military Order of Saint Lazarus was founded by Crusaders in 1119 as a leper hospital in Jerusalem and its original aim was to care for lepers and protect pilgrims in the Holy Land. It operated a leper hospital at Melton Mowbray, and perhaps one in Soho Fields. In 1629 the close formed part of the jointure settled on Queen Henrietta Maria by her husband Charles I. In 1661 the queen leased the close to the Earl of St Albans, who in 1673 sublet it to Joseph Girle, a most active Soho speculator, who in 1683 let land to James Pollett. Through all these manoeuvrings the land remained Crown freehold, so in 1698 William III was able to grant it to his favourite, the Earl of Portland.

COLMAN HEDGE CLOSE

This was a six-acre field bounded on the east by Colman Hedge Lane and on the north by Doghouse Close, on the west by Windmill Field and on the south by the north side of what is now Brewer Street. The close had been owned by a religious establishment, probably the Dean and Chapter of St Paul's Cathedral, until 1455, when it was sold to a brewer. Consequently at the time of the Dissolution, being already in private ownership, it was not confiscated by the Crown.

In 1572 the close was acquired by a goldsmith named John Denham, who soon sold it on to a brickmaker whose family sold it in 1630 to Sir Edward Wardour, an official in the Exchequer. By 1685 there was a scattering of buildings over the close, particularly along the western edge abutting Colman Hedge Lane. The close's building potential, combined with the progress being made in the development of Soho Square, encouraged Sir Edward's grandson in 1685 to grant a lease on it to a consortium of builders who undertook to 'improve it by building'.[13]

The leading, and most interesting, member of the consortium was James Pollett, a cook turned speculating builder. Pollett had already acquired leases on parts of Doghouse Close and neighbouring Little Gelding's Close, which also abutted Colman Hedge Close. As a Catholic he had suffered the loss of certain rights and civil liberties, but the brief reign of James II offered him unprecedented business opportunities. In 1685 he started building in Edward Street, running west off Wardour Street – no doubt named in honour of Edward Wardour. But it was Berwick Street that was to be Pollett's greatest achievement. It was planned as a fine and noble street, the houses at the centre of its east side being given arcaded ground floors in order to form one edge of a spacious and architecturally impressive marketplace, as at Covent Garden Piazza. Unlike most of his contemporary speculators Pollett was thinking big and was intent on giving this part

of Soho a significant urban ornament that could also be
a money-spinner. In 1687 he obtained from the king the
rights to the hay market then held in nearby Haymarket
Street, and the following year obtained a second royal grant
allowing him to transfer the hay market to his leasehold
land in Soho, which would be 'fitt to receive the ... Carts,
wagons or Waines of hay and straw and for the keeping of
the said market'.[14] This gave Pollett a valuable monopoly
and he wasted not a moment. He managed to get the
south portion of Berwick Street under way the year he
received the first royal grant, and by the choice of name
made his allegiance most clear. The Duke of Berwick was
James II's illegitimate son, so by honouring this minor
scion of the royal family Pollett was presumably hoping
to hitch himself firmly to the Catholic-friendly court of
his king and patron. But Pollett had made a big mistake.
With the accession of the Protestant William and Mary
he found himself persecuted for being a 'professed papist',
and in 1690 both market grants from James II were can-
celled. This, predictably, led to the collapse of the Berwick
Street hay market. But evidently works had started by
1690, because thirty years later John Strype, in his *Survey
of the Cities of London and Westminster* of 1720, noted that
'about the Middle of this street is a Place designed for a
Hay Market ... with some Houses built Piazzo wise, and
sustained by Stone Pillars'.[15] Presumably it was in order
to accommodate this proposed marketplace that Broad
(now Broadwick) Street, when it was subsequently laid
out, was – for Soho – so extraordinarily broad. It is not
known when the fragments of this ruined project were
finally cleared away, but to judge by existing buildings all
must have gone by the 1820s.

But the accession of William and Mary did not com-
pletely destroy Pollett's ambitions for his leasehold land
in Soho. In 1689, on part of Little Gelding's Close, he laid
out Poland Street, with building starting during the first
decade of the eighteenth century. Pollett named his new
street not after a royal patron but after a famous inn that
stood nearby on Oxford Street.[16] Pollett died in 1703, but
his vision for Berwick Street and Poland Street did not
die with him. His executors completed Poland Street, the
eastern part of Broad Street and, in 1707, pushed Berwick
Street north to the Tyburn Road from the arcaded buildings of the abandoned market, working in conjunction
with the new estate owner, the Duke of Portland. It must
have been this portion of Berwick Street that John Strype
had in mind in 1720 when, in his *Survey*, he described it
as 'a pretty handsome strait Street, with new well built
Houses, much inhabited by the French'.[17]

THE MILLFIELD

The eleven and a half acres known as the Millfield –
located between Swallow Street/Regent Street on the
west, Little Gelding's Close on the east, Foubert's Place
on the south and Tyburn Road/Oxford Street on the
north – were part of a large amount of land in and
near north-west Soho that had belonged to the Mercers'
Company until the Reformation, when it passed to the
Crown. The Millfield was presumably named after a mill
on the nearby Tyburn River or Brook.

The Mercers' former estate included several parcels of
land which subsequently fell under the control of various
freeholders and leaseholders who in the seventeenth and

eighteenth centuries played key roles in the making of
Soho. Most significant among their creations was Great
Marlborough Street.

The Millfield formed part of the former Mercers' land
that William Maddox, a Merchant Taylor, purchased in
1622 from a City brewer. In 1664 it was settled on Maddox's son Benjamin, who in 1670 leased it for sixty-two
years to James Kendrick, who immediately started
granting subleases on the Millfield to speculating builders. Things seemed to have moved fast, especially along
existing routes through the field; for example, the ancient
footpath between Marylebone and Piccadilly (now Kingly
Street), part of which formed the eastern border of the
Millfield, was soon lined with houses.

Less accessible portions of the estate languished a
little, but James Pollett's exertions to the east and south
acted as a great stimulus. An investor named James Steel
had leased five acres at the east end of the Millfield that
adjoined Pollett's leasehold land, and in 1704 he subleased
these five acres to a carpenter and speculating builder
named Joseph Collens. This was a wise move. Collens
was one of Pollett's executors and cut from the same
cloth. He promptly laid out Great Marlborough Street,
wide and majestic and intended to be one of the finest
streets of west Soho. It was also, subtly but significantly,
intended to improve the status of the neighbouring leasehold estate formerly owned by Pollett for which Collens
had partial responsibility. Indeed, a plan emerged to
develop the two estates jointly – and in fact the extreme
east portion of Great Marlborough Street was built on
land controlled by Pollett's executors.[18]

LITTLE GELDING'S CLOSE

Little Gelding's Close was also, until 1536, part of the large estate owned by the Mercers' Company. It was bounded by Tyburn Road to the north, and included the south side of the Tyburn Road frontage, running down to Broadwick Street and encompassing the land forming that street's south frontage. The close was very narrow and from west to east stretched little more than 150 feet. In 1671 it was purchased by James Collens. Things now become a little complex. Collens almost immediately leased the ground to John Allen, a Soho bricklayer and speculating builder, for a term of sixty-two years. But in April 1679 Collens and his son William sold the freehold of the close to Sir Benjamin Maddox, whose interest was subject to Allen's lease. Although Allen did not build, neighbouring building initiatives in Soho no doubt gave his lease an enhanced value and it was taken over by James Pollett, who laid out Poland Street. By his will of 1715 Maddox left the freehold of the close to his grand-daughter Mary Rudland and his other land in St James's Parish to his daughter Mary Pollen. This is typical of the complex web of interests by which late-Stuart and early-Georgian London was developed by ambitious but often under-resourced speculating builders, usually working on a shifting mosaic of small freehold or leasehold estates.[19]

PAWLETT'S GARDEN

Pawlett's Garden, named after the ubiquitous James Pollett (or Pawlett), once formed the western portion of Little Gelding's Close. During the late-Stuart and early Georgian development of west Soho the garden was treated as essentially an independent entity, yet it shared its early history with the close. From 1590 to 1691 it was part of the leasehold estate held from the Crown by the Pulteney family, who in 1694 regained control of the garden, along with part of Windmill Field, when the Crown granted the family's trustees the freehold of the land. There was a condition: they had to set aside part of the land as a burial ground.[20] By this time Pollett had acquired an interest in the land and sold a sublease on an acre at the north end of the garden to the vestry of St James's, Westminster, for that purpose. In 1694 the vestry acquired the freehold of the ground from the Crown. By 1733 the burial ground was full, with part of it in use since 1725 as a site for the parish workhouse. Curiously, a workhouse or poorhouse survived on the site, in various manifestations, until 1913, when its wards were used during the early part of the First World War by Belgian refugees. Apart from the burial ground and workhouse, the significant features of the garden are Dufour's Place, initiated in 1719 by Paul Dufour, and the terrace of houses, built in 1722–3 (now numbers 48–58), forming the west end of the north side of Broadwick Street (see p. 319).

WINDMILL FIELD

This ancient parcel of land extends around modern Great Windmill Street. In the 1580s the ground to the east of that street was in the possession of Widow Golightly; no one now knows how she acquired its ownership. The strip of land measured nearly 600 feet by 100 feet and was probably a memory of the 'medieval open field system of cultivation'.[21] The ground to the west of Great Windmill Street, as far south as Coventry Street, had been owned by the Mercers' Company and was acquired by the Crown in 1536. In 1559 it formed part of the large area in Soho granted by Queen Elizabeth to William Dodington, who in 1561 sold it on to a brewer named Thomas Wilson. The windmill, after which the fields were named and which is shown on the 1585 survey of the area (see p. 20), stood on the site of what is now Ham Yard. By 1700 or so the windmill had gone.

In the 1570s James Poultney (*sic*) became a subtenant of a portion of the Manor of St James and during the following century obtained control of various additional parcels of land, so that by 1660 Sir William Pulteney was in possession of several closes or fields. These included the northern part of Windmill Field, on which Great Pulteney Street and Little Windmill Street and Cambridge Street (now Lexington Street) were built and the Laystall Piece or Knaves' Acre at the east end of the south side of modern Brewer Street. Mulghay Close, or Dog Field, was to the west of Warwick Street. Construction started on parts of this newly assembled estate in the 1660s and continued into the 1720s. Great Pulteney Street became the estate's showpiece, being of a higher style than anything the Pulteneys developed on their estate east of Wardour Street.[22]

SIX ACRE CLOSE AND PESTHOUSE CLOSE

Other small estates in west Soho included Six Acre Close, now with Carnaby Street and part of Kingly Street as its main thoroughfares, and Pesthouse Close, on which parts of Marshall Street and Broadwick Street now stand.[23]

Six Acre Close was defined to the north by what is now Foubert's Place, to the west by the west side of Swallow Street, to the east by Newburgh Street and to the south roughly by Beak Street. According to the *Survey of London*, 'the close was probably formed soon after 1590, when two small adjoining fields until then in different occupation, both came into the leasehold possession of Thomas Poultney'.[24] The freehold of this land had passed during the Dissolution to the Crown, from which in 1668 Sir William Pulteney obtained an extension of his lease to 1723. Soon afterwards the close reverted to its identity as two fields, separated by the ancient path connecting Marylebone to Piccadilly, both under Pulteney control but laid out and developed separately. Much of the land forming the western portion of the close was subleased in 1671 to Roger Looker, a gardener, who built himself a house here and laid out an adjoining market garden. He died in 1685 and his widow quickly sold her sublease to a bevy of purchasers. In 1692–3 the Pulteney family sold its interest in Six Acre Close to pay debts and legacies left by Sir William; the majority of the interest was acquired by William Lowndes.[25]

The story of Pesthouse Close is emblematic of the odd manner of Soho's growth, where small estates evolved in almost insular manner at different times, often with wildly differing aspirations and histories. Having belonged to the Mercers' Company until the Dissolution, the close was open land in 1665 when, during the Great Plague, the Earl of Craven obtained possession for the construction of a pesthouse and burial ground. Subsequently becoming known as Pesthouse Close, the land is now defined to the north by the rear elevations of the buildings on

the east end of Foubert's Place; to the south by the rear
elevations of the buildings on the south side of the west
end of Broadwick Street; to the west by the west side
of Newburgh Street; and to the east by the west side of
Dufour's Place.

Lord Craven, a soldier by profession, was also a Fellow
of the Royal Society. He decided to stay in London as
the plague raged and became involved in a commission
set up to consider the best way to prevent the epidemic
spreading. It was known that the disease was contagious
and that exposure to the dead could prove fatal, so victims were isolated when they displayed symptoms and
the corpses of those who died were treated with extreme
caution and disposed of as quickly as Christian decency
would allow. Craven recommended the construction
of pesthouses – essentially isolation wards – and that
plague pits be removed from human habitations as a
better alternative to shutting victims in their own homes
and cramming bodies into the generally packed parish
churchyards, usually surrounded by houses. Craven's
model pesthouse in the fields of west Soho consisted
of thirty-six small houses for the reception of the sick
and accommodation for a physician and surgeon, all
set within a walled compound. The burial ground was
located on what was to become the junction of Marshall
Street and Beak Street. Some thousands of bodies were
said to have been buried here and the relevant volume of
the *Survey of London* records that 'the discovery in more
recent years [1921] of human bones buried behind no. 41
Beak Street confirms the existence of such a plague pit'.[26]
Number 41 had been the painter Canaletto's lodgings in
the 1740s (see p. 331), and this discovery was made when

his former top-lit studio in the rear yard was demolished in 1921. Curiously Canaletto, when in London, had been working over a plague pit and within the atmosphere of ancient death and decay – a fittingly Venetian experience.

In 1671 Lord Craven bought the freehold of the site of his pesthouse and burial ground from James Baker, whose family had owned the land since 1619. Craven's aim was to keep his buildings intact and the plague pit available for use by St James's, Westminster, and neighbouring parishes if they 'hereafter at any time happen to be visited with the Plague'. But the tide of history in Soho was turning against the preservation of this useful but most gloomy facility. By the 1720s Lord Craven was dead and his 'lazaretto' surrounded by buildings – mostly houses – as neighbouring estates were laid out and built up new streets. This of course meant that the pesthouse's key role as a place of isolation during the visitation of contagious diseases was fatally compromised. Clearly the institution had to go, but there were complications over ownership and the money various institutions and parishes had invested in the place. Also, as houses sprang up around the lazaretto the value of Pesthouse Close increased as building land. Parliamentary approval was required to close and remove the lazaretto, but initially this was not forthcoming. When the Bill was presented by the new Lord Craven there was still a fear that the plague might return and that such buildings and burial pits might yet be needed. It was not until 1733 that Lord Craven made a second attempt, by which time fear of the plague's imminent return had abated; and no doubt residents of houses around the pesthouse – horrified by the thought of it coming back into use – were only too glad to put their weight behind its removal. Lord Craven's second Bill received Royal Assent in April 1734, but only after it was agreed that a replacement pesthouse for the relevant parishes be built in the remote fields of Paddington.

The presence of the pesthouse meant that this land had not, like neighbouring estates, been covered by streets and houses. When the Bill received Royal Assent Craven pushed ahead to build, but the small size of the close and the tardiness of its development presented him with problems. The only option was to lay out streets that connected with the grids already established on neighbouring estates, but since these grids obeyed no overriding or unifying logic, all that could be done was to knit the disparate pieces together in the most elegant way possible. However, this carried additional complications and special agreements had to be made with two of the estates. As the *Survey of London* observes, this was 'unusual in this area of generally haphazard building'.[27] An obvious decision was to continue Broadwick Street west on to Pesthouse Close, but to do this Craven had, in 1735, to persuade William Pulteney, the lessee of the adjoining portion of Broadwick Street, to remove the bar he had erected to separate the two estates. This communication was arguably of equal convenience for Pulteney's tenants, although some sense of privacy was clearly lost, and presumably this is why Craven was obliged to pay the annual tribute of 'one fat buck'.

The Pesthouse Close land was leased by Craven in 1733 and 1734 to two London carpenters who erected houses to generally match – in scale and quality – those built to the west on the Pulteney land of Pawlett's Garden. One of these houses – number 74 (originally 28) – became in 1757 the birthplace of William Blake. Set at right angles to this terrace, on the east edge of the close, Craven organised the construction of a terrace of six houses looking into Dufour's Place that had been initiated in 1719 by Paul Dufour on Pawlett's Garden. Built in the mid 1730s, this handsome terrace survived until the mid 1960s.

The other agreement Craven made was with the executors of William Lowndes, who in the early 1690s had purchased the Pulteney estate's interest in Six Acre Close. Here Craven wanted to extend the existing market, constructed about ten years earlier on the eastern part of Lowndes land, onto Pesthouse Close. Since this was to the mutual advantage of all involved, the market extension took place.

Another obvious decision for Craven was to extend a wide, blind court running north off Silver Street (now the central and east part of Beak Street) to form his estate's main north–south thoroughfare, named Marshall Street after the family's seat at Hamstead Marshall, Berkshire. 'A New Plan of the City of London, Westminster and Southwark', published in 1720 in John Strype's *Survey of the Cities of London and Westminster* (see p. 25), shows this Silver Street court – unnamed – most clearly, as it does the still-open land to its north, described as 'Pest House Ground', surrounded by newly built houses.

During the late eighteenth century the Craven family extended its Pesthouse Close estate to the west by purchasing portions of the Lowndes estate on Six Acre Close. By the 1820s the Cravens owned most of Carnaby market, and the east side of the central portion of Carnaby Street. In 1821 the market and adjoining buildings were demolished and during the following five years handsome if modest uniform terraces of houses and shops were erected on

Ganton Street, leading to Carnaby Street, along the west side of Marshall Street (formerly the west edge of Carnaby market) and on both sides of a newly created street, now Newburgh Street, running parallel with Carnaby Street. In addition, the Craven Chapel was built at the north end of Marshall Street, where it turns to the west to become part of what is now Foubert's Place. Completed in 1821, the brick-built box of a building survives in mutilated form.

GELDING CLOSE

The field that gave west Soho its most significant architectural legacy was Gelding Close, because on this stretch of boggy land Golden Square, one of the principal urban ornaments of the parishes of St James's and of St Anne's, was laid out in the 1670s.

The design of the square was probably the work of Sir Christopher Wren (who signed off a drawing of its plan), advising a consortium of entrepreneurs headed by John Emlyn and James Axtell, who gained royal consent to build in September 1673 and then entered into complex and confrontational legal disputes and mortgage arrangements with the ruthless property developer, speculator, entrepreneur, brickmaker and gambler Isaac Symball and the speculating builder William Partridge, who together erected many of the initial houses, intended to 'accommodate gentry' (see p. 341).

Soho's spatial contrasts

To this day the spatial experience of walking around the west part of Soho is entirely different to that of exploring the area to its east. Soho Square, Dean, Frith and Greek Streets epitomise the classical city ideal of the seventeenth and eighteenth centuries – straight, broad and long streets, an orthogonal grid and dramatic vistas. By comparison the narrow and irregular courts, alleys and cul-de-sacs of west Soho and the Pulteney estate along Wardour Street feel positively medieval. This is, of course, partly due to the fact that the Wardour Street area was developed gradually and in irregular manner from the very early seventeenth century, whereas Soho Fields to its east was pristine until laid out in a grand and coherent way in the 1670s. But the difference must also, in part, be due to the contrasting attitudes of the estate owners. The Soho Fields/Portland estate had the scale to be expansive. The Pitt and Pulteney estates on and near Wardour Street were pinched in scale and, it seems, over the years also pinched in imagination. In 1720 John Strype, in his *Survey of the Cities of London and Westminster*, observed that the houses on Wardour Street were 'very ordinary and ill inhabited'.[28]

In the mid 1960s Ian Nairn well expressed the differences in Soho's character. The area east of Wardour Street, with its 'chequerboard of streets ... hard to tell apart', he called 'High Soho' – a place 'as formal as a minuet though far less innocent'. Soho west of Wardour Street was 'Low Soho ... cosier, shabbier, more winding and more mixed up – council flats and old-established business amongst the *trattorie* and nude bookshops'.[29] Many things have changed in Soho during the last fifty or so years, including the growth of 'Chinatown' around Gerrard Street. But also – thank goodness – much remains the same.

Soho's Social Decline

Soho's slow social decline can be dated to the 1720s and 1730s, when large late-seventeenth-century houses and gardens started to be replaced by smaller houses and courts of modest buildings. This was a gradual process, occasionally contradicted by individual initiatives such as the construction in the mid 1730s of palatial houses in the centre portion of Dean Street (see p. 256). But in the very late eighteenth and very early nineteenth centuries change accelerated, with trade and manufacturing increasing and the area becoming a place of refuge. This was nothing new of course, since, as we saw, Huguenots fleeing France had settled in nascent Soho from the 1680s and created a valuable precious-metals trade. The main difference was that the waves of nineteenth-century immigrants were more desperate and less well equipped to prosper. They were attracted by the low rents charged in some of Soho's multi-occupied houses in its more crowded and less salubrious districts, by the casual employment offered by its manufacturing industries and by its growing cosmopolitan atmosphere as a place of entertainment, with restaurants and markets providing other potential sources of income.

Charles Dickens captures some of the atmosphere in Soho in the 1830s, as it retreated from gentility to trade, manufacturing and multi-occupation. In *Nicholas Nickleby*, published in 1838–9, Dickens describes the lodgings of the

erratic Newman Noggs, a bankrupt and alcoholic, who
was presumably, in the readers' estimation at least, a typical denizen of Soho's backwaters. The lodgings – in either
Beak Street, Carnaby Street, Cambridge (now Lexington)
Street or Broad Street – were 'in that quarter of London
in which Golden Square is situated' in 'a bygone, faded,
tumble-down street, with two large irregular rows of tall
meagre houses, which seem to have stared each other
out of countenance years ago'. Dickens also encapsulates
the social history of these 'sombre streets ... where the
houses were once fair dwellings in the occupation of
single families, but have, and had, long deteriorated into
poor lodgings let off in rooms'. The 'common staircases'
of such houses, were, observed Dickens, 'like a tributary
channel to the street'.[1] Dickens knew Soho well because
as a child he used often to visit his uncle, Thomas Culli-
ford Barrow, who lived at 10 Gerrard Street.

The cholera outbreak of 1854 in and around Broad/
Broadwick Street reveals the poverty and overcrowding
of the west part of Soho. This street had long been poor,
on the periphery of a large eighteenth-century slum bordering Swallow Street. This ramshackle area had been
reduced in scale by the construction of Regent Street
during the 1820s and by various contemporary rebuildings
around Carnaby Street, notably Newburgh Street and
its environs (see p. 358). But the cholera outbreak, at the
time reported and analysed in detail, made it clear that
poverty remained deeply ingrained there. The analysis
was confirmed by Dr John Snow, a surgeon and pioneering epidemiologist based at 44 Frith Street, who held that
cholera was largely waterborne and not the result of a
mystic miasma of 'tainted' or noxious air, as many at

the time believed. Snow was puzzled by the fact that the people living around Broad Street were particularly hard hit by the disease. He investigated the circumstances, observed they were using the same public pump in Broad Street and deduced that it was the corrupted water from the pump that was spreading the disease.

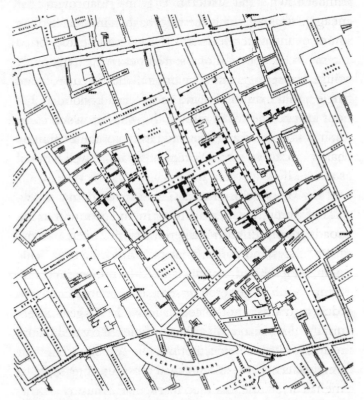

John Snow's map locating outbreaks of cholera in west Soho in the autumn of 1854.

The map Snow produced, documenting the outbreaks of cholera, offers a portrait of the Broad Street slum.

Many – probably most – of the poorer households in the vicinity used the Broad Street pump and Snow's map reveals that many of these were located at the west end of Broad Street, in Marshall Street, in the courts and alleys between Marshall Street and Carnaby Street, and in Berwick Street and the narrow streets around it. Snow managed to get the Broad Street pump disabled and the epidemic decreased dramatically. He then investigated the source of the water dispensed from the pump and found it came from a portion of the Thames particularly badly polluted by sewage. Snow's work in Soho led to profound changes in the disposal of waste water in London and in cities around the world, and in the ways in which clean water was sourced and protected from contamination by sewage or decaying bodies in tightly packed urban burial grounds.

A few years before the 1854 cholera epidemic a new wave of immigrants started to arrive in Soho, to join the poor Irish and English clustered mainly in the narrow streets, alleys and courts west of Wardour Street. This group, which has done much to form the character of modern Soho, largely comprised Italian political and economic migrants who started to arrive in large numbers from the 1840s as a result of the turbulence created by the struggle for Italian unification and liberty. But, rather than being just economic and political refugees, they seem to have had an artistic – or more particularly musical – bent. Most of them were from the south and they carried their deep-rooted traditions with them into the streets and courts of Soho. Many found employment in the hotel and restaurant industry and in 1886 were in a position to promote and protect their work by establishing the

Società Italiana Cuochi-Camerieri in Gerrard Street, a club that offered members convivial gatherings, helped them find jobs and provided financial aid if they fell ill.

Social, political and military upheavals in Europe during the second half of the nineteenth century all made their mark on Soho, which became a favoured London location for foreigners seeking refuge. The Franco-Prussian War of 1870 provoked a wave of refugees, as did the collapse of the Paris Commune the following year, which ultimately drove the poets Paul Verlaine and Arthur Rimbaud, locked in a deadly affair, to seek solace, in the winter of 1872–3, in the bars at the west end of Old Compton Street. In these, absinthe was readily available, as were their drugs of choice, opium and hashish.[2]

During the 1880s Soho's Jewish population – which had had a synagogue on the Pulteney estate from 1761 and a Free School at 60 Greek Street from 1853 – was rapidly enlarged by an influx of Jewish families fleeing persecution in Russia and Russian-occupied Poland. These families settled around Berwick Street, which was a Yiddish-speaking area by the 1890s, with 70 per cent of its shops and businesses Jewish-owned or -operated, cohabiting with but replacing the slightly earlier Italian market community. What remains of the Berwick Street market, now just a huddle of stalls at the south end of the street, is a memorial to the arrival and residence of these foreign communities in Soho. At their height, in the late nineteenth and very early twentieth centuries, the street market and shops in Berwick Street possessed great vitality and were famed as the only place certain exotic foreign fabrics and foods could be found in London. It was the epitome of the cosmopolitan.

Berwick Street market also, of course, had its dark side – most obviously the cut-throat competition and the poverty just lurking below its colourful and confident veneer. A manifestation of this dark side was the desperate 'schleppers' who haunted the street and who, for some, made shopping there a harrowing experience. The word is Yiddish and once meant a Jewish peddler, but in Berwick Street, from the 1880s, it meant a forceful, fast-talking tout positioned outside a shop whose sole goal was to drag passers-by inside in the hope of making a sale. Thelma Benjamin explained the experience of falling among schleppers in her 1930 London shopping guide: 'if you stop and look in the window, you will find a hand on your arm and a persuasive voice in your ear, and, unless you are very firm, you will be led into the shop, from which there seems to be no escape except by purchase!'[3] And if a purchase was not made, or a solicitous tout ignored, it was more likely than not that the hapless female shopper would be bombarded with insults of a most personal nature. It is significant that when Gordon Selfridge opened his vast shopping emporium on Oxford Street in 1909, one of his selling points was that female customers would be able to wander all day, at their leisure, through his store without being importuned in the slightest by his staff. This was clearly seen, at the time, as something to boast of.

Charles Booth in Soho's mean streets

A portrait of the condition of life in Soho's streets and courts in the 1880s is offered by the 'poverty maps' produced by the social reformer and philanthropist Charles

Booth that were published in 1889 with his *Life and Labour of the People*. The maps colour-code London streets according to the economic status of their inhabitants and, to a degree, their physical condition. Booth devised seven categories, gold denoting 'Upper-middle and upper classes' who were 'Wealthy' and, at the other extreme, black the 'lowest class', which Booth described as 'vicious' – probably meaning not savage but sunk in vice – and 'semi-criminal'. Between came, after black, dark blue indicating 'Very poor, casual. Chronic want.' Then light blue for 'Poor 18 shillings to 21 shillings [income per] week for a moderate family'; purple for 'Mixed. Some comfortable, others poor'; pink for 'Fairly comfortable. Good ordinary earnings', and red for 'Middle-class, well-to-do' (plate 8).

On the Soho streets and courts bounded by Regent Street, Charing Cross Road, Oxford Street and Leicester Square no gold was shown on Booth's map. There was red, but mostly along the periphery of Soho – on Regent Street, Oxford Street and a few small groups along the south edge of Soho around Piccadilly Circus and Leicester Square. The only area of red in the body of Soho was the south side of Great Marlborough Street. A lot of Soho was coloured pink, including Soho Square and Golden Square and much of Frith Street, Dean Street, Gerrard Street, Great Pulteney Street and Brewer Street.

Soho contained no areas of black, but there were some 'very poor' areas marked dark blue, notably west of Broad Street, around Marshall Street and Carnaby Street, east of Greek Street, in a stable-yard immediately south of Meard Street and to the north-west end of Poland Street. The rest of Soho, in extent about equal to the area coloured pink, was coded light blue and purple, which denoted areas where the inhabitants were poor but largely in work or where the streets and houses were of 'mixed' occupation, with the reasonably 'comfortably' off living in very close proximity with the poor. Light-blue, or 'poor', streets included St Anne's Court and Noel Street. Purple-coloured streets were numerous and included Lexington Street, Broadwick Street, Berwick Street, most of Poland Street, Greek Street, parts of Old Compton Street, Richmond Buildings, Meard Street and much of Wardour Street and the Newport market area.

Booth resurveyed Soho on 5, 7 and 23 October 1898 to see if his colour-coding of nine years earlier needed to be revised. He walked the streets in the company of a local policeman, PC A. Gunn, who acted as guide and, to a degree, informant and guardian; and the detailed notes and observations he made – seemingly written up in situ by his unpaid secretary, George Herbert Duckworth – were used for the third edition, by now entitled the *Life and Labour of the People in London*, which appeared between 1902 and 1903 as a multi-volume publication.[*]

Booth's and Duckworth's succinct observations of 1898 flesh out the information on his maps and throw a vivid light on aspects of life in late-nineteenth-century Soho. A recurring theme in Booth's street-by-street observations is the large numbers of 'foreigners' and Jews living in the area, the rich mix of activities and the huge number of restaurants and 'foreign clubs'. The foreigners were presumably mostly Italians and French and Polish and Russian Jews with perhaps a few Greeks, continuing the

---

[*] Booth's notebooks are preserved in the Booth Archive in the London School of Economics.

tradition of the Greek community that had constructed an Orthodox church in Hog Lane as early as 1677.

In Lisle Street, on 23 October, Booth and Duckworth noted 'many foreigners, especially at its east end', along with 'French chefs and Scullery men'. They also recorded numerous 'small wholesale shops working for West End houses'. Booth confirmed the street as pink, 'as in map'.[4] In Leicester Square they noted 'houses with tailors', and Booth downgraded it from red to pink. Leicester Place, they observed, contained the Hotel de Paris, the Queen's Hotel and the Hotel de l'Europe, and was 'a street where foreigners playing at the music halls lodge' and where 'you will see troupes of dogs ... or dancing bears come out of the house doors'. Little Newport Street had a 'much better character now than formerly' because a 'Vestry man with a keen scent for brothels has driven prostitutes to the east side of Charing X Road & Shaftesbury Avenue, and out of the parish [of St Anne's, Soho]'. So this street Booth upgraded to pink from purple. Nearby Newport Court, however, remained a street of 'poor' lodgers – 'rough and some thieves' – living over shops occupied by 'general dealers'. The road, noted Booth and Duckworth, was 'dirty', which Booth usually took as an indication not just of poverty but also of moral decay. Of Gerrard Street the pair did little more than comment that it contained many 'societies and clubs', but in Macclesfield Street, which used to have 'well known brothels on both sides', they noted that it 'looked as if there was one still'.[5] Greek Street apparently had 'no poor', was 'better than formerly' with 'a good class' living above its shops and, like Frith Street, contained 'many chefs'. Booth upgraded the street from purple to pink. Kettner's restaurant was the most significant feature for Booth in Romilly Street (in 1898 still known as Church Street), but they also noted 'brothels', although most had been 'driven out' during the previous ten years to the 'Tottenham Court Rd district'. Frith Street was 'mixed', with 'many prostitutes and bullies', and indeed 'a noted restaurant for bullies [prostitutes' protectors] on east side'.[6] Along the north end of Frith Street – which was 'better' than its south end – were tailors, watchmakers and jewellers.[7] Dean Street contained a mixture of 'wholesale firms & dwelling houses', and while there were 'some reputed brothels' there were 'fewer clubs than formerly' and its 'character ... a little better' than that of Frith Street. A bit more detail was added later in the survey. The mixed trades in Dean Street included 'jewellers, printers', with the rent of 'front' rooms being '9 shillings or 10 shillings and 14 shillings for a first floor room'. In Old Compton Street there was also 'a large proportion of foreigners ... shops and restaurants' with 'houses off ... used by prostitutes'.[8] In Bateman Street there were silversmiths. Meard Street, they noted, 'has become a Jews haunt ... has been so for the last 4 or 5 years', some having 'come here from Whitechapel and some from abroad', with 'a great many children in the street, well fed, dirty, well clothed'. Booth decided to downgrade this street to purple and light blue rather than just purple as before.[9] Richmond Buildings was 'a colony of waiters who come home late, make fair but rather uncertain money, gamble a great deal & never seem to go to bed'.[10] St Anne's Court was 'rough', with 'the buildings holding many casuals' and 'rough looking women at the entry, cock-

ney Irish'.[11] Exploring this section of Soho led Booth and
Duckworth to note that 'back cottages are a feature of
Soho and many workshops and dwellings are built ...
whose existence would not be guessed from the street
front'.[12] Soho Square was 'the only square in London
with four corners!' observed Booth with, seemingly,
some excitement – 'the streets run out of the centres of
the sides instead of the corners'. It contained 'hospital
and business houses' but very few people living in it.[13]

He also pondered why Soho Square, along with
Golden Square nearby to the south-west, was not
'opened to the children of the neighbourhood' since
there was a 'great want of open space' in Soho, the
only appreciable area being the 'small churchyard of
St Anne's'. Clearly, in 1890s Soho the old practice of
limiting access to squares to all but a small number of
key-holders – usually those living around them – continued. So essentially Soho's squares remained private
places for the privileged few.

Of the west and south-west portions of Soho, which
Booth and Duckworth inspected on 6 and 7 October,
they noted that the hotels and restaurants at the junction
of Great Windmill Street, Coventry Street and Arundel
Street were 'for outsiders' and 'patronised by foreigners
... largely ... this last year by Americans'. After stating
that the husband of 'Marie Lloyd [the then internationally
famous music-hall star who had been born in Hoxton] ...
one Courtney keeps a public house on the west side' of
Rupert Street, Booth and Duckworth seemingly quote
PC Gunn: 'She's a shady lot & in with the bookmakers.'
Gunn goes on to reveal that in a raid the previous night
on a betting club in Denman Street police had expected

to take Courtney in, 'but for a wonder he was not there'.
Marie Lloyd, her family and some of her friends were,
seemingly, part of the upper-end gangster fraternity of
London's 'swell mob'.*

Booth and Duckworth recorded that in Rupert Court
there were 'many French', and although once a renowned
'den of prostitutes', many had moved out although 'some
still remain'.[14] Green's Court had 'very many Jews' and
the 'smell of fried fish'; Little Crown Court was 'all
foreigners',[15] while Berwick Street was 'mixed', with 'a
restaurant' at the north end being a brothel. There were
also 'many silversmiths, platers, engravers' and its southern
portion was 'a street market' with 'barrows and shops'.[16]
In Denman Street were 'two noted brothels – now empty',
while in Ham Yard were to be found a 'soup kitchen &
hospice founded in 1846, rebuilt in 1883', with none living
in the yard 'except those over the soup kitchen' and the
rest of the buildings 'factories & advertising agents offices'.
After these entries on the different streets of Soho Booth
and Duckworth offered some 'General Remarks', including on the presence of many foreigners, the 'in and out'
habits of the area's prostitutes, the 'many Jew children' to
be seen but 'few of other nations', and the 'late hours &
gambling habits of waiters'; but all in all they concluded
that there was 'less roughness' than ten years earlier. PC
Gunn added a comment on the district's Jewish inhabitants.
He claimed that there was no longer any 'overcrowding' in

---

* Marie Lloyd had married Percy Charles Courtney in November 1887
and by May the following year the couple had a daughter. The marriage
proved unhappy. Courtney and Lloyd's families and friends shared a
mutual dislike. He became addicted to alcohol and gambling and was,
when drunk, violent and threatening. By 1894 the pair had separated.

Soho 'except among the Jews', who 'will always occupy all four corners of a room & take in a lodger to fill the centre'.

It is possible to delve deeper into the curious pattern of life suggested by Booth's, Duckworth's and Gunn's colourful observations by reference to the census returns for 1891. These, in fact, evoke a yet more startling image of life in Soho. Take Richmond Buildings, for example. Most of numbers 3, 4, 5 and 6 – among the five-storey 1730s houses demolished in the early 1970s – appear to have operated as a single common lodging house. These institutions, if improperly run, were the bane of Victorian London, often squalid and sometimes little more than low brothels. But if properly organised they provided cheap although cramped accommodation for working people with low earnings who lacked the means to acquire more permanent or private lodgings. The 'head' of this lodging house may have been Martin Rosenberg, a Swedish-born thirty-eight-year-old who gave his trade as a 'tailor' – certainly he is listed before the 'lodgers' in the census for 3 Richmond Buildings, but it is possible the lodging-house keeper lived nearby. Rosenberg was married to a thirty-four-year-old London-born woman named Amelia and they had four children aged one to seven. Their 'household' also included two young and single female servants – one born in Denmark, the other in London. In number 3 Richmond Buildings seventeen lodgers are listed; in numbers 4 and 5 there are another seventeen lodgers and in number 6 a further eleven. All were male, suggesting an air of propriety, and all were single. In number 6 there was, in addition to the lodgers, another family consisting of a sixty-nine-year-old widow named Sarah Anne Olden, a servant, a seven-year-old grandson and what appears to be this family's own lodger – a twenty-three-year-old 'Taylor Coat maker'. It is possible that Sarah Anne Olden was the lodging-house keeper. Certainly this was a job often undertaken by elderly, but presumably still robust, widows. The forty-five lodgers listed as being in residence in these four houses on the night of the census offer a fascinating vignette of an aspect of Soho life in the last decade of the nineteenth century. Most are in their twenties and thirties, with only a few in their fifties. Most – seemingly fourteen – came from Sweden and around ten from Germany, but they also hailed from Denmark, Switzerland, France and Guernsey. Very few were London-born. The occupations they pursued were varied but generally humble. There were many tailors and coat makers, but also jewellers, a watchmaker, a billiard-table maker, a cook/confec-tioner, a photographer, a few carpenters, a hotel porter and three waiters. But this may well not have been the total number of lodgers in these four houses. There is also a list included in the census after the inhabitants of number 6 Richmond Buildings have been enumerated. It says '4 and 5 R' – an afterthought? – and the names, ages, occupations and origins of another seventeen male lodgers have been added, including six more Swedes and a number of Germans.[17]

Can sixty-two lodgers and two 'families' totalling twelve people really have lived in these four five-storey houses, each with a maximum of sixteen or seventeen rooms if basements, closets and garrets were occupied, and perhaps a dark and dingy outbuilding or two? With people sharing rooms – even beds – as was usual in the poorer type of common lodging houses, the answer is certainly – and sadly – yes, although it is hard to imagine quite how the sanitary arrangements were managed. Many people existed like this in late-Victorian London; and indeed a similar picture is revealed in the censuses of 1891 and 1901 for the still-surviving early-eighteenth-century houses in nearby Meard Street (see The Walk, p. 152). It's no wonder Booth and Duckworth observed much coming and going in Richmond Buildings, where the occupants never seemed 'to go to bed'. Many, perhaps, didn't have beds they particularly wanted to go to and preferred to walk the streets or spend most of the night sitting in Soho's seedier gaming or drinking establishments.

Soho in the twentieth century

Soho's history in the early twentieth century was varied, and in many ways represented a world of almost staggering contrasts. Poverty, neglect and desperate sweated industry combined with almost equally desperate frivolity made it a most extraordinary place. As haunt and home of several communities of foreigners, the area from time to time attracted intense interest from the press and the police. For example, in October 1906 the *Illustrated London News* dubbed Greek Street and its environs the 'foreign quarter of London' and the 'haunt of choice rascaldom'.[18] At the same time Inspector McKay of the Metropolitan Police, giving evidence to a Royal Commission, denounced Greek Street as 'the worst street in London'. The Commission was investigating accusations against the police of corruption and bribery related to gambling, prostitution and the persecution of foreigners. When pressed to explain what he meant by this

somewhat surprising statement, McKay stated that
'crowds of people gather there nightly who are ... some
of the vilest reptiles in London'. McKay was not thinking
just of pimps, prostitutes and thieves but also, presumably, of politics. From the 1870s anarchists of foreign
birth – notably Italian and Russian – had settled in Soho
and had become of increasing interest to the government
and police.

McKay's startling accusation started a fight. The Reverend J.H. Cardwell of St Anne's Church took the remark
very personally. He responded with a stout defence of the
hard-working foreign residents of Greek Street, attacked
McKay's 'absurd calumny' and asserted that 'there is not
a single disreputable character in Greek Street'; indeed,
he argued, 'there is scarcely one in the whole of Soho'.[19]
Both these extreme statements were, of course, not
quite the truth. This Cardwell knew well because, while
defending Greek Street's honour, he was also involved
in the battle against Soho's sex industry. He had noted
how respectable workers were 'literally being driven out
of house and home to make room for the traders in vice
who can afford to pay exorbitant rents', and argued that
one house in six in Soho was a 'disorderly house' – a
rather quaint term for a brothel.[20]

Another perspective is offered by Joseph Conrad.
Although an émigré with a fondness for Soho's bohemian life (as revealed by his regular attendance at the
literary dining club in the Mont Blanc restaurant in
Gerrard Street), Conrad had no sympathy for émigré
revolutionaries or anarchists and was no typical bohemian. So his portrait of Soho and adjoining districts as
anarchist enclaves in *The Secret Agent* is most interesting.

The novel was published in 1907 and tells a complex and sleazy tale of political intrigue, espionage for a nameless foreign power, raw terrorism and tragic human nature. Most of the anarchists are not only foreign but also live off the money and compassion of women, while the main character, Adolf Verloc, has a shop in Soho selling pornography and contraceptives. Soho and Fitzrovia are depicted as places of physical, moral and ethical decay – neither picturesquely bohemian nor dramatically criminal – to match the seedy condition of the novel's protagonists. The book was inspired in part by a real Fitzrovia and Soho anarchist, the Frenchman Martial Bourdin, who in 1894 and in most hapless manner blew himself up in Greenwich Park, by mistake and with his own bomb, while making his way to his target, the Royal Observatory.

In the same decade as these differing views of Soho were expressed there started to emerge a certain romance, an *élan* about the area that was, in large measure, to define it for much of the twentieth century. This attitude is reflected in a froth of well-meaning and would-be socially aware publications about what were generally regarded as the tantalisingly wicked and 'foreign' quarter of London. A few are perceptive, many contain nuggets of fascinating information, but most are fairly trite. Typical are *Living London: its work and its play, its humour and its pathos*, published in 1901 and edited by George R. Sims,[21] and Thomas Burke's quasi-autobiographical *Nights in Town*, published in 1915. Burke is good on Soho: 'Soho – magic syllables! For when the respectable Londoner wants to feel devilish he goes to Soho, where every street is a song. He walks through Old Compton

Street and instinctively he swaggers, he is abroad; he is a
dog ... has peeped into the places that are not ... Quite
... you know.'[22] This magic attracted Arthur Ransome,
who in 1904 made a pilgrimage to Hampstead, Chelsea
and Soho to discover and savour London's own bohemia. He was delighted by what he found, particularly
in Soho. Not only 'dark eyes, dark skin, sallow-skinned
faces every where' and a babble of foreign languages, but
also adventurous young Englishmen 'from conventional
homes determined to live in any way other than that to
which they have been accustomed', and who haunted the
area's 'merry' restaurants.[23]

A popular focus for the appreciation of Soho's special
cosmopolitan character was Berwick Street market.
It held spellbinding attractions for many observant or
sensitive early-twentieth-century Londoners, mesmer-
ised by its foreignness. Sophie Cole, in *The Lure of Old
London*, published in 1921, was enthralled by the fact that
the market was 'never dull' and took 'strangers into its
confidence' and, carried away on a wave of romance,
explained that 'the costers' barrows of fruit and flowers
making splashes of colour ... might have stepped straight
out of an Italian canvas'.[24] Virginia Woolf was another
devotee. In her diary for 1915–19 she wrote that 'the stir
& colour & cheapness' of Berwick Street market pleased
'me to the depths of my heart', and she used the experience a few years later in her novel *Jacob's Room*, published
in 1923. Here she writes of the market being 'fierce with
light' in which 'blaze ... raw meat, china mugs and silk
stockings', while 'raw voices wrap themselves round the
flaring gas-jets'. Somewhat awkward imagery perhaps,
but reasonably evocative.[25]

By the mid 1920s Soho had started to benefit from its central position in London's growing theatreland as grander restaurants established themselves, for example *Quo Vadis*, under the inspired direction of Pepino Leoni, from 1926 in Dean Street. Most were owned or operated by Italians, but also in 1926 a demure Belgian lady opened a Brussels-style tea room and cake shop in Frith Street. Her name was Madame Vermeirsch and her establishment was called Patisserie Valerie.

Although in its way dashing, romantic and even beguilingly mischievous, Soho was not generally perceived as stylish or glamorous in a glitzy way like other West End haunts. There remained about it an air of poverty and a sense of darkness, degeneration, mystery and even danger. Horace Wyndham, writing in 1926, struck a rather cynical and world-weary tone when describing Soho in his survey titled *Nights in London*, which claimed to reveal where 'Mayfair makes merry':[26]

> I always think Soho is a corruption of So Low. Yet there is an odd glamour about the district, just as there is about ... the Caledonian Market [but] personally I find Leather Lane more attractive, and better food and drink procurable in the New Cut. Wherever they have their premises – Old Compton Street, Dean Street, Frith Street, Lisle Street, or Wardour Street etc. – the majority of the Soho restaurants affect exotic names, This, of course, is due to their origin, for the proprietors hail from the Balkan States and the United States, from Belgium, France, Greece, Germany, Italy, Palestine, and Switzerland.[27]

Despite this variety, Wyndham proclaimed that 'with

regard to menus and prices, all these places are much of
a muchness'. This dismissive and supercilious attitude
presumably reflects, in authentic manner, the opinion
Mayfair grandees held of 1920s Soho – a strange little
place full of pretentious and artful foreign 'johnnies'.
Wyndham especially had it in for London's attempt
at bohemia: 'nowadays there is no actual Bohemia in
London', although, he conceded, 'there is still a fair
imitation of what passes for one'. For Wyndham, bohemia meant merely 'a community not hide bound by
ordinary conventions. Further, it has no settled address,
but is scattered from Chelsea to St John's Wood, from
Hampstead to Soho.' 'Bohemians' were, according to
the exquisitely patronising Wyndham, 'actors, artists, and
musicians . . . authors and journalists and people generally living "by the sweat of their quotation marks." All
of them are poor, and most of them are comparatively
honest.' The 'rallying points' of this community were
'various restaurants and grill-rooms and clubs and pubs
and beer halls round Shaftesbury Avenue and Leicester
Square', including 'dingy little cook-shops (masquerading
as "restaurants") established in Soho and the purlieus of
Berwick Market'.[28] A good example of a bohemian club
was, according to Wyndham, the Hambone in Ham Yard,
off Great Windmill Street and near Piccadilly Circus: 'it
is very typical of a dozen others in this neighbourhood,
and serves as a convenient port of call for "slips" (as I
have heard them called) that pass in the night', but, in
the opinion of this jaundiced critic, it was 'an entertain-
ing enough haunt, with cabaret concerts much above
the average, given in a big room [reached by means of]
narrow stairs . . . where dragons sprawl on yellow papered

walls'. The membership of the Hambone was 'distinctly catholic', with Sir Woodman Burbidge and Lord Dewar being 'patrons', probably with 'Gordon Selfridge ... together with a host of actors and artists and authors and musicians'. Wyndham also describes the club's setting: 'For some reason I have never fathomed, Ham Yard appears to be rather a haunt of coteries which do most of their business towards the small hours. Thus, in addition to the Hambone itself, the Windmill and the Last Club are also established cheek by jowl.'[29]

Soho's atmosphere, real or imagined, of decadent 'Bohemia' and of danger and decay must have kept a number of travellers and tourists at bay – as well as evidently provoking the amused contempt of superior West Enders. This darkness and bad reputation no doubt derived in part from the 'naughty nineties', when the far-fallen Oscar Wilde – whose disgrace was still a recent memory and warning for some in the 1920s – was known to have frequented male brothels in Rupert Street and to have often dined in louche company at Kettner's in Romilly Street and at the Café Royal, on the edge of Soho in Regent Street.

Keeping all and sundry at arm's length no doubt helped preserve Soho's peculiar character. But Soho was not just about decadence and decay; it was also home to literary and dining clubs, the most famous early example being The Club in Gerrard Street, which flourished in the 1760s and 1770s and whose members included Sir Joshua Reynolds and Edmund Burke (see p. 189). Also in Gerrard Street, but much later, was the dining club in the Mont Blanc restaurant, where writers such as Joseph Conrad and William Galsworthy used to gather (see p. 190). A

trifle later Quo Vadis in Dean Street became home to
the Grubb Club, where writers would meet and artists
would show their work, encouraged by food or 'grub'
vouchers issued by the enterprising proprietor, Pepino
Leoni. This was all good publicity, as revealed by a puff
in the *Daily Express* in 1929 announcing that, with Quo
Vadis and the Grubb Club, Soho had acquired its own
'Academy'.[30] And there were political clubs – some rather
odd. In December 1917 Virginia Woolf's husband Leonard
founded the 1917 Club, based at number 4 Gerrard Street.
Despite its dramatic-sounding name, which was indeed
inspired by the October Revolution in Russia, this was not
a Bolshevik club, more a gentlemen's club on the cheap
for socialists, some of whom were also members of the
Bloomsbury Group.

Soho at war

Physically Soho escaped the Second World War largely
intact, although some stunning buildings were lost – such
as the nave of St Anne's Church, the late-seventeenth-
century Carlisle House, which closed the west end of
Carlisle Street and the western vista from Soho Square,
and a group of good houses (notably 25 and 26) dating
from 1720 in Great Pulteney Street. Indeed, it was during
the war, as bombs wrecked and demoralised large parts
of London, that Soho, with its decaying and overcrowded
Georgian houses and courts, fully realised its potential
as London's vibrant and marginally wayward social
heart. It was now that Soho displayed its sturdy and stoic
character – its 'bottom', as a Regency gentleman might
have observed, its admirable staying power. In its way

it became emblematic of war-torn London. It was not good enough just for life to go on – that was taken for granted – it had to go on with a sense of humour and a sense of style. And that's what happened in Soho.

Carlisle House, built in 1685 in Carlisle Street and destroyed in 1941.

The streets and buildings in south-west Soho, near Piccadilly Circus, became particularly lively and in many cases lurid. As London burned, Soho and its habitués – including many RAF fighter pilots and, later on, members of the US 8th Air Force – enjoyed a prolonged party, fuelled by sex and alcohol. During 1940 RAF pilots and Canadian troops favoured meeting in the Regent Palace Hotel, just north of Piccadilly Circus (recently largely rebuilt but with its fine Art Deco basement bars retained and restored – see p. 311), which became known as the 'Canadian Riding School'. As Tom Clayton and Phil Craig explain in *Finest Hour*, the 'Canadians were not the only boys to get riding lessons there. Up the side streets were clusters of cafes, restaurants and bars.' In Denman Street was a restaurant and nightclub called Chez Moi that was a 'favourite with fighter squadrons', its walls covered with caricatures of pilots drawn by the establishment's resident cartoonist.[31]

Chez Moi survived the war, as did the Regent Palace Hotel, although the latter was hit twice by bombs. What did not survive the war, or certainly did not survive it unscathed, was the nearby and more sophisticated Café de Paris. This restaurant and nightclub opened in 1924 in 3–4 Coventry Street, on the southern edge of Soho near Leicester Square. In the early years of the war it was popular with a smarter set – Guards and cavalry men, RAF and Royal Navy officers from the nearby Admiralty – and had been a haunt in the 1930s of the Prince of Wales, the Aga Khan and Cole Porter when he was in London.

The Café de Paris was in a basement and, when war started, it was believed to be relatively safe, so as bombs fell the bands played on and the smart set continued their revels – no doubt escapist rather than purely hedonistic in nature. The tragic fate that befell the Café seems to epitomise Soho's frantic wartime life. People could drink, chatter, flirt and dance – display humour and style – but there was, in the end, no sure escape from the dreadful reality of brutal and arbitrary death. On the night of 8 March 1941 it was hit in quick succession by two high-explosive bombs. It was packed with people, many of them officers on leave; thirty-four were killed and eighty injured. Among the dead was the bandleader Ken 'Snakehips' Johnson. One of the bombs, after penetrating the upper floors, had detonated just in front of him. The Café was blasted, not burnt, and was restored to look much as it did before the bombs fell. It did not reopen until 1948 and, having weathered numerous post-war vicissitudes, remains in operation.

Although bomb damage was not intensive, Soho was a sad sight when the war ended. Much of its fabric was damaged or even more run down, many houses were overcrowded or contained a wide mix of unlikely uses. But on the west side of Soho the wartime atmosphere of excess continued and by the early 1950s had confirmed Soho as London's intoxicating if seedy clubland. It was a place of wild, louche, often illegal and sometimes dangerous entertainment and also notorious for petty crime and gangsterism. There were the 'Maltese Mafia' and characters such as the Whitechapel Godfather Jack Spot and his partner Billy Hill applying muscle and blade. Most of the crime centred on the growing and ever more organised sex industry, but with drug-'peddling', as it was then called, increasing in scale. These factors were related, of course, and helped to give Soho

a curious sense of identity: a wayward, licentious and
exotic atmosphere that helped fuel its famed phase in
the 1950s and 1960s as London's anarchic quarter, a place
for hard-drinking eccentrics, outsiders and ornery artists
looking for their particular muses. Extraordinary establishments – outlandish and often literally underground,
or at least cavernous in feel – emerged to cater for these
habitués of Soho. Many such bars and drinking clubs are
noted in Jack Glicco's *Madness After Midnight*, published
in 1952, which 'lifts the lid' on Soho's clubs and sex life
in the years just before and immediately after the Second
World War. So racy and explicit is deemed the content
of this little portrait of interwar and post-war Soho
that it's still necessary, when perusing it in the British
Library, to sit at the desk reserved for 'special material' (a
euphemism for pornography and all manner of sadistic
and masochistic publications) beneath the steely gaze
of a librarian.

Glicco was a musician and the clubs with which he
was familiar were clustered around Great Windmill
Street, Denman Street, Kingly Street and Gerrard Street.
In Denman Street, Chez Moi seems to have given way
to the jauntily named Mazurka. Many of the names
of the clubs were predictable – the Ragtime and the
Frivolity – others more strange and suggestive, for
example the Morgue in Ham Yard and the Gestapo Club
(surely a Glicco invention) at the junction of Beak Street
and Kingly Street. Some clubs aimed to serve specific
communities or ethnic groups. The Nest in Kingly Street
'was a favourite haunt of all the famous coloured stars',
but in Glicco's somewhat unfortunate words became
'infested' with a 'number of white women who became

infatuated with some of the negroes'. Another 'coloured club' was the Jigs in Wardour Street, near St Anne's Court, and the 'few white people who went there were', sneered Glicco, 'mostly of low class'.[32]

Ham Yard still thrived in the early post-war years but seems to have shed a good deal of the bohemian affectation that had annoyed Horace Wyndham. Presumably the war years, with their flourishing black market and atmosphere of desperation and exploitation, had introduced an element of viciousness so that, according to Glicco, by 1952 Ham Yard had become known as the Blood Pit. He described it as 'a tiny mews, reached through a narrow entry' and confirmed what Wyndham had noted about the yard's strange nocturnal habits:

> By day it looks sleepy and dilapidated ... But in those years between the wars a strange transformation came over Ham Yard as the clocks struck 11 p.m. From ten rooms in ten houses music would blare forth into the night ... and through the night they played until four in the morning, in the Avenue Club, in the Pavilion, the Oak, the Top Hat, the Hambone, Mother Hubbard's, the Morgue and others. And into Ham Yard ... came the motley crew of West End night-lifers. There were smart people in evening dress and jewels; prostitutes and their clients and prostitutes seeking clients; toughs and roughs ...[33]

Ham Yard survives but all its old buildings have gone, replaced by recently completed and somewhat bland architecture that has transformed this part of Soho's old bohemia into just one more West End backwater, complete with rather corporate-looking hotels and restaurants. It's not terrible – in fact, with its trees and York-stone paving it's rather congenial – but despite being rebranded 'Ham Yard Village' it lacks any distinct Soho character. All that survives from the old days is the Lyric, a rather good late-Victorian public house purveying 'independently brewed ale, porter, stout and lager' on the corner of Ham Yard and Great Windmill Street.

The 43

The most famous of the interwar Soho clubs was, according to Glicco, the 43 at 43 Gerrard Street which, in its libertarian and unconventional management style, certainly seems to have provided something of an inspiration for later, wayward nightclub entrepreneurs. The establishment, which opened in 1920, was owned and run by Kate Meyrick, who, according to Glicco, 'made the 43 Club the greatest night club in British history'. Meyrick's nightclub career lasted just over a decade – she was dead by January 1933 – but, says Glicco, she was 'known to the whole world' because of her audacious behaviour. She was a 'dowdy-looking' middle-aged Irishwoman who was the mother of eight children. But 'half a million pounds flowed through her hands' and she became 'a legend' because she ran a series of clubs – including the 'up-to-date' Manhattan Club that opened in Denman Street in 1925 and the Silver Slipper in Regent Street in 1927 – often selling intoxicating liquor after hours or occasionally without the bother of obtaining licences at all. She 'paid thousands of pounds in fines' and was jailed five times for divers offences including bribing police officers, but remained afloat financially because the glamour of her activities and establishments attracted customers who were willing to pay the large sums she charged for drinks and for entry. Crime, it seems, did pay Mrs Meyrick rather handsomely and she became something of a heroine for good measure.[34] She was also the matriarch of an extraordinary dynasty. Most of her daughters were pretty and bright – at least one seems to have gone to Roedean and Cambridge University – several became noted club owners in their own right and at least three were married to aristocrats: Irene to the 6th Earl of Craven, whose family had been Soho landlords from the mid seventeenth century (see p. 88); Mary to the 14th Earl of Kinnoull and Dorothy to the 14th Baron de Clifford.

Much, but presumably not all, is revealed in Kate Meyrick's memoir, *Secrets of the 43 Club*, published in 1933, just after her death. According to legend, the manuscript was so hot that it was impounded by the police, acting presumably for some influential agency, to check for potential libels and to ensure that certain elevated patrons of the club were not compromised. The memoir reveals many things. For example that Meyrick started her career in London's nightlife with the subterranean Dalton's Club in Leicester Square in 1919, when all was 'hectic ... with everyone still trying to forget the War';[35] that Lord Kinnoull was a most unfortunate-looking young fellow whose intemperate life (he was declared bankrupt in 1926, divorced from his first wife in 1927 and died aged only thirty-five) was engraved upon his face; and that 1925 was a wonderful year 'all round' that brought 'innumerable distinguished guests' to the 43 including 'Lord Loughborough, indulging in that period of wild gaiety which preceded his suicide ... Prince

Christopher of Greece [and] Sophie Tucker ... a really wonderful genius, [and] whenever Rudolph Valentino was in London the "43" was the very first night-resort he always visited'. Mrs Meyrick confides to her readers that she 'could go on naming celebrity after celebrity *ad nauseam*' – and that is precisely what she does, page after page,[36] revealing that 'one of our most frequent Royal visitors was Prince Carol of Roumania – now King Carol II', who to the appreciative Mrs Meyrick 'did not seem at all the dissipated figure that some of the sensational newspapers have represented him to be'. Mrs Meyrick's riches were fleeting, but not her love of London and its nightlife – 'It is at night that people become alive and real to me' – and what, she asks on the final pages of her memoir, 'is the message of this life of mine ... "Queen of the Night Clubs?" To what end? ... I began with little, and so I stand at the present time. The wheel has swung its full cycle. [But] I still have my ambitions. I want to make money, to win back the great fortune which once I had and lost. What does the future hold in store? It may hold disappointment, perhaps. But one thing it never, never can take away from me, and that thing is the love of life, real life, brilliant and pulsating'.[37]

But the future held nothing. Not in this world anyway. Within a month or so of writing these words Kate Meyrick was dead, aged fifty-eight. But the memory of the 43 lived on, at least in artistic imagination. Evelyn Waugh clearly had it in mind when evoking the Old Hundredth Club – overseen by Ma Mayfield – in his 1945 novel *Brideshead Revisited*.

Number 43 Gerrard Street still stands – a large and well-constructed building of 1901 – but it now houses the

Loon Fung Supermarket; and its cavernous interior, once the haunt of party-going crime bosses and fun-seeking royalty and aristocrats, is now packed with shelves selling exotic Oriental foods.

Far from heroic for Glicco were the Soho drug dealers. The most infamous was Brilliant Chang from Hong Kong, 'who was once Britain's biggest dealer in drugs'. Glicco evokes a haunting image of Chang in the early 1920s:

> strolling nonchalantly out of Shaftesbury Avenue into Regent Street, a lovely blonde on his arm, [he] was a Chinese of maybe five-foot-six or seven tall, immaculately dressed in Western clothes, a fur-lined overcoat buttoned neatly, pince-nez perched on his nose ... Brilliant Chang was a fabulous man in those days, a name to be spoken in whispers and with awe, [the] king of the dope-peddlers, the man through whose fingers ran the bulk of the cocaine then being sold in enormous quantities to the drug addicts of London.[38]

Chang owned, as a front, a number of restaurants in Soho in which young blonde women had a habit of dying of drug overdoses, one of whom included Freda Kempton, a hostess from the 43.[39] Naturally this eventually caught the attention of the police, who investigated Chang and started to collect evidence. Chang retreated from Soho to the relative obscurity of Limehouse but was finally charged, tried and imprisoned for unlawful possession of drugs and in 1926 deported. By this time, according to Glicco, Chang had fallen victim to his own products and left Britain a jittering wreck.

The Gargoyle Club

Although seemingly exhaustive in his Soho survey Glicco omits important clubs, particularly in east Soho. Many of these were smarter or of a more artistic and bohemian nature than those places – frequented by razor-wielding gang-men and drug peddlers – known to an itinerant bandsman like Glicco. There were, for example, on the north side of Meard Street the Gargoyle Club and the Mandrake Club, the latter really no more than a semi-private drinking establishment with a very well stocked bar, and elsewhere a scattering of homosexual or lesbian clubs and pubs that seemed to have generally passed Glicco by. However, he noted the Ham Bone Club near Ham Yard, which had been in operation below the legal radar since the 1920s, as had the Festival in Dean Street and at least half a dozen more.[40]

The Gargoyle had been opened in 1925 by the socially eminent David Pax Tennant, a son of the 1st Lord Glen-conner. It was located on the upper floors of 69 Dean Street, a much-altered 1730s house with its front door on Meard Street. The club, when still a stunning London novelty, was lovingly described by Kenneth Hare in *London's Latin Quarter*, published in 1926. As Hare explained:

The Gargoyle, like so many other night clubs, holds its revels in 'Dark Soho'...Turn into Dean Street and then – why then just fade away into that seemingly negligible and wholly unobtrusive alley, which is as shrinking as the primrose, indeterminable as air, and elusive as Will-o'-the-wisp. Do not go too early. The alley does not materialize before about 9.30 p.m. It just *happens* at about that hour and has no real existence before ... This alley will conduct you to a Lilliputian lift which will just hold four ... and step out into the Elizabethan kitchen ... the open fire of mellow red brick, oak tables, oak dresser, oak rafters ... window curtains with their yellow, green and red stripes, and yellow lanterns suspended from the mouths of gargoyles ...

At the centre of the club's rooftop garden was a slightly raised dance floor, framed by Christmas trees in pots and with all the neighbouring chimney-stacks 'painted a brilliant red, doubtless without their owners knowledge' to create a Venetian image 'with the poor chimneys' serving as campanili to create the illusion that 'the whole city hangs in the heavens and fairyland is before us'.[41] Members of the club – who were obliged to pay four guineas per year for the honour – were likely to meet 'people of note', burbled Hare, such as Noël Coward, Arnold Bennett and George Belcher, the *Punch* cartoonist and painter. The club also, quite naturally, included cabaret, in the early days organised by – indeed, featuring – Tennant's wife the actress Hermione Baddeley.

Founding members of the Gargoyle included Augustus John and Clive Bell, and among its honorary members was, rather surprisingly, Henri Matisse, who did much to give distinction to the Gargoyle's interior. The story of Matisse's involvement is extraordinary. The artist had been in London twice before the Gargoyle opened, first in 1898, for his honeymoon, and second for several weeks in October and November 1919 when collaborating with Diaghilev and Stravinsky's Ballets Russes performance of *Le Chant du Rossignol* at the Empire Theatre, Leicester

Square. In 1898 Matisse had been an impoverished and
obscure young artist, but in 1919 he had reputation and
money and stayed at the Savoy Hotel, along with Diaghilev. It's possible that it was during this visit, preparing
costume and set designs, that Matisse acquired a taste
for interior decoration and a familiarity with the streets,
courts and atmosphere of Soho. Whatever the case, when
the moment came, Matisse was ready. And the moment
came, as such moments do, through the collision of
random circumstances.

Years before launching the Gargoyle, Tennant had
become friends with Matthew Pritchard, an exquisite
academic and amateur occultist, 'sometime Byzantine
scholar and putative philosopher'.[42] Pritchard, who had
befriended Matisse in Paris in 1907, was to prove pivotal
in the creation of the Gargoyle's interior but he was not
the man who brought club owner and artist together.
This was the work of Georges Duthuit, a friend of
Tennant's who happened to be the husband of Matisse's
eldest daughter, Marguerite. Sometime in 1924, when
with Duthuit in France, Tennant met Matisse, and what
would normally have been a brief and formal encounter
between a young man in his early twenties and an artist
in his mid fifties became intimate when Matisse discovered that Tennant was a 'disciple of Matt Pritchard'.[43]
Tennant's forthcoming business venture was discussed
and, it seems, Matisse warmed to the topic:

> [Tennant] had explained that he was having an elaborate
> coffered ceiling, à la Alhambra, made ... which was to
> be painted with twenty-two carat gold leaf. An excellent
> complement, Matisse suggested, would be to have the

walls entirely covered with a mosaic of mirrored tiles. He knew of an eighteenth-century chateau whose contents were about to be sold. Included were some immensely tall looking-glasses ... When cut into thousands of small squares and set into the walls, these tiles of subtly imperfect glass would produce *un effet éclatant*.

Tennant 'was so elated by this inspired concept ... that he made Matisse an honorary member on the spot'.[44] The mirrors were duly purchased and the works executed as Matisse had advised to create the club's 'ballroom' ceiling. The result was – and remained – sensational. Francis Bacon remembered the first impression the interior made on him: 'I didn't go up to the Gargoyle until after the war – about 1947 – and it's true to say that when one arrived quite late most people, including oneself, were generally half drunk. But they looked for moments like birds of paradise coming down this beautiful gold and silver staircase into the multiplicity of small mirrors made into a very beautiful room. I've never been a great admirer of Matisse, but this room really worked as a setting.'[45]

The club's initial Tudor look and 'ye oldness' described by Hare was rapidly diluted and largely replaced with a sharper, smarter, contemporary and arty ambiance, expressive, as Anthony Powell put it, of 'go-ahead culture'.[46] This change of atmosphere and aspiration was not just because of the Matisse-inspired ballroom ceiling, but because Tennant had made two very important purchases. When in Paris he had visited Matisse's St Michel studio and, from racks of canvases, selected and bought two for the modest sum of £600. These, as it happened, turned out to be two of the most important paintings of the twentieth century and by 1925 were hanging on the walls of the Gargoyle. They were *The Red Studio* of 1911 and *The Studio, Quai Saint-Michel* of 1916. These paintings hung in the dining room (some accounts say one was in the ballroom), and their dominant presence (*The Red Studio* measures 2.1 metres by 1.8 metres and *The Studio, Quai Saint-Michel* 1.5 metres by 1.1 metres), along with a set of twelve lithographs by Matisse showing dancers, elevated the Gargoyle from a mere upper-crust nightclub to a cultural shrine.

The Gargoyle survived – even thrived – during the war but then ran out of steam. The vivacious 'Bright Young Things' for whom it catered were no longer bright, nor young nor, in many cases, alive. By the late 1940s the Gargoyle's charms had tarnished, and it became famed not for its style or its glittering socialite customers but as a ready watering hole for Soho's growing band of eccentric and forever inebriated social outcasts and outsiders. The fact that this disparate and dissipated band included artists and poets who were to become some of the most notable of the period – Francis Bacon of course, but also Lucian Freud and Dylan Thomas – did not prevent the Gargoyle's steady decline.

By the late 1940s Tennant had sold the Matisse paintings. *The Red Studio* was taken out in June 1940 when, after Dunkirk, the Gargoyle was closed because a German invasion seemed imminent or, at the very least, London would be smashed by bombing. The club was reopened in June 1941 just, by chance, when Germany invaded the Soviet Union and the war took a new turn; the club soon became a meeting place for Britain's new émigré Soviet allies. But by then *The Studio,*

Quai Saint-Michel had also been removed. Both paintings were soon sold: *The Studio, Quai Saint-Michel* is now in the Phillips Collection in Washington DC; *The Red Studio* hangs in the Museum of Modern Art, New York.

As the club faltered, an ill-fated theatre was installed in an attempt to attract custom. It did no good – the times were against it. Tennant died in 1968, but by then the Gargoyle was being managed by others, and in the late 1970s it slipped into oblivion. A comedy theatre and a strip club took over much of the building and by the early 1980s, according to Michael Luke, 'the Matisse mirrored ballroom walls, the oak Tudor Room and all the interiors' had been stripped for conversion to 'a sophisticated studio complex'.[47] In 2009 the upper part of the house was united with the lower floors to form the Town House bar, a restaurant and hotel operated by the Soho House group. The building can be visited, the ghosts of the Gargoyle can be evoked, and even fragments of 1730s panelling and a fine staircase can be inspected. It is smart once more, but not glamorous as in the old days.

Soho in the 1950s: the Colony Room

The most famed of Soho's post-war clubs was not the once-grand Gargoyle but the Colony Room, located almost opposite in Dean Street. The Colony also offered escape and solace in the form of all-day drinking and non-stop conversation, but with an added sense of danger and adventure. Sadly, I did not know the Colony Room well, and when I did go I was much too late to observe its finest moment as the new drinking haunt of Francis Bacon, Lucian Freud and Frank Auerbach – weaned away from the faltering Gargoyle – and a flurry of actors and exotic Soho drunks and posers. But in 2008 I became embroiled in a last-ditch attempt to save the Colony and, as a result, witnessed a demise that was as bizarre and eccentric as the club's sixty-year life.

Muriel Belcher had founded the club in December 1948 and for thirty or so years presided within its first-floor rooms in an autocratic and sometimes malevolent way, insulting many of her hapless guests in artful, studied and usually obscene manner, calculated to make the most pompous appear the most ridiculous. One of her favoured and admirably economical jokes was to refer to all men as women. This sexual game, when played on particularly masculine or self-important males, had the effect of immediately making them appear absurd. Muriel's barbed greetings were a test of moral fibre and fortitude. You either laughed it off, gave as good as you got, or felt deeply insulted and flounced away. It was an initiation that separated the old goats from the prissy interlopers and became a Soho institution. Indeed, Muriel's inventive mastery of four-letter words became something of a leitmotif among her Soho entourage. The habit survives yet in some quarters, as I was reminded during a talk given in recent years at the Chelsea Arts Club by Colony Room veteran Molly Parkin. Needless to say, the Chelsea Arts Club is not the Colony Club, but neither is it squeamish or reserved. But in her choice adjectives and descriptive phrases Miss Parkin paid homage to Muriel and certainly commanded attention.

The immediate post-war Soho decades are evoked brilliantly by Daniel Farson in *Soho in the Fifties* published in 1987. Farson was one of Soho's leading figures at that time and no one was better qualified to tell the story of its streets, drinking haunts, peculiar characters and compelling atmosphere. As George Melly explains in his introduction to the book, the tale Farson tells 'is really about a love affair', about 'a dreamlike decade when everything seemed possible and time alone appeared an irrelevance'.[48] Farson explains that when he first came to London after Cambridge, 'I knew little about Soho apart from the vague impression that it was a villainous spot. Like all outsiders, I was mistaken. In the fifties, Soho was blessed with innocence, [it] has always attracted eccentrics rather than criminals [and], to the young especially, Soho is irresistible, for it offers a sort of freedom.'[49]

When Farson arrived in Soho in 1951, 'London was suffering from post-war depression and it was a revelation to discover people who behaved outrageously without a twinge of guilt and drank so recklessly.' The structure of Farson's exploration of the escapist world of Soho – 'haunted' by 'trapped lost souls' like Jeffrey Bernard[50] – takes the form of a day-and-night perambulation during which, as in Dante's tour of the Inferno, some very rum characters and locations are encountered. There was the Caves de France, a club on Dean Street next to the Colony that, with its dark, smoky and cavernous interior, was 'in many ways ... the most astonishing place in Soho and the closest to Bohemia'.[51] And there were Soho's famed 'queer pubs', as they were called then: the Fitzroy off Charlotte Street to the north and not in Soho proper, and the Golden Lion at 51 Dean Street – a charming neo-Tudor pub of 1929 – into which a married couple might wander by mistake and leave 'swiftly when they discovered that they were surrounded by strange men'.[52]

The faded Gargoyle also gets a mention. It had, observed Farson, 'known grander days' but was still in the 1950s a place of legend. Farson tells tales that are partly fact and partly drink-fuelled fantasy: 'The most astonishing aspect of the Gargoyle was the fact that the room was designed by Henri Matisse and executed by the architect Sir Edwin Lutyens. Originally it contained two magnificent Matisse murals but one was sold to America for less than £1,000 and the other was bought by Kenneth Clark for £600 and subsequently drifted to America as well.' These 'murals' were presumably the two Matisse paintings that once hung in the dining room or ballroom.

Lutyens was, apparently, responsible for the club's 'leather curtains with an African motif'. These curtains were not approved by Matisse. According to Courtenay Merrill, 'who worked at the club from the outset [and] remembered Matisse', the eminent artist was 'shocked by the curtains and their African motif' and thought them 'the work of a fanatic'.[53] No other chroniclers of the Gargoyle mention a Lutyens connection but it's possible that the great man, renowned for his playful streak, would have relished designing a nightclub. Farson was also impressed by the grandeur of the club's early days. He managed to get a glimpse at membership books from the mid 1920s and observes that on 'one evening there were two princes, three princesses and the king of Romania' enjoying the pleasures of the club, to which 'the Duke of Windsor was [to become] a regular visitor'.[54] But by Farson's time a new clientele had started to drift in, 'upsetting the older members with their own brand of rowdiness'. The change is expressed, writes Farson, 'by two names in the membership book for 1951: Guy

Burgess, who joined on 8 May, and Donald Maclean who signed it three days later'.[55]

Farson dedicated his book to 'Ian Board and the members of the Colony, and for Muriel Belcher who started it' and naturally includes, in his tour around Soho, a portrait of the Colony and its hostess. He remembers that 'she was so rude to John Braine, crying out "There's plenty of room at her top!", that he started legal action against her until his solicitor urged him not to be so silly, and 'she was so insulting to Barry Humphries ... that he never set foot in her club again'.[56] As Farson admits, 'all of this makes her sound like a monster', but since he was one of her favourites Farson naturally concludes that Muriel 'could be immensely kind and perceptive'. In an attempt to sum up Muriel's contradictory qualities, Farson quotes Paul Potts, a 'Soho personality' and writer. She was, suggested Potts, 'a kind of non-ecclesiastical cardinal or perhaps a delinquent saint. She is a natural procurer whether it be the bacon for the eggs or a date for a girl friend. The relatively small room which is her domain and where she is an absolute sovereign must be one of the most unique rooms anywhere ... it is the sort of place where you can't get much for ten bob but you can get an awful lot for nothing.'[57]

After Muriel died in 1979 the club was taken over by her long-time barman Ian Board, and after his death in 1994 by his veteran barman Michael Wojas. This was continuity, and so all should have been well. Sadly, Wojas became increasing unwell and parted with paintings that had over the years been donated to the club by various artists, and in 2008 parted with the lease. Members, who believed they owned the club, were astonished and outraged that a Soho institution could be dismantled in this manner. An attempt was made to save the club by getting it listed as 'a building of historic or architectural interest'. One morning I witnessed English Heritage historians inspecting the club. It was pointed out that parts of the interior clearly dated from the early eighteenth century, and that the bar had been one of the cultural beacons of post-war Britain. Admittedly the interior – with its famous bilious-green walls and sticky floor and bar top – had that morning-after look and was clearly recovering from an overnight hangover. On the whole, I thought the inspection went well. But with hindsight I realise that the serious historians should only have been let in at night, when the green glowed, conversation flowed and no one noticed the sticky floor. English Heritage, keen to avoid controversy, refused to recommend the club or the building housing it for listing (plate 9).

The building – 41 Dean Street – survives, but its soul has fled. It's now a melancholy sight. From Blacks Club opposite it is just possible to get a glimpse into the first-floor room that housed the Colony. But this can be most disconcerting. Instead of shadowy green walls, a red glow of dimmed light and the motion of carousing figures there is – nothing. A few partitions, painted white, dividing up the bar area, and a bright light. Is it someone's flat? It looks like a morgue.

The last days of the Colony Room are a parable, a case study that seems emblematic of the demise of much of Soho's life. Virtually nothing now survives of that bohemian era. Not just the Colony Room, but the other quintessential Soho clubs and bars have also gone – and the pubs and restaurants that still exist have now changed

1. Corner of Brewer Street and Great Pulteney Street in the early 1970s when all was derelict. The terrace (centre and right) dates from 1719–1720.

2. The same view in 2019. All the late Georgian buildings on the corner with Brewer Street (left) have been demolished, but the earlier houses have been repaired. They are now once again in residential use.

3. Number 21 Great Windmill Street. A modest late Georgian house demolished in late 2019. In March 2020 the site remains cleared with contractors at work. The proposal is to construct a building with a façade that replicates the lost original, topped by a two-storey mansard roof.

4. The former Turk's Head tavern at 9 Gerrard Street. Built in 1758 and now a Cantonese delicatessen.

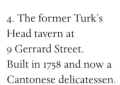

5. Numbers
1–9 Meard Street
built in 1732.

6. The centre and east end of the north side of Lisle Street, from 1792–5,
partly on the site of Leicester House and its garden.

7. Soho Square looking south in *c*.1725. In centre is Monmouth House, to left – running south from the square – is Greek Street, and to the right is Frith Street.

8. Charles Booth's 'Poverty Map' of 1889. Red and pink indicated homes and streets that were 'fairly comfortable' and 'well to do'. Dark blue showed homes that were 'very poor' and inhabited by families in 'chronic want'. Light blue identified the homes of the 'poor', while purple marked homes and streets that were 'mixed' – the poor and comfortably off.

9. Interior of the Colony Room a few days after its closure in 2008. The scene is still set for convivial evening gatherings that were, alas, to be no more.

10. The Coach and Horses, Greek Street, right and – to the north – Maison Bertaux.

12. The north side of Soho Square showing, from left to right, numbers 13 (painted green with first floor pediments), 14 and 15.

11. 'A Bazaar', by George Cruikshank in 1816, generally taken to be the Soho Bazaar at 4–6 Soho Square.

13. Number 1 Greek Street, built 1746–54, with, second on right, number 3.

14. Detail of the entrance hall of 36 Gerrard Street, built 1737.

15. Numbers 17–19 Lisle Street, built 1792–5, despite the panel in the pediment being dated 1791.

their natures. The Golden Lion at 51 Dean Street remains in business, although now without the character or clientele observed by Farson, and threatened by Crossrail 2 (see p. 247). The 'queer pub' banner has been transferred triumphantly to the Admiral Duncan in Old Compton Street, which is now Soho's unchallenged highway of homosexuality.

Quo Vadis in Dean Street and Kettner's in Romilly Street are also still in operation, although Kettner's has been absorbed by the Soho House empire and, along with its club building on the corner of Greek Street and Old Compton Street, was in the summer of 2018 reborn from a cocoon of scaffolding and hoardings, but seemingly very little changed. L'Escargot in Greek Street, founded in the late 1920s by Georges Gaudin, also survives, but here changes are significant. Gaudin – who raised his edible snails in the basement – retired in the late 1970s, since when the restaurant has passed through several hands and in its current manifestation – still located in its fine 1740s house – is visually somewhat garish.

Soho sanitised

During the last thirty-five years the sex industry has been largely driven out of Soho east of Wardour Street as a result of legislation introduced in the early 1980s. And even in west Soho there is now only a small and very regulated 'public face' on show, at the junction of Wardour Street, Brewer Street, Rupert Street and Walker's Court, with shops or newsagents requiring local-authority-issued licences if they intend to sell 'adult' material. As has often been observed in recent years, the old Soho has been sanitised – and to a degree homogenised, to the point of near-obliteration. The last days of Soho's more loosely regulated and rambling sex industry are documented, in a very personal manner, by John Wortley in *Skin Deep in Soho*, published in 1969. Wortley opens his book by reminding readers that although the 'subject of Soho has been "done to death" [there] is yet ... still no detailed guide-book to modern Soho or comprehensive record in photographs of the extraordinary, kaleidoscopic square mile'. He then reveals that his 'Soho adventure began in 1964' and that his 'romantic obsession for the place ... is summed up in a quotation from John Galsworthy: "Of all the quarters in the queer amalgam called London, Soho is perhaps the least suited to the Forsyte spirit ... Untidy, full of Greeks, Ismaelites, cats, Italians, tomatoes, restaurants, organs, coloured stuffs, queer names. People looking out of upper windows, it dwells remote from the British Body Politic."'

Wortley's adventure 'developed', he confides, 'after an encounter with a circuit strip-dancer'. For Wortley, in 1969, 'brash, visual stimulus' remained the 'core of modern Soho'. But he could sense the way the wind was blowing. Has Soho's special character declined? he asks. And concludes no: 'for me it remains the appetite centre and place for foreigners which it has always been'.

The 'thesis' of Wortley's book is straightforward: to demonstrate that in England 'strip dancers ... are treated too solemnly by a Puritan tradition which despite the surface free-wheeling of a younger generation still deeply equates sexuality with sin'. The book is dedicated to a stripper named Tina Maria who, in various stages of undress and in diverse postures, appears throughout its pages. The portrait Wortley offers of the geography, customs, characters and institutions of sexual Soho in the 1960s is enthralling:

> I went to Jean Straker's Academy, No. 12 Soho Square, a dedicated – and I think honest – French fighter for pubic hair in nude photography. Ruskin should have taken Effie there, I thought ... At Raymond's Revuebar in Walker's Court [I] was impressed by Paul Raymond: sharp suit; clever disciplinarian and knack with nudes ... One of his girls stripped from a live horse. It commuted from Reading ... I went into a Dean Street club ... Lager with the coke and coffee at the bar. There was a superbly clumsy act which billed itself as a salacious duo, a coloured girl having a row with her boyfriend, a white girl dressed as a man, and the two lovers make it up after the man has punished the curtain a couple of times to simulate beating the negress. They undress for further reconciliation in bed ... another girl was a tassel dancer. 'Swinging London they call it' said the commentary ... the audience of twenty-two men and two wives, average age twenty-eight ... five-thirty in the afternoon and a freezing day ... the dancer ... coughed a winter cough and stood naked in her boots; incongruous tableau with her audience which to me is fundamental Soho.

And even in the Swinging Sixties Soho was, for Wortley, a domain characterised by history that offered

> [a] chance to bind together past and present ... A hosier's son, William Blake, was born at 28 Broad Street and writes *Song of Innocence* [sic] round the corner in Poland Street

lodgings. Gainsborough finds a model for his *Blue Boy*, in an ironmonger's son from Brewer Street. Nelson, before Trafalgar, collects his coffin from a shop in Brewer Street, made from the wreck of a French ship sunk in the battle of the Nile ... Mrs Siddons embroiders her new home at 54 Great Marlborough Street ... the first recorded Soho tart burns down a house in 1641 ... 'Queen of Midnight' Kate Meyrick, marvellous lady, dies in 1933. Taxi drivers and dance band leaders stop for a two minute silence. 'The Englishman,' she once said, 'may take his pleasures sadly but he does not take them in a niggardly fashion.'[58]

In the early 1970s, just before Soho's sex industry started to be regulated into relative invisibility and reduced in extent, the Chinese community began to arrive in large numbers and, around Gerrard Street, eventually created a lurid version of New York's Chinatown, complete with a Chinese-style street arch. The food in Chinatown is mainly Cantonese and generally good – or at least good value – the atmosphere lively, and the 'Town' has become a popular London tourist attraction. I suppose, at the very least, it illustrates Soho's ability to accommodate change and to thrive as a place of contrast, with Gerrard Street's surviving and once-grand early Georgian houses now containing restaurants and shops, their fine panelled interiors the backdrops to bustling commerce.

Soho reduced

Although Soho escaped the Second World War with relatively little damage, it did not escape greedy and heartless post-war demolition and rebuilding. Not only was

Richmond Buildings lost but also terraces of the 1730s in Livonia Street and, in 1967, the entire early-eighteenth-century south side of St Anne's Court and the tall, robust St Anne's Building of 1864 by William Burges. The post-war despoliation had started early. In 1953 the magnificent early-eighteenth-century 54 Great Marlborough Street, with its sensational staircase, was destroyed. A little later a significant portion of early Georgian Berwick Street was demolished, including in 1960 the splendid number 63, with its columned, panelled and plaster-embellished first-floor front room. A particularly brutal demolition came in 1965, when the fine house of 1734 in which William Blake had been born, what had been 28 Broad Street, on the corner with Marshall Street, was swept away for a grim and out-of-scale civic block that includes – perched disconcertingly on a two-storey podium that relates not at all to Soho's terrain – a fifteen-storey tower of local-authority flats. These are named, with bitter irony, William Blake House. At the same time, in adjacent Dufour's Place, six charming early-eighteenth-century houses with wonderful panelled interiors were also destroyed. A trifle earlier the superb and palatial 24 Great Pulteney Street had been replaced by a characterless commercial redevelopment, as had 12 Great Marlborough Street, a most generous house of 1707 with a magnificent staircase. The sad work continued in the 1970s, when two fine houses forming the centre of a bold 1737 terrace on the south side of Gerrard Street were demolished after fire damage, and when early terraces in Brewer Street, each side of the corners with Great Pulteney Street, were lost, including the mid-eighteenth-century 40–44 Brewer Street. Also demolished at roughly the same time were the outstanding 1720s

8–13 Great Pulteney Street, 42–44 Broadwick Street of 1706, with splendid panelled interiors, and groups of good early houses in Wardour Street and D'Arblay Street and 17 Soho Square of 1800. These are all shocking losses, displaying a profit-obsessed insensitivity to history and beauty that remains heartbreaking. But one of the losses that was not only shocking but almost inexplicable was that, in the early 1970s, of St Thomas's Church on Kingly Street. It had been built in 1702 under Sir Christopher Wren's supervision and was in reasonable condition at the time of its unforgivable demolition.

East elevation of St Thomas's Church, built in 1702 and demolished in the early 1970s.

17 Soho Square during demolition in the early 1970s.

But what has changed more in Soho than its physical presence is its spirit. The profound oddness that still characterised Soho in the early 1970s – when I first got to know it well – that strange sense of romantic abandonment and decaying Georgian grandeur combined, somewhat paradoxically, with an almost village atmosphere, has almost entirely gone, replaced by mainstream consumerism, commercialism and tourism. The array of very individual and one-off bars and restaurants – like Jimmy's in Frith Street, which since 1948 served a splendid mix of Greek and English food and the largest chips I've ever seen – have mostly been driven out by ever-rising rents. Also long gone is the once-magical Bianchi's in Frith Street, an Italian restaurant of relaxed and Continental charm overseen by Soho's star *maître d'*, Elena Salvoni. It was my favourite Soho restaurant in the early 1970s – as it was for many – because it was utterly individual and because Elena made all feel welcome. In most cases these characterful and splendid places have either gone entirely or been replaced by restaurants, cafés or bars that are chain endeavours familiar from any high street, serving not Soho eccentrics, outsiders or would-be *bohèmes* but tourists and out-of-towners seeking a lager and a noisy night out.

Survivors

But not all is – yet – absolutely lost. A very few older establishments do survive in more or less unaltered form and with their atmospheres still partly intact. The Coach and Horses at the south end of Greek Street and the French House (properly the York Minster) at the south end of Dean Street were at the heart of bohemian Soho and they are still in operation – physically little altered and most rewarding if you catch them before the hordes arrive. The Coach and Horses became the local of Jeffrey Bernard, who finally came to a sort of feckless fame (or at least notoriety) as a columnist with an alcohol-honed acerbic wit and could be found at the bar most evenings until his death in 1997. This pub still has its moments, even though the Soho 'low life' that gave it distinction (Bernard's phrase, not mine, and the title of his column in *The Spectator*) has been dispersed. But even this diluted version of Bernard's Coach and Horses might not be with us long. In June 2019 the characterful tenants did not have their lease renewed and the brewers now run the pub as a 'managed house'. Sounds too corporate for Soho where hostelries have flourished because they were run by characters, such as Kate Meyrick in the 1920s and Muriel Belcher in the 1950s (plate 10).

The Gay Hussar, at 2 Greek Street, was founded in 1953 by Victor Sassie and in its early days served fine Hungarian fare in an intimate setting to leading poets and politicians, whose photographic portraits were used to decorate the walls. But in the summer of 2018 the Gay Hussar shut its door for the last time, and by the end of the year its once-mysterious but welcoming ground floor frontage was derelict and plastered with the usual array of fly-posters. Death, in Soho, is often abrupt. But in June 2020 builders were in and by early 2021 housed a wine-bar named *Noble Riot*. All might be well.

A survivor that, thank goodness, continues to thrive is Ronnie Scott's Jazz Club at 47 Frith Street. It started in Gerrard Street in 1959, moved to Frith Street in the mid 1960s and continues business much as usual. But perhaps most uplifting is Maison Bertaux, a patisserie founded in 1871 which occupies an early-eighteenth-century pair of houses at the south end of Greek Street (plate 10). Its main building has scarcely changed in the thirty or so years I've been going there and, despite the now familiar rent and rates increases, it remains full of vitality and character – and still doggedly serves *café au lait* as its drink of choice, although I notice that, bowing to the tastes of the times, cappuccino has crept onto its menu.

Bar Italia at 22 Frith Street is a reminder of a most characterful Soho story of which virtually no physical trace remains. Bar Italia is virtually unaltered in appearance since it was opened in 1949 by the Polledri family, which owns it still, and business looks good, so the bar goes on doing what it does best – being itself, and a thing unmoving in a rapidly changing world. Not that it's static: the family has recently expanded its business into the adjoining premises, once occupied by Bianchi's restaurant. Soon after Bar Italia opened, a fashion flared up in Soho for a type of establishment that was to flourish during the coming couple of decades before withering rapidly to near-extinction. The often arty coffee bar emerged early in the 1950s, to become a gathering place for youth and for those seeking to pass the time in characterful and convivial manner. The Bar Italia, being a more serious coffee establishment – especially for night-time Soho workers or residents – never quite fell into the arty coffee bar category.

The coffee-bar revolution

It is now hard to imagine how novel the coffee bar was when it first appeared in London, almost certainly in Soho. This novelty was in part based on technology. A coffee bar, if it was fully to live up to the expectations of its customers, had to possess one of the newly available espresso coffee-making machines so it could dispense coffee topped with the frothy milk that had suddenly become so desirable.

At one level the coffee bar gave young people – who emerged as a significant and commercially valuable constituency in London's economic and social life during the 1950s – a place to meet that was exotic and not a pub. Not being a pub meant several things: first, it was where those too young to get into a pub could gather, but, perhaps more significantly, the coffee bar was a place where single women or groups of women could go and feel safe, free from intimidation or the presumption that they were there to be picked up. Also, homosexuals felt safer closeted in a coffee bar than in the usually fiercely hetero London pub, and so coffee bars formed part of the emerging 'gay scene' at a time when to indulge in certain aspects of homosexuality was still illegal.

The origin of the post-war Soho coffee bar is now, to a degree, lost in myth, but there seem to be a few generally accepted facts. The Maka Bar, at 29 Frith Street, opened in 1953 and housed London's first Gaggia-made steam-pressured espresso machine, and so was among the pioneers of Italian-style coffee. This was soon followed (probably also in 1953) by Moka Ris and Les Enfants Terribles. Both were in Dean Street (Moka Ris at number 10), although they were different in character. Moka Ris was architect-designed, and so a rather upmarket style statement; Les Enfants Terribles was far more informal. All of these establishments offered their customers music, jazz being preferable, but also skiffle and folk when it became popular with the younger generation in the early 1960s. This fashion spawned new clubs like Les Cousins in the basement of 49 Frith Street, a place that burned bright for a few years as the centre of London's 'folk scene' but, as the spirit passed on, closed in 1972. And even when live music was not available, that other marvel of the modern age – the juke-box – helped ensure that most coffee bars were distinctly musical places.

The connection between coffee and music was taken to a higher level by the 2i's Coffee Bar at 59 Old Compton Street from 1956 to 1970. A plaque now fixed to the building claims it was 'the birthplace of British rock 'n roll and the popular music industry'. Hyperbole no doubt, but not without some truth. Famously, it was here that the filing clerk Harry Webb metamorphosed into Cliff Richard. These music-oriented coffee bars themselves mutated into the late-night music clubs for which Soho became notorious in the 1960s and 1970s, most inhabiting large-scale former industrial or commercial buildings in Wardour Street – the Flamingo (from 1957 until 1967 at 33–37); the Whisky A-go-go (which inherited the Flamingo buildings); and the Marquee Club (from 1964 to 1988 at number 90).

Some early coffee bars were themed, in a way that now seems painfully self-conscious. For example, in the basement of 23 Meard Street was located Le Macabre, with its coffin-shaped benches and illuminated skull lamps. It must have lasted into the 1970s because I just about remember it – dark, lots of black paint, dilapidated by that time and not a little absurd. And, Soho being Soho, there were also 'political' coffee houses, notably the Partisan Coffee House at 7 Carlisle Street, opened in 1958 by the Marxist historian Raphael Samuel. It was a place of political debate more than a place of business, and sadly soon closed.[59]

The coffee bars are long gone, as have many of Soho's most characterful establishments; but, in contrast, there have been some relatively recent arrivals that continue or that revive Soho's traditional qualities. Charles Booth and George Herbert Duckworth remarked in 1898, when conducting their re-survey of the area and updating Booth's poverty map, on the number of clubs in Soho. In this respect, at least, the area has not changed. Some, like the Groucho Club in Dean Street and Soho House in Greek Street and in Dean Street, cater for the media or – more alarming still – 'celebrities'. But Blacks, also in Dean Street, and the Academy Club, above Andrew Edmunds's excellent restaurant in Lexington Street, are clubs that seem more in the spirit of old Soho – literary rather than media, mixed in their membership and even, at times, a trifle eccentric, certainly most tolerant of oddballs and outsiders. Admittedly, Blacks has changed somewhat in the last few years along with its ownership, becoming more mainstream; but, to be fair, its peculiar character has managed to survive the transition. So, in contrast to the higher-profile members' clubs, Blacks and the Academy remain places where convivial souls gather over a drink to chat, and are not merely establishments in which to be seen or in which to indulge in a frisson of exclusivity. So, despite everything, some aspects of Soho endure and ensure that it remains one of the most charming and intoxicating places in Britain.

Overleaf: Section of Richard Horwood's London map of 1799–1819. Some street names have changed – for example, Silver Street has become Beak Street and Cambridge Street has become Lexington Street, but the essential street pattern of Soho survives so this map should help to guide – and inform – the walk. The outline of Oxford Circus and Regent Street are shown to the west and were under construction by 1819. Regent Street defines both the western edge of Soho and its character. The Parliamentary Bill of 1813 to construct Regent Street states that it was to provide 'a boundary . . . between the Streets and Squares occupied by the Nobility and Gentry' to the west and the 'narrow Streets and meaner Houses occupied by mechanics and the trading part of the community' that by then were the dominant community of Soho.

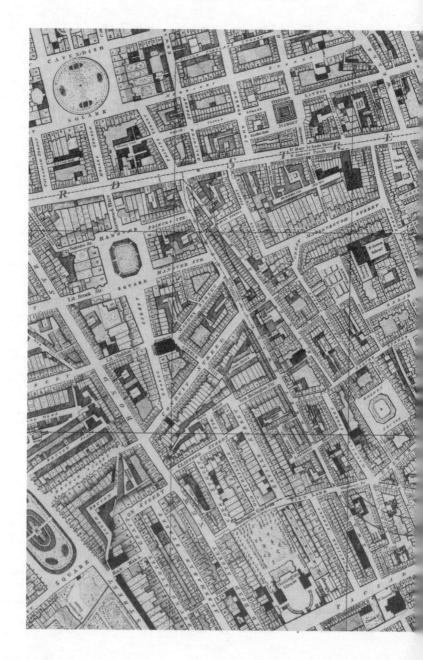

The Walk

Soho is now – and for the purposes of this walk – defined by Charing Cross Road on the east, Oxford Street on the north, Regent Street on the west and – a little more subjectively – Coventry Street, Leicester Square and Cranbourn Street on the south. The walk might perhaps more accurately be described as a Soho gazetteer, but one organised geographically and not alphabetically. It starts at Soho Square, then the route is as follows:

Soho Square; Greek Street (excursions into Manette Street and Romilly Street); Gerrard Place; Gerrard Street; Macclesfield Street; Newport Court; Newport Place, Lisle Street; Little Newport Street; Shaftesbury Avenue; Wardour Street (south) (excursion into Rupert Street and Rupert Court); Coventry Street; Old Compton Street (excursions into Moor Street and Charing Cross Road); Frith Street; Carlisle Street; Dean Street (excursion into St Anne's Court); Great Chapel Street; Meard Street; Wardour Street (north); D'Arblay Street (excursion into Portland Mews); Berwick Street (excursion into Walker's Court); Brewer Street (excursions into Great Windmill Street, Archer Street, Sherwood Street and Denman Street); Lexington Street (excursion into Silver Place and Ingestre Place); Broadwick Street (excursions into Poland Street and Dufour's Place); Marshall Street; Beak

Street (excursions into Great Pulteney Street, Warwick Street, Golden Square, Lower John Street, Lower James Street); Carnaby Street; Newburgh Street; Ganton Street; Foubert's Place; Kingly Street; Great Marlborough Street; Argyll Street; Oxford Street Underground station.

Soho Square

Soho Square remains one of London's most atmospheric and charming squares, despite the fact that most of its early buildings have been demolished, many during the interwar years. Sadly, the more recent buildings lack architectural distinction, although happily their blandness has failed to utterly overwhelm the square's established character. This is perhaps due largely to the open and relaxed nature of its central garden, essentially an informal lawn divided into four quarters by paths with a sheltering fringe of shrubs and a scattering of trees. At its centre is a quaint, arcaded, picturesque and wonderfully inappropriate timber-framed structure that looks like a theatrical rendering of the witch's house in *Hansel and Gretel*. It is in fact a tool shed that was erected in the mid 1870s and, in the process, dethroned the statue of Charles II that had presided over the square since at least the 1680s. The statue was returned to the square in 1938, but not to its original and dominating position, perhaps because a bomb shelter had been constructed below the square and the shed had a vital role as an emergency exit. Now weather-beaten, the armour-clad, po-faced figure, with head turned intimately to one side, loiters at ground level on a path in a most casual pose, as if propositioning passers-by. Interestingly, the general layout of the square is much like the original scheme, except that then the planting was formal, the paths and lawns more regular in size and all was contained within an outer path which allowed a promenade around the square but within the garden's railings. In 1954 the garden was opened to the public. Until then it was, as with the gardens in most London squares, for the enjoyment primarily of those occupying buildings around the square.

The story of the square starts in the 1670s when Soho Fields, also known as Kemp's Fields, were leased in April 1677 by Joseph Girle, brewer, to Richard Frith, brickmaker (see p. 57). It was already called Soho Square on Rocque's map of 1746. By 1691 forty-one houses had been built around the square – loosely uniform but not organised to form a coherent unified composition. The houses were generally three storeys high and three windows wide, with string courses and wood modillion eaves cornices.

The uniformity of the brick construction and scale of the houses, and the simplicity of their elevations, gave the original square a visual harmony. But, evidently, from the 1740s architects and speculators rebuilding houses around the square became obsessed. Like few other locations in London, Soho Square evolved into something of a monument to what is known as the Venetian or Serlian window. This is a tripartite affair in which the central window is the widest, has an arched top and is flanked by two lower and narrower straight-topped windows. This motif makes an appearance in Sebastiano Serlio's highly influential *Tutte l'opere d'architettura et prospetiva* published from 1537. It was favoured by the influential Renaissance architect Andrea Palladio and promoted in his *I quattro libri dell'architettura* of 1570, and was seen and admired in

Venice and Vicenza by British Grand Tourists.

The first of Soho Square's houses with elevations dominated by huge Venetian windows was number 7. This rebuilding of 1745–8 was by George Weston, a Soho-based plasterer, on a lease from the Portland estate. The design was perhaps by Sir Robert Taylor, a skilful architect of grand West End terraces and country villas. The composition is memorable. The front door was part of a tripartite arrangement formed by a central pediment over the door itself and rising from a frieze and architrave that extended over the windows on each side. The door was framed by Doric columns and the entire composition flanked by pilasters. Above the door at first-floor level was the Venetian window – the central arched window framed by Ionic columns – and on the second floor, above the Venetian window and of the same width, a semicircular lunette. Both Venetian window and lunette were set within a wide and shallow arched recess – a motif derived from Palladio – with the entire elevation crowned by a wide pediment. It's to be eternally regretted that this wonderful building was demolished in 1929 for a seven-storey-high Art Deco sliver of a building that is sadly nondescript.

The next manifestation of the Venetian window came in 1758–9, and this time the project featured not one but two large windows. The leading amateur architect Sir William Robinson of Newby Hall, Yorkshire, designed and built 25 and 26 Soho Square, the execution of both houses being undertaken by a Soho carpenter and surveyor named Thomas Dade. Robinson was an ardent admirer and copyist of the works of Palladio, so the huge first-floor Venetian windows of each house were set within a large relieving arch. This was a composition taken directly from a Palladio design that had been acquired in the very early eighteenth century by Lord Burlington and which inspired a whole series of British Palladian architects and buildings – including William Kent's Horse Guards and Vardy's Spencer House. Number 25 was demolished in 1937, leaving number 26 as the sole survivor of the Venetian-window houses.

The last of the Venetian-window-dominated Soho Square houses to be built was number 32, constructed between 1773 and 1775 by a banker named Sir George Colebrooke. Once again, the architect might have been Sir Robert Taylor, who had worked on Colebrooke's country estate at Arnos Grove, Middlesex. This house was, arguably, the quintessence of the Venetian-windowed terrace house. The main door was a tripartite composition featuring a huge fanlight set in a wide, shallow arch and crowning the door and its flanking windows. At first-floor level there was a tripartite window the same width as the door composition, and immediately above this – at second-floor level – was a huge Venetian window. Its width and central arched window corresponded to the key dimensions of the central window and door below it. The vast size of the fanlight and the windows above it, combined with the unity of the entire composition, made the front of the house read as a veritable wall of glass, and since it faced east the interior would have been flooded with sunlight on cloudless mornings. The final touch was, in fine Palladian manner, to set all windows within a brick relieving arch.

32 Soho Square, built in 1773–5, in the 1920s. It was demolished in 1937.

During the construction of this house Colebrooke's bank ran into difficulties and in about 1777 he sold it to the botanist Joseph Banks. Banks, who had accompanied Captain James Cook on his 1768–71 voyage of scientific experiment, observation and discovery to Tahiti, New Zealand and the east coast of Australia, owned and occasionally occupied number 32 until his death in 1820. The house, which had a rich and fantastic neoclassical interior, was demolished in 1937.

Needless to say, the loss of three out of four of these beautiful and architecturally vigorous houses is a ghastly tragedy.

Early or interesting surviving buildings around the square are:

Number 2 The first house on this site was built in about 1680. The existing building was constructed in 1735 by John Sanger, a St James's carpenter. In 1744 it was occupied by Sir John Phillips of Picton Castle, Pembrokeshire, who – as a baronet, Tory MP and Jacobite – confirms that in the mid eighteenth century the square's residents remained grand and interesting. After Phillips's departure the house became, in 1748, the home of the envoy of the Venetian Republic.

Sanger's house survives fairly intact, although the street façade has been rendered and lined out to simulate ashlar, a shop front has been added, the first-floor windows have been lengthened and the Doric-pedimented doorcase, although handsome, is a late-eighteenth-century addition. The interior is good, with panelling in the ground-floor front room, probably originally the dining room, and in the adjoining back room where the fireplace is flanked by niches in which finely carved scallop shells form their half-domed tops. These niches must have been designed to house large statues or marble-topped buffets. There is a top-lit staircase placed towards the middle of the plan (decidedly a novelty in the mid 1730s, but found also in 48

Greek Street) and many richly detailed cornices survive.

Numbers 4, 5 and 6 were erected in 1801–4 and tell an extraordinary story. They were built, as we have noted, by John Trotter, the head of a firm of army contractors, who had acquired the late-seventeenth-century 4–7 Soho Square and demolished all but number 7 for the erection of a warehouse – an early, and most dramatic, expression of the changing nature of Soho around 1800 from residential to manufacturing, trade and commerce. Looking at them now, with their modulated window proportions and generous floor-to-ceiling heights, it is surprising that they were built as a utilitarian warehouse. But presumably Trotter was obliged to make his building harmonise as far as possible with the surrounding and architecturally respectable houses. The rear elevation at 6 Dean Street – with wide windows and a carriage entrance – is handsome but looks far more like industrial architecture.

After the Napoleonic Wars he turned the building into the Soho Bazaar, an enterprise that had the declared primary aim of encouraging 'Female and Domestic Industry'. Trotter was attempting to mix commerce and trade with morality and philanthropy. The Bazaar, or market, was to be an institution, explained a breathless supporter named the Reverend Joseph Nightingale:

founded on ... benevolent and patriotic principles [in which] the industrious ... may hope to thrive; reduced tradesmen may recover and retain their connexions; beginners may form friends, connexions and habits, before they encounter more extensive speculations; and artists, artizans, and whole families, employed at home,

although infirm or in the country, may securely vend
their labour to advantage by proxy.

So the enterprise, among other things, sought to help
humble war widows and even genteel but impoverished
military families by offering goods at moderate prices and
the opportunity for selling items – perhaps the produce
of family sewing evenings – in a discreet and respectable
manner. Nightingale hinted at another of the institution's
aims. By providing young country women, for whom
London often exercised a fatal attraction, the opportunity
for trade and income through honest toil they could be
saved from being driven into prostitution through des-
titution. And thus, as Nightingale explained, the Bazaar
would do its bit to stop the country pouring 'its happy
and innocent virgins into the common sink of London'.[1]

The Bazaar opened in February 1816. Nightingale
describes the interior. The ground floor was one large
room hung with red cloth and mirrors and provided with
mahogany counters, with two rear rooms – the grotto
and the parterre – decorated with climbing plants. There
was also a kitchen to supply hot food, stoves to provide
heat and even a ladies' changing-room. The Bazaar was
evidently a pioneering enterprise. In fact it sounds rather
like an Edwardian department store in which shopping
was organised to be a pleasing and prolonged experience
(plate 11).

The goods sold in the Bazaar consisted mostly of
millinery, gloves, lace, jewellery and plants – essentially
artefacts for ladies and which ladies could make or provide. There was also a stall selling painting materials and
paper, where the very young Turner bought colours and

sold his sky paintings – the smallest for 1s 6d each. The vendors hired their pitches by the day and all business was conducted on 'the fairest and most liberal plan', with prices being fixed and the goods marked with a price tag.[2] The pitches were regulated and 'watched' by constables, behaviour was to be decorous, and the Bazaar even employed a matron to minister to the needs of its lady customers.

The Bazaar was an instant success and continued to function in this building until 1889, when it was altered to house a firm of publishers, Adam and Charles Black, and the existing continuous shop front was added. The Soho Bazaar reopened at 77 Oxford Street and was in 1893 described by Charles Dickens junior in his *Dictionary of London* as 'the best and oldest bazaar in London, chiefly devoted to the supply of the requirements of ladies and children'.[3]

Numbers 8 and 9 were developed in the late 1680s and early 1690s. Sir Richard Onslow, who became the Speaker of the House of Commons and the 1st Baron Onslow, lived at number 9 from 1691 until his death in 1717. The fact that Onslow chose the square as his London home confirms that the initial aspirations of the Soho development as London's new aristocratic quarter were realised. Both houses were replaced by the existing French Protestant church. Although French Protestants have a long association with Soho, their connection with this site dates only from 1891 when the existing church was built. The architect was Sir Aston Webb, who later designed Admiralty Arch on the Mall and the east front of Buckingham Palace. Architecturally the church is curious since it has little to do with French Protestant artistic traditions and nothing at all to do with the established architectural character of Soho. The building is, rather, a vehicle for the architect to display his own tastes and demonstrate his awareness and mastery of then current fashions in ecclesiastical design. The church is in a rather free Franco-Flemish Gothic manner perhaps more associated with Catholicism than Calvinism, with just enough additions in other historic styles, notably Romanesque, to make the building appear original and not just a slavish copy of an historic model. Much terracotta is used – in the late nineteenth century a fashionable material that was both robust and capable of carrying fine detail. The group of buildings created by Webb comprises not just a church but a vestry, library, schoolroom and living quarters for the pastor. So, like Catholic and Evangelical urban missions, the church complex – which continues to function as intended – is a small world entire of itself, a bastion of French Protestant faith embedded in the heart of Soho.

Number 10 This is one of the only two houses in the square that retain a significant amount of original late-seventeenth-century fabric. The other is number 15. Number 10 was built in the mid 1680s by John Steele under a lease from Frith and Pym. It was two separate houses but united in 1696. Eminent early occupiers included Lord Berkeley, who lived here until 1716, then Lady Buckley until 1732 and Lady Montague until 1734. The brick front – although greatly altered, with windows lowered and the ground floor reconstructed – is essentially late-seventeenth-century. Inside, little survives beyond the basic floor plan, which includes a pair of rear closets, but there is still a magnificent and very robust open-well staircase with massive square newels, large and fat balusters and a broad handrail. A rare survival, and a really good example of late-seventeenth-century joinery.

Number 13 This house was built in 1768 along with the now demolished number 12. The front, with its rather grand details, must have been stuccoed in the mid nineteenth century, but inside some good early details survive. The main staircase is placed in the centre of the house, between front and back rooms, and is wrought of stone in minimal manner with slender balusters of wrought iron – very sculptural. In the first-floor rear room, which has a half-hexagonal bay facing the garden, there is a delicate plaster ceiling of Rococo design and panelling.

Number 14 A house that itself tells the chequered building history of the square. The first house on the site was built by Frith and Pym soon after 1677. And the floor levels of that house seem to have been preserved in later rebuildings and alterations, so the ghost of the late seventeenth century continues to lurk within the current and rather unpromising building. The first major reconstruction seems to have taken place in the mid 1790s, and since then the top storey has been rebuilt, as has the ground floor, and the remainder of the elevation has been over-restored and reconstructed. The house's most famous past resident was, according to an English Heritage blue plaque, Mary Seacole, the Jamaican-born nurse who did good work in the Crimea during the war in the 1850s.

Number 15 Here, as with number 10, a good deal of the late-seventeenth-century fabric survives, notably the brick elevation. There also still lingers inside – unlike in number 10 – a strong sense of the original house, for here it is possible to imagine what the interiors of the first Soho Square houses were like. The plan survives, including back rooms with chimney breasts set in the rear corners, deep closet wings and a compact dog-leg staircase, still with its stout square newels and robust balusters. Panelling with heavy bolection mouldings survives in a number of rooms, and even an original bolection moulded chimney surround. The first inhabitants were the family of the Earl of Mountrath and in 1766 Sir Stephen Janssen, then the Lord Mayor of London (plate 12).

Number 21 The existing building was erected *c.*1838 for Edmund Crosse and Thomas Blackwell, whose company – selling canned, bottled and dried food – subsequently expanded to the north and in the process occupied and then replaced the splendid number 20, designed in the 1770s by Robert Adam. The site of number 20 is now occupied by Crosse & Blackwell's purpose-built and over-large stone-faced office block, completed in 1926. Number 21 is interesting because it illustrates a building type emerging, but in a most uncertain manner. It was built as an office, or merchant's counting house, store room and shop, but still looks domestic – as, to a degree, did the slightly earlier Soho Bazaar. This was perhaps out of respect for the still largely residential nature of the square in which domestic architecture was dominant. But it must be said that the long and remorselessly utilitarian brick elevation to Sutton Row rather gives the game away. This industrial-looking building was the jam and pickle factory, with the bottling plant and the labelling department being housed within the splendid rooms of the Adam house.

Before Crosse & Blackwell's rebuilding of number 21, the old house on the site had some fame – or at least notoriety – as the White House Hotel. This establishment was kept from the late 1770s until 1801 by Thomas Hooper.

As far as it's known, the hotel functioned primarily as a brothel of a highly picturesque and escapist sort. It had a number of exotically decorated rooms, many with their walls inlaid with large mirrors, that seemed to mix the erotic with the horrific. Rooms included a 'Painted Chamber', a 'Grotto', the 'Coal Hole' and the 'Skeleton Room', where a machine-operated skeleton could be made to step out of a closet. What the skeleton did next, or the role it played in the greater scheme of things, has not – sadly – been recorded with any certainty.[4] However, in the 1850s the indefatigable Henry Mayhew, who had evidently gained some second-hand knowledge of the long-lost but still 'notorious place of ill-fame' from 'street-patterers' (storytellers), offered a little more information about this strange place of exhibitionism, magic, sex and horror:

> Some of the apartments, it is said, were furnished in a style of costly luxury; while others were fitted up with springs, traps, and other contrivances, so as to present no appearance other than that of an ordinary room, until the machinery was set in motion. In one room, into which some wretched girl might be introduced, on her drawing a curtain as she would be desired, a skeleton, grinning horribly, was precipitated forward, and caught the terrified creature in his, to all appearance, bony arms.

Other dimly lit chambers were ornamented with a coffin or furnished with a sofa that 'was made to descend into some place of utter darkness; or, it was alleged, into a room in which was a store of soot or ashes'.[5]

Number 19 St Patrick's Church. From 1685 to 1791 the site was occupied by Carlisle House, which, in about 1760, came into the possession of the exotic Venetian Theresa Cornelys. She fitted up the house in grand style and used it for public receptions, assemblies and masquerades after the completion in 1761 of a major addition in adjoining Sutton Street. There was a charge for admission, and cards, dancing, dining and operatic performances were available – but most importantly it was a place of fashionable parade which also offered the opportunity for profitable encounter. Stylish courtesans seeking clients and men willing to pay for their pleasures could use the rooms to mutual satisfaction. During the 1760s Mrs Cornelys's rooms played an important and productive role in London's well-oiled and lucrative sex industry. But all things come to an end, and due to a mix of circumstances Mrs Cornelys's famed establishment closed in 1772, when she found herself insolvent and a bankrupt bound for a debtors' jail. She returned to Carlisle House in 1775 as manageress for her creditors, slid back into debt and died in 1797 while in the Fleet Prison. Carlisle House was demolished in 1791 and replaced by a pair of houses fronting on Soho Square.

The 1760s assembly room on Sutton Street was converted into a Roman Catholic chapel, whose congregation in 1866 acquired the pair of adjoining 1790s houses on the square. In 1891 the chapel and the northerly of the two 1791 houses were demolished for the erection of St Patrick's Roman Catholic Church.

This building makes its presence felt in dramatic manner. The site of the house is occupied by a tall, Italianate tower while the former assembly room was replaced with a somewhat gaunt and cavernous nave lined with numerous small chapels. It is decidedly Italian in feel, and its foreign and solemn atmosphere and lofty interior are in exotic and striking contrast with the worldly bustle of the square. The architect was John Kelly.

Number 21a The Presbytery. The building was erected in 1791–3 on the southern portion of the site occupied by Carlisle House. It is a very fine example of late-eighteenth-century domestic design with tall and elegant first-floor windows, a good fanlight and many original interior details. It seems to have been built as a superior lodging house – it was certainly in divided occupancy from the start – until acquired by St Patrick's in 1866.

Number 26 This is the last house in the square with an heroic Venetian window, originally one of a pair built in 1758 to the designs of the amateur Palladian architect Sir William Robinson. The house is tucked into the corner of the square, with a narrow elevation that suggests only half its volume. So entering it is quite a surprise, with a large, stone-built staircase appearing to the right, its presence concealed from exterior views. The interior, although much altered, remains one of the best in Soho. The stone staircase is set behind a screen of Ionic columns and furnished with fine wrought-iron balusters; one of the ground-floor rear rooms has a rich cornice and a high-quality fitted and pedimented bookcase, which could well be the work of Thomas Chippendale, who is documented as having decorated the house for Sir William. Within there is still a considerable quantity of carved joinery and mahogany-veneered doors, which are no doubt Chippendale's work. The ground-floor elevation was removed in the mid nineteenth century to create commercial accommodation and has recently been rebuilt, with the front door set within a squat, tripartite composition to match the Venetian window above. This design was inspired by John Tallis's view of Soho Square in his *London Street Views* of 1838–40.

Number 36 The front of the house dates from the late eighteenth century but its plan, with a closet wing to the rear, suggests that much of the fabric might well be late-seventeenth-century. The interior details, like the front, date from the late eighteenth, with some additions of the early nineteenth century. There is an especially good marble fireplace of *c.*1775 in the ground-floor front room incorporating a frieze inlaid with a large-scale Greek key pattern, rendered in red/brown marble. Very beautiful. Well worth getting inside.

Number 37 This house, with number 38, frames the entrance into the square from Carlisle Street. Both these houses, although far from reading as a pair, are large and handsome, both have visually powerful and very architectural shop fronts and canted bays on their Carlisle Street elevations. Number 37 was built *c.*1690 and rebuilt *c.*1766, from which time some good details remain, including the serpentine wrought-iron staircase balustrade and a fine plaster ceiling of Rococo design in the main first-floor room. The shop front, embellished with Greek Doric engaged columns, is a most solemn and splendid affair. It appears to have been installed for Messrs Dulau and Company, foreign booksellers, who occupied the building from 1800 and through the entire nineteenth century. During the first decade of that century part of the house was also used for public entertainments and was known as Dulau's Rooms. Perhaps this shop front doubled as a portico to allow customers to enter in style.

Number 38 The house seems to have been built in 1735 by James Sanger, who also built the adjoining numbers 1 and 2 Soho Square. But Sanger's work has been greatly altered. The most memorable features now are the two-storey canted bay, carried on Doric columns at street level, which faces onto Carlisle Street, and the handsome mid-nineteenth-century shop front facing onto the square. This, as if to complement the Doric shop front on 37, also incorporates a colonnade, but formed with Corinthian columns, which are far richer in detail.

Greek Street

The street has carried its current name since it was laid out in the late 1670s and was no doubt named in honour of the Greek Church that had been built in 1677 in a court off the west side of nearby Hog Lane (now part of Charing Cross Road). This church was taken over by a French Protestant congregation in 1682 and is described simply as 'French Church' on Rocque's map of 1746, when St Martin's Almshouses are shown on the west and north sides of the court (see p. 26).

Number 1 One of the finest mid-Georgian houses in London. The existing building was constructed in the mid 1740s, but its superb interior – richly decorated with Rococo plasterwork and high-quality joinery – was completed a little later.

The first house on the site was built in 1678 and in 1740 acquired by John Smithers, a bricklayer and speculating builder. He demolished it in 1742, but went bankrupt before he could rebuild. His creditors acquired the site and passed what remained of the lease to two other speculating builders, Joseph and George Pearce, who seemed to have erected the shell of the new house by

1746 and – perhaps – started to fit out the ground floor. At this point the landlord, the Duke of Portland, granted a new eighty-seven-year lease to Joseph Pearce. The house remained at least partly a shell until in 1754 Pearce's executors sold the remainder of the lease to Richard Beckford, for the large sum of £2,500.

Beckford was a wealthy Jamaica trader who made a fortune from sugar planted, picked and processed by slave labour. His brother was 'Alderman' William Beckford – a City of London grandee and twice Lord Mayor – and his nephew was William Beckford, who became notable as a connoisseur of advanced architectural and artistic taste and eventually a social outcast and recluse in consequence of his alleged homosexual predilections.

Richard Beckford moved into 1 Greek Street for Christmas 1754, by which time most of the rich interior, with its profusion of high-quality Rococo plasterwork on walls and ceilings and its fine joinery must have been completed (plate 13). Towards the end of 1755 Beckford left the house, never to return, dying in France in December that year. In April 1756 Beckford's trustees sold the house and leasehold interest to Sir James Colebrooke for the colossal sum of £6,300. This suggests that Beckford's improvements – notably the exotic Rococo plasterwork – cost around £3,800. Some idea of the high value of this house is suggested by the fact that in the mid eighteenth century a London journeyman tradesman would earn little over £1 a week and, according to Isaac Ware in 1756, a 'common' London house (three windows wide and five storeys high) cost '£600 or £700' to build.[6] Colebrooke lived in the house until 1761, when it was sold to George Cruickshanks for only £4,000. Perhaps Soho's changing status, as it became more commercial and less aristocratic, or waning enthusiasm for its sumptuous Rococo interior, made the house less valuable. Cruickshanks lived there until 1765, at which point it went into a social decline that reflected accurately Soho's altered character. By 1811 the house, no longer a desirable residence for a fashionable tenant, was taken by the Westminster Commissioners of Sewers and so went into institutional and office use. In 1855 it was occupied by the Commissioners' successor, the Metropolitan Board of Works (MBW). The main rooms were maintained, but some alterations and additions were made to permit the house to function as the nerve centre of the organisation that was to create Victorian London's new roads – for example the Embankment, Charing Cross Road, Shaftesbury Avenue, Commercial Street in Spitalfields – and infrastructure, notably new sewers. It is curious that the mighty works intended to make London a healthier and more efficient modern city were planned within the gorgeous Rococo rooms of this merchant palace.

In 1861 the MBW removed to larger premises and the house was sold for £6,400 – essentially its value in the 1750s – to the House of Charity, which owns it still under the name of the House of St Barnabas-in-Soho. This charity had been established for the 'relief' of the destitute and homeless poor in London, and the fact that it chose to locate itself in Soho says much about the social complexion of the area in the 1860s. As with many Victorian charitable institutions, it was not just the physical but also the spiritual welfare of the poor that was of interest. The House of Charity aimed to 'have a Christian effect on the poor population',[7] and to this end in 1862 built a splendid chapel in the garden, designed in a powerful early-Gothic style by a little-known architect named Joseph Clarke. When glimpsed from Manette Street, and seen in the humdrum setting of modern Soho, this chapel – with its array of French-style curved apses – is a most surprising and pleasing evocation of the romance of the Middle Ages.

Despite this preference for the Gothic style, and despite the pressing demands of its function as a refuge for the poor – particularly the 'fallen' women of Soho – the house was well preserved. Its main rooms – with their classical mouldings and flamboyant Rococo decoration, which must at times have seemed grotesquely out of step with the charity's pressing social concerns – were suffered to survive. The only significant loss was the sale of three ornate fire surrounds, probably to raise funds to complete the chapel. The house no longer functions as a refuge but serves as an office and money-spinner for the charity. It has even recently participated in the creation of a smart members' club within its fine rooms to help generate funds for its charitable aims.

What this means is that one of London's finest Georgian houses is, with certain constraints and conditions, open for exploration. The house offers a circuit of reception rooms on the ground and first floors, reached and connected by the large entrance hall, containing a generous open-well staircase of considerable grandeur, with stone treads and ornamental wrought-iron balusters. The ground-floor rooms have bold panelled walls and pedimented overmantels, still in the Palladian style. These perhaps date from the mid 1740s. The first-floor rooms are far more ornate, with their Palladian wall ornament augmented by Rococo ceilings wrought in plaster and papier-mâché. The first-floor room on the corner of Greek Street and Soho Square is the best, with its action-packed ceiling including writhing dragons that may be a fashionable touch of Chinoiserie or a reference to the City of London connections of the Beckford dynasty. These Rococo refinements probably date from the mid 1750s.

Number 3 This is a deceptive house. Its outside is plain and, with its applied-stucco window architraves, it looks mid-nineteenth-century. But on closer inspection the brickwork is earlier, with good pointing, and the original brick arches are just visible above the architraves. The house was built in 1744 by Joseph Pearce, on a lease from the Portland estate. Pearce had worked on the construction of 1 Greek Street and built number 3 as a pair with the now lost 2 Greek Street. The interior is well preserved above ground-floor level, including a panelled first floor with an enriched cornice, a panelled second floor and a fine original staircase set at the end of a panelled entrance passage. The existing shop front is puzzling: the central window with its glazing bars and radial corners suggests an early-nineteenth-century date, but the cement brackets topped with wreaths framing the façade appear mid-nineteenth-century. So I suppose it is a mixture of both.

Excursion into Manette Street

This was called Rose Street until 1895 and was first developed in the early 1690s. The dominant historic building is number 14 and its large size suggests this was no ordinary house. It is in fact a rare survival of a most emotive building type. It was built in 1770–71 as the St Anne's parish workhouse and was designed by James Paine, a notable architect of the day, famed for his country houses and town mansions. This is the place where select paupers of the parish would have been housed, monitored and put to work to make their lives – financed by parish ratepayers through the Poor Laws – modestly profitable and far from comfortable. An extra storey was added in 1804, which explains the flattish early-nineteenth-century pediment that now adorns the centre of the building. As the *Survey of London* explains, 'the lot of the paupers [here] seems to have been a hard one',[8] with a population of 240 adult paupers in the winter of 1818 crammed into ninety-seven beds. In 1837 the responsibility for maintaining the poor of the parish was transferred from St Anne's vestry to the Guardians of the Strand Union and the building fell empty. Its survival is remarkable. Extended upwards and to the rear, coated with stucco, it is now a somewhat ungainly monument to a bleak past; but it endures and now seems to be in jolly and gainful employment as offices and studios for the media industry.

There are other buildings in the street that are of interest. Number 16, to judge by its front, dates from the late eighteenth century but its rear elevation suggests it was part of the original development of the street. Number 17 is also of eighteenth-century origin and has an early second-floor workshop, possibly built to house one of Soho's industries; perhaps it was the home and workplace of a silversmith.

Return to Greek Street

Numbers 11, 12, 13 and 14 These houses form a fascinating group that, due to stucco and mass-produced moulded decorations, is easy to dismiss as a late-nineteenth-century rebuilding of little interest. In fact, numbers 12 and 13 are, in essence, a very large, seven-window-wide house built in the mid 1680s. The squarish proportion of its windows suggests its date, and a photograph taken in 1914, before it was stuccoed, shows a fine brick elevation with square panels in the parapet which no doubt replaced a fine timber-eaves cornice. By the early twentieth century the house was divided in two, but was originally known as Portland House and was the largest house in the street.

The history of its occupation is a history of Soho in miniature. In 1685 it was lived in by Lady Wolstenholme, and so reflected the initial aspiration of Soho's landlords and developers to create an aristocratic quarter. In 1691 it was occupied by the Huguenot Abraham Meure, who, rather than working in precious metal, took up the task of educating young men of Huguenot descent. The house became an 'academy' or boarding school and achieved such a good reputation that English aristocrats and grandees – including the Earl of Montagu and Thomas Pitt, the owner of the nearby estate – sent their sons there. In 1715 the house became the residence of the Savoyard ambassador, who was probably a tenant of Viscount Chetwynd, who then held the head-lease. In the 1720s the house was the home of the viscount's brother, John Chetwynd, who was an MP, an envoy to Spain and a Lord of the Admiralty. But gradually its status and its occupants changed, as did the nature of Soho itself, and by the mid 1760s the house had descended the social scale from aristocratic home to place of work and entertainment. In 1766 the leasehold interest passed to James Cullen, an upholsterer who was associated with the notorious Mrs Cornelys of Carlisle House, Soho Square fame. In the opinion of the *Survey of London*, the pair 'joined in a similar undertaking in Greek Street',[9] and this house – for which Mrs Cornelys paid the rates until her bankruptcy in 1772 – became a place of 'assemblies' and part of Soho's subtle but growing sex industry.

After the failure of Mrs Cornelys's business ventures Cullen let Portland House in 1774 to Josiah Wedgwood, who turned it – and its extensive back premises – into the London warehouse and showroom for his firm's pottery. This use as a place of somewhat refined trade was typical of late-eighteenth-century Soho. In the late 1790s the Wedgwood Company moved from Portland House, after which it was occupied by a coach maker, and then divided into separate accommodation, becoming a studio and exhibition space for various artists. By the early twentieth century Portland House had become Wedde's and Piemonte Hotel and restaurant.

Sadly, nothing of age or interest appeared to remain within Portland House, and its courtyard buildings had been rebuilt and renamed Wedgwood Mews. And if by any chance any old interior fragments did survive, they are all gone now because by the summer of 2018 Portland House had been reduced to no more than a façade, propped up on Dean Street while building works took place on the large site behind.

Numbers 11 and 14 now frame Portland House in symmetrical manner. Their generally matching stucco façades are presumably mid-nineteenth-century but their histories, of course, stretch back far earlier. Number 11 had in 1701 housed the King's Square Coffee House and until 1772 had been Mrs Cornelys's 'Little House', perhaps her own home.

Number 17 was built in the late 1680s, and survived into the late twentieth century. It has now been crudely rebuilt in a poorly detailed Georgian manner but retains a shop front (heavily restored) from the mid 1820s that is a very rare survival of elegant late-Georgian commercial design and that was probably made for the carver and gilder Michael Tijou, whose firm operated from the house between 1803 and 1832.

Number 18 A handsome early-nineteenth-century building with a pleasing brick front. The somewhat heavily detailed, stone-built shop front, in a peculiar and indeterminate early Renaissance style, was designed in 1862, probably by the architect A.H. Morant. In 1864 the upper part of the house became the headquarters of the Central Council of the International Working Men's Association.[10] The association had been recently formed following a meeting at St Martin's Hall that had been attended by a variety of radical, revolutionary, socialist and communist groups including Italian republicans, Irish and Polish nationalists, trade unionists and German socialists. Karl Marx was present but did not address the meeting. The aim of the gathering was to organise and unite working men throughout Europe so that they could argue more forcefully for increased liberties, civil rights, security of employment and improved working conditions and wages. Marx joined the twenty-one-strong committee that formed the First International, which gathered at 18 Greek Street. So this humble building became one of the cornerstones of the revolutionary politics that in Russia in 1917 started a process which changed the world.

Number 20 Built in 1842 for Thomas Hopkins and H.C. Purvis, colourmen, who remained in occupation until the late twentieth century. The shop front is an excellent and robust affair – little altered since the building was constructed – with thin Doric pilasters defining the shop windows and the doors to the shop and the house. All the glazed openings retained their external shutters when I photographed the house in the early 1970s. There is no sign of them now. Also early and surviving is a hand-operated swivel hoist that, fixed at ground level, was used to move drums of paint between the ground floor and the basement. Until recently the ground floor operated as a Pizza Express, with customers seated outside, below the hoist, like well-stuffed parcels waiting to be lifted skywards. The restaurant, in April 2001, is empty.

Number 21 A good early-nineteenth-century yellow-brick façade with the curious and unusual detail of timber lintels fixed above the upper-floor window arches. Their purpose is uncertain, but presumably structural rather than ornamental. They were possibly inserted to spread the load of the upper floors away from the window arches and onto the flanking brick piers. Perhaps at some point the upper floors carried unusually heavy loads; or the lintels could have been intended as fixings for some type of blind. At ground-floor level is a fine early-nineteenth-century shop with elongated Greek Revival Ionic pilasters. Until about 2014 this house remained in traditional twentieth-century Soho use. On the ground floor a rather tired newsagent's, off licence and general store was in operation, with 'working girls' active above. This was one of the few houses east of Wardour Street where the euphemism 'models' was still pinned to a usually open front door, complete with a small red lamp. This relative discretion continued the practice of the area's eighteenth-century sex industry, where the prostitutes tended to work from home rather than patrol the streets. By the summer of 2018 things had changed. The façade had been painted dark grey and the lintels obscured – a surprising mutilation and presumably a misguided attempt to give the house a smarter appearance. The store had been upgraded, with a standard fascia virtually obscuring the Ionic capitals. The red lamp and 'models' sign were nowhere to be seen, suggesting that the 'working girls' had been moved on.

Numbers 17–21 Greek Street form, with their good shop fronts and reticent but well-wrought brick elevations, one of the most satisfying early-nineteenth-century groups in Soho.

Numbers 26, 27 and 28 form a group of much-altered and re-fronted late-seventeenth- and early-eighteenth-century houses. Numbers 27 and 28, clad with stucco and with first-floor pediments, house Maison Bertaux, the excellent and long-established Soho patisserie; number 27 retains a staircase located between the back and front rooms, which is a late-seventeenth-century form.

Number 29 The Coach and Horses public house, also stucco-fronted, but its storey heights are slightly higher than those of its Greek Street neighbours. The quadrant corner suggests an early-nineteenth-century date. In early 2019 a threat to the pub's future emerged. It's colourful tenants were not to have their leases renewed by Fuller's, the pub's owner, and there were even rumours of it being turned into a 'theme pub'. The proposal was being fought by the landlord, loyal patrons and locals. To draw publicity to his fight, and to demonstrate the artistic and historic importance of the pub's unchanged interior, the landlord did the brilliantly obvious thing. In June 2019 he staged, within the pub, performances of Keith Waterhouse's 1989 play *Jeffrey Bernard Is Unwell*, which is set within the pub. Since Bernard was a stalwart regular it is clear that the pub already has a theme – Jeffrey Bernard and Soho from the 1950s into the 1980s – in which case the pub should be left as it is to tell its own story. The brewers run it as a 'managed house' and say they will keep it unchanged, because 'themed pubs are not Fuller's' thing'. But in early 2020 it closed for 'restoration' with re-opening scheduled for April. A year later it reopened – physically unchanged.

Numbers 34, 35a and 35 form, with 4 Romilly Street (see p. 183), a very altered group dating from *c*.1735. The corner building, 35, appears to have been entirely rebuilt in the late nineteenth century and now houses the Y Ming restaurant. According to Jonathan Fryer, in his book *Soho in the Fifties and Sixties*, this building housed David Archer's bookshop after it moved to Soho from Bloomsbury. Archer, the 'great unsung hero of Soho', held salons in the shop – with Henrietta Moraes serving the buns – attended by the local 'literati'. Beverage was all-important, so the party usually ended up in the Coach and Horses. Archer had an eye for talent and was an early champion of Dylan Thomas. Number 35a retains much of its original façade, although the brick arches appear rebuilt. It also retains some panelling and its original dog-leg staircase. Number 34 has been crudely re-fronted, perhaps entirely rebuilt. All are currently under threat of demolition for the construction of Crossrail 2.

Numbers 37 and 39 Kettner's restaurant occupies these houses, and four others in neighbouring Romilly Street. Kettner's was established in 1867 and so was arguably Soho's oldest surviving restaurant until it closed in 2015. It reopened in 2018 under the ownership of Soho House and is now part of an hotel, the main entrance being at 29 Romilly Street. Still closed in mid April 2021. All the houses are eighteenth-century in origin although all have been radically altered – more, perhaps, inside than out.

Number 47 This house dated from the late seventeenth century, although the front and back walls had been rebuilt in the late eighteenth. It retained its original staircase with square newels, and a bolection moulded fireplace in the first-floor rear room appeared to be original. The house's first occupant was Lady Ingoldsby, again confirming the aristocratic aspirations of Soho in its early days. In the early 1970s I photographed the exterior of the house. It was derelict and generally unloved and, with the blinking of an eye, passed away, unchampioned and unmourned, as was so often the case with historic buildings at the time, not only in Soho but in all of Britain's towns and cities. Such losses are not only sad in themselves but invariably dilute what is left behind.

Number 48 One of Soho's finest Georgian houses. It was built in 1741–2 on a sixty-five-year lease from the Portland estate. The speculating builder was Thomas Richmond, who some years earlier had developed Richmond Buildings, off Dean Street, and the palatial 75, 76 and 77 Dean Street. The house was first occupied by George

Chardin, presumably a Huguenot. The exterior, although only three windows wide, possesses more than usual grandeur, with its windows framed by stone architraves, and those to the first floor having, in addition, pulvinated friezes and cornices. This was all very fashionable in the 1740s, and imitated aristocratic Palladian mansions in St James's Square and Grosvenor Square. The plan of the house is usual for Soho terrace houses – a front room, a rear room and a closet half the width of the rear room and projecting beyond the rear wall. But there are subtle but significant differences that add greatly to the building's spatial excitement. The staircase is not squeezed into one corner of the ground plan but occupies a generous volume within the centre of the site, with its majestic flights of beautifully turned balusters and Doric newels ascending around an open well. But most striking – certainly unusual for such a house – is the fact that the staircase is top-lit, so it reads rather like a Roman atrium. This was pioneering indeed for a three-window-wide London terrace house of the early 1740s and anticipated the coming neoclassical fashion by over twenty years. The ground floor has been altered, although many original details survive; but the first- and second-floor rooms, and all the closet rooms, retain their panelling – and this is generally very good indeed. There are also delightful details to see, including a white marble fire surround in the first-floor front room, which also retains a fine Rococo ceiling, certainly now a rarity in a London terrace house of the period. Most of these details can be seen with relative ease since the building houses L'Escargot restaurant, which has been here – in one form or another – since the 1920s.

Number 50 This house is nearly as good as number

48 and, although less ambitious and more usual in its plan-form, has a splendid front elevation distinguished by an arched and centrally placed first-floor window, a bold stone cornice and the substantial remains of a fine Doric doorcase. The house also retains a good staircase and much panelling. It was erected in 1736 on a sixty-three-and-a-half-year building lease by William Frith, carpenter, of St James's parish. The lease was not granted directly by the Portland estate but by a consortium that had already obtained a Portland lease on the land. The first occupier was George Crowle, the MP for Hull and consul at Lisbon, yet another reminder that, in the 1730s, Greek Street remained a desirable residential location. The interior cannot easily be seen. The building is currently the home of the rather exclusive Union Club, whose members are 'carefully selected' and include people of 'business' and managerial types in the media industry.

Number 51 Like its long-lost neighbour, number 52, this house was built in 1733 by Nicholas Saunders. The two houses replaced a single late-seventeenth-century mansion, a move that reflects Soho's changing character when, during the eighteenth century, houses of a more humble type were in demand. Inside, a good original staircase survives.

Excursion into Romilly Street

Until 1937 this was named Church Street. The first houses were built along its length in 1678, with most of the street complete by the late 1680s. None of these early houses survive in any significant manner.

Number 4 This house, with its horrid plastic windows

and scrubbed yellow brickwork, is not now much to look at. But it was built in 1735, on a Portland estate sublease to the speculating bricklayer Francis Drewitt and carpenter John Moore. Its small size presumably reflects the modest ambitions of those redeveloping Romilly Street in the early eighteenth century. Inside, some panelling and a dog-leg staircase survive. The satirical artist Thomas Rowlandson exhibited here in 1775. It is now occupied by the 'Man Clansmen Association', a Chinese workmen's society. The building is currently threatened with demolition for Crossrail 2.

Numbers 19–24, together with 37–41 Frith Street (see p. 232) form one of the most evocative Georgian groups in Soho. The houses – dating from the 1730s to the 1780s – are much altered, some mutilated with a sense of jolly unconcern, and the group is most informal. But this is the point: it offers a happy balance of variety of detail within general uniformity of scale and form, a quality that characterises much modest Georgian street architecture. But – above all – the generally ad hoc repairs and alterations are not brutally offensive and help to record the passage of time, expressing vitality and giving the buildings a wonderful sense of authenticity.

Number 19 Built in 1763. Much altered inside and out but now memorable for its two-storey-high canted bay window, a most handsome and unusual detail in the street frontages of London's eighteenth-century houses, although there are a couple of other examples surviving around Soho Square. The bay was probably added *c.*1790, when a painter named William Sherlock occupied the house.

Numbers 21 and 22 A good pair, built in 1738 on a

lease from the Portland estate. Number 21 was built by a Soho tallow chandler named Thomas Cuthbert and 22 by Jane Allam, a spinster and descendant of one of the initial developers of Soho Fields – so a businesswoman with good local contacts. Both fronts have been altered or obscured by paint, but the interiors in 21 are good – the *Survey of London* claims that they are the best in the street – with much enriched panelling and a fine staircase. The staircase also survives in 22. Number 21 is now occupied by Gautier's restaurant, so it's possible to get a glimpse of the ground-floor interior.

Number 24 Built in 1781, under a ninety-nine-year lease from the Portland estate by a local upholstery named Timothy Goulding. It forms a group with 37 and 38 Frith Street, which date from the same time. The flat and simple elevations and construction of yellow brick (now soot-stained) contrast with the more richly detailed earlier houses, often built of brown, purple and red bricks and with elevations enlivened with string courses. The blank windows in 37 are a typical no-nonsense Georgian speculator's solution to the thorny problem of how to detail a terrace house of standard plan for a corner site.

Numbers 28 to 31 The hotel incorporating Kettner's restaurant occupies this entire group of houses, plus two in adjoining Greek Street (see p. 181). They are a mixed bag of much-altered early-eighteenth-century houses which, despite later ground floors and painted brick elevations, still form an attractive group.

Number 34 This house, only two windows wide, confirms the modest aspirations of at least some of the early-eighteenth-century builders operating in the street. Its exterior is painted and architraves were added to its windows in the nineteenth century, but it clearly dates from the early eighteenth century. In mid 2019 it still operates as a 'walk-up' – one of the few in east Soho – with the front door open and in the hall bells by which contact can be made with 'Sexy Ruby' or 'New Samanta' waiting in the rooms above. The open door also means the staircase can be viewed, which is well worth doing because its bulbous balusters and closed string form suggest a construction date for the house of c.1718.

Numbers 37–39, on the corner with Moor Street The Spice of Life, a late-nineteenth-century pub with the remains of a good interior.

Gerrard Place

This small street was formed in 1732 when the houses to the west of Devonshire House were demolished. This new street, originally called Nassau Street, connected the existing Gerrard Street with King Street (now replaced by part of Shaftesbury Avenue). Devonshire House, built in the later seventeenth century for the Earl of Devonshire, stood on the site of what is now the block forming the east side of Gerrard Place. The house fronted west, with its garden to the east. Devonshire House was also demolished in 1732, its destruction related to the construction of a block of speculative houses named Whetten's Buildings, after their builder, a Soho bricklayer called John Whetten.

Number 3 Gerrard Street presents a side elevation on the south-west corner of Gerrard Place. It was part of Whetten's Buildings and built in 1733–4 by Whetten on a lease granted by John Jeffreys (see p. 188). The side elevation of 3 Gerrard Street is an impressive composition intended to ornament the prospect of Gerrard Place. It is three windows wide – all widely spaced – with, in the centre of the first floor, a blank arched recess containing a handsome pedimented tablet inscribed 'Nassau Street in Whetten's Buildings 1734'. Now stucco-clad.

Number 2 Gerrard Place is immediately to the north. Also built by Whetten in 1733–4, it is now somewhat mutilated and rebuilt, but remains handsome and suggests the architectural ambitions of Whetten's conception for the street. On the left side of the elevation is a bold pilaster strip (presumably echoed on the long-lost house to the north of the group) and a large Doric cornice set above second-floor level, which means that the top floor (now poorly rebuilt) would have read as an attic on a Roman triumphal arch. What survives of the house's interior, or certainly what is currently visible, suggests the high quality of the finish. The entrance is very fine, with fluted Doric pilasters, a dentilled cornice and a seat recessed into the panelling on which footmen could rest while awaiting orders.

Gerrard Street

Despite the almost overwhelming paraphernalia associated with the street's quite recent manifestation as the heart of Soho's Chinatown, despite neglect and the crass intrusion of commerce into wonderful early interiors and onto fragile historic façades and – most of all – despite some serious demolition, Gerrard Street remains one of the most rewarding Soho streets to explore, still rich in buildings of intense interest. It was laid out in the mid 1670s on the Military Ground, part of which had been acquired on lease from the Crown by Baron Gerard of

Brandon. The story is told on p. 70.

Gerrard Place, number 2 on the right, and Gerrard Street in c.1974.

Number 3 (See Gerrard Place above).

Numbers 4, 5 and 6 all formed part of Whetten's Buildings, constructed in 1733–4. However, these three houses are lower in height than number 3 and their elevations stuccoed and much altered. From 1917 to 1932 the 1917 Club, founded by Leonard Woolf, was based in number 4 (see p. 116).

Number 6 is probably the least altered, with segmental headed windows and a band course above the second-floor windows.

Early panelling survives in portions of these houses –

for example in the entrance passage of number 5.

Number 9 was the Turk's Head, built in 1758 and one of London's only few surviving purpose-built eighteenth-century taverns. It is a splendid building, two rooms wide and two rooms deep, with a large rear assembly room at first-floor level reached by a wide, robust and well-detailed staircase. Much panelling survives but it is generally concealed behind shelves lined with food, for the building currently houses a Cantonese delicatessen. The façade was rendered in the early nineteenth century. It was in this tavern that The Club dining club met from 1764 to 1783 (plate 4).

Numbers 10 and 11 date from the start of construction of the houses in the street, *c*.1680. Both are much altered – particularly number 11 – but they are remarkable survivals. Number 10 still has its brick front, although it is painted heavily, with square-headed windows and a flat string course above the second-floor level. These are typical details of the period. No doubt both houses would originally have had timber-eaves cornices.

Number 12 was also built in 1680, but probably re-fronted in 1848 when stucco and crudely detailed giant Ionic pilasters were added that now, in rather ungainly and pompous manner, flank this modest two-window-wide elevation.

Number 16 was rebuilt *c*.1730 by John Meard and it is Meard's house, it seems, that survives today, although much altered with crude architraves framing the windows and a shop or restaurant front at ground level. The most striking thing is that it's taller than its late-seventeenth-century neighbours because, although the same number of storeys, it has more elegant rooms with higher ceilings, as became increasingly the fashion during the eighteenth century. Despite the alterations it is clear that the façade is significantly different to those built at approximately the same time by Meard in Meard Street (see p. 265): notably, here the window heads are segmental, not flat. In the nineteenth century this was the location of the Mont Blanc restaurant, which was a favourite meeting place for literary men. Here dined, and met – before and just after the First World War – Joseph Conrad, John Galsworthy, G.K. Chesterton, Hilaire Belloc, John Masefield, Edward Thomas, Ford Maddox Ford and W.H. Davies.

Number 17 has a façade similar in character to number 16 but its storey heights are lower. This suggests that this is a late-seventeenth-century house re-fronted in the early 1730s. There is a straight joint between it and number 16, revealing that – if it was indeed re-fronted in the 1730s – this was a project separate from Meard's work next door.

Number 18 appears to be a house of c.1680 re-fronted in the early nineteenth century – as suggested by the wide window spacing – when it was stuccoed and decorated with charming and characteristic details, including cast-iron window guards at first-floor level, and the giant paterae that frame the façade just above the level of the first-floor window heads. James Gibbs, the eminent architect, lived at number 18 from 1720 to 1726, when he was designing St Martin-in-the-Fields.

Number 27 also appears to be a house of c.1680 but the *Survey of London* records that the existing house dates from 1783, presumably largely reproducing the late-seventeenth-century design.[11] It served as an hotel from 1874 to 1917 and from 1918 as a restaurant. The brick corbelled cornice must date from this period of commercial use. The *Survey* records that in the mid 1960s the building retained parts of its Art-Nouveau-style ground-floor restaurant frontage, including cresting of wrought iron and flower-pot holders. This has all been swept away for a minimal, modern look.

Number 30 was built in 1778, replacing a house of 1683. It is a fine house for its date, if a trifle old-fashioned in its details. It's fronted with yellow bricks – very well wrought – and the façade has fine and precise proportions. The first-floor windows are of roughly double-square proportion – an ideal at the time and signifying lofty first-floor ceiling heights. The second-floor windows are of slightly shallower proportion, while those of the third floor are set above a Roman-style dentilled cornice and are almost square in shape.

The doorcase is especially fine, its Doric pilasters with guilloche-ornamented shafts (a detail particularly popular with Palladian designers in the early decades of the eighteenth century) supporting large consoles that in turn support an open pediment. Set between the scrolls and within the pediment is a fine arched fanlight. Elements of this design are reminiscent of ones published in the 1720s and 1730s by Soho residents James Gibbs and Batty Langley.

Number 31 dates from *c*.1683 so is one of the few, and arguably the best preserved, of the street's original houses. However, it is far from being unaltered. The façade is rendered and the ground floor modern. The house is large, so representative of the more generous houses in the street, three windows wide, four storeys high above a basement, with windows proportioned to reflect the standard hierarchy, the first floor being the piano nobile. There are string courses between floor levels and there would originally have been a timber eaves cornice, not a parapet. Little remains inside, apart from the original – or at least early – staircase, which has carved console step ends and Doric-column newels at lower levels and stout balusters at upper levels. But there might be more – the window shutters are visible and look early. Until 1966 the house retained its original panelled front door and ground-floor elevation. The door has now gone and the ground floor has been obscured in an almost baffling manner.

Numbers 36–39 (consecutive) were built as a roughly uniform group in 1737, replacing two of the street's larger, late-seventeenth-century houses on a sixty-one-year building lease from John Jeffrey to Joseph Buckoke, a local carpenter. Presumably Buckoke was the architect of this noble group as well as the leading speculator behind its construction. The group fared reasonably well until the mid 1970s, when numbers 37 and 38 were damaged by fire. I remember going to see the pair soon after the blaze. The upper parts had been badly damaged but most of the façades survived, along with the lower areas. They could have been saved if action had been taken quickly. But it was not. The ruins were propped, initially occupied, then seemingly abandoned, reduced to ground level only and finally rebuilt in a facsimile manner but, sadly, with details not up to scratch. So numbers 37 and 38 are no longer of any architectural interest. But that is far from the case with the two survivors.

37 and 38 Gerrard Street, built in 1737, in the early 1970s after fire damage, photographed during Chinese New Year festival.

Number 36 is probably, architecturally, the most impressive building in the street. Like its fellows, it has a four-storey façade of noble proportion, with pronounced first-floor windows, a third-floor attic storey set above a masonry cornice, and stone cills supported on brackets to all windows. Buckoke attempted – and achieved – a powerful and generally unified elevation that was not just minimal speculative building. Like the best Soho builders, he created a notable composition that made a significant contribution to the enjoyment of the street as a whole.

But the real and individual glory of number 36 is its interior. Its large-scale entrance hall and staircase are truly superb. The front door, with its early-nineteenth-century fanlight, leads to a wide entrance passage with boldly detailed panelling of three-quarter height, flagged with Portland-stone slabs and diamond-shaped insets of Purbeck stone. Most oddly, many of the diamonds are not placed at the junctions where four Portland slabs meet, as is usually the case, but in some cases are inlaid into the slabs. At the end of the hall is a pair of fluted Doric piers, topped by blocks of triglyph Doric frieze supporting a cornice. Beyond is the generous staircase compartment, panelled and with a pediment-topped door surround set on axis with the entrance passage. The stair stands at right angles to this axis, and is only visible once the compartment has been entered. Like all the joinery it is boldly detailed and scaled, with a sweeping handrail, fine balusters and carved tread ends. This broad staircase is – or was originally – top-lit by a roof lantern, because the balustrades on the half-landings are set in from the party wall to allow natural light to filter down the full depth of the staircase, from roof to basement. A lovely detail. The balustrade to the basement is formed with stout late-seventeenth-century balusters, evidently reused, in an out-of-the-way location, from the previous house on the site. Adjoining the foot of the staircase at ground-floor level is another pedimented doorcase leading into a rear room. The ground- and first-floor rooms are also fitted with panelling of very high quality.

This glorious entrance passage and staircase hall (plate 14) can generally be inspected because the building is in multiple occupation, with a retail space on the ground floor. It's not a gentle – or suitable – use for this marvellous building, but it does mean that parts of the interior are, at certain times, accessible. Enjoy it, but tremble as you do so because it's hard to know how much more tough usage this inherently fragile interior can take.

Number 39 is the other survivor of this 1737 group. It has been stuccoed externally and radically altered internally.

Number 40 was rebuilt in 1799, replacing the 1680s house in which the goldsmith Paul de Lamerie lived in the early eighteenth century. The current house is a fine example of its date, elegant and minimal with a simple arched doorway.

Number 41 dates from c.1680, or a little after, but has been much altered, with its façade stuccoed and a large restaurant window inserted into its ground-floor frontage.

Numbers 42 and 43 were rebuilt in 1901 as a commercial building, which survives. A plaque states that this is the site of the house in which the poet John Dryden lived for the last fourteen years of his life, partly as part of his plan to escape the attentions of his wife. As Dryden put it in her epitaph:

Here lies my wife: Here let her lie!
Now she's at rest, and so am I.

In fact Dryden, who died in 1700, probably lived at number 44, also now lost.

Number 45 The existing house was built in 1878, replacing a house that – until 1770 – was occupied by the carver Thomas Speer. Strangely, the existing building is adorned with the remains of a splendid eighteenth-century pedimented doorcase, delicate and exquisite in its carved details. Presumably this was reused from the eighteenth-century house on the site and is the doorcase Speer lovingly carved for his own home. It is – or was – a wonderful piece of work. When recorded by a drawing in the 1966 *Survey of London*[12] it had Doric pilasters supporting an intricately carved frieze topped by an open pediment. Over the years I have witnessed, with sorrow, the neglect and gradual erosion of this admirable piece of work and been taxed to know what to do about it, beyond recording it in photographs. Such gradual, natural and subtle decay is generally beyond the reach of conservation laws. Now most of the carved frieze has gone (one inner face alone survives), as have the Doric capitals, and all is covered by an obscuring layer of dark grey paint. Honest change I suppose, and the wear and tear of daily life. But it's evident that for many a year no one has loved this once thoughtfully preserved fragment. However, the pediment survives intact, with its delicately carved mouldings and modillions. Enjoy it while you can.

Number 47, with its simple brick elevation and cill band at second-floor level – now painted – appears to date from the 1730s.

Macclesfield Street

This street was laid out in the 1670s as part of the Gerrard Street development.

Numbers 2 and 3 were built between 1729 and 1730, on leases granted by John Jeffreys to the Soho speculating builder John Meard (see p. 267). Both are now much altered, number 3 being stucco-clad. The third-floor central window on number 2, suggesting a gable, is an oddity – presumably an addition, perhaps an artist's or engraver's studio. During the eighteenth century many painters, particularly of miniatures, gave their addresses as Macclesfield Street.

Number 11 is a public house and, with its wide, stepped gable and rich detailing, is a wonderful and full-blooded example of Dutch or 'Flemish' Renaissance revival. It was built in 1890 to the designs of the pub architects Saville and Martin as the Macclesfield. There had been a tavern on this site from at least 1690. It was called the Horse and Dolphin, a name which is commemorated in the adjoining yard and mews. Fortuitously, given the building's seventeenth-century Dutch look and narrow, deep plan, it has long housed the De Hem Dutch pub, bar and oyster buffet – indeed was designed for De Hem. If Dutch beer is what you like, along with a plate of *bitterballen*, served at a long marble counter, then this is the place for you. George Sims, a journalist, playwright, social observer and author in 1889 of *Horrible London*, seems to have been a fan and was even driven to verse by the place:

When oysters to September yield, and grace the grott'd
    Mecclesfield,
I will be there, my dear De Hem,
To wish you well and sample them.[13]

Numbers 12 and 13, with gaunt fronts and widely spaced windows, must date from the early nineteenth century; number 13 has a simple round arched front doorway.

*

Dansey Place, just off Gerrard Street, contained a most rare 'Webb's Patent Sewer Gas Destructor'. Dating from the mid 1890s, the device was a lamp, plumbed directly into the sewer, that destroyed smells and dangerous gases by consuming them at 700 degrees Fahrenheit. If gases built up, sewers could simply explode. This clever device – invented by Joseph Webb – not only cleared the sewer below of potentially explosive noxious fumes but at the same time illuminated the street above. The lamp featured in 1957 in a BBC series called *Stranger Than Fiction* but, sadly, has been removed. Another survives in Carting Lane, off the Strand.

Newport Court

Numbers 21–24a (originally probably three separate houses of unequal size) are a remarkable survival and the only place where it is possible to get an idea of the appearance of the late-seventeenth-century development of the 'Newport Ground' in Soho as masterminded by Nicholas Barbon.

The site of these houses was leased for sixty years in May 1688 by Nicholas Barbon to Henry Webb. Although the ground floors are all modern, the upper parts of the house have been relatively little altered and are a rare and wonderful demonstration of what the modest architecture of late-Stuart London looked like.

These are not grand houses of the rich and powerful but small houses, in a narrow court, that were the homes and places of work for relatively humble Londoners. What is striking is their sophisticated simplicity and uniformity. All first-floor windows are the same size and on the same level and they are slightly deeper in proportion than the similarly regimented second-floor windows. This arrangement makes it clear that the first floor was the piano nobile, containing the best and loftiest rooms. All windows are topped by segmental arches, wrought simply in brick. This is quite an early use of a form that became ubiquitous in London from the second decade of the eighteenth century until the early 1730s.

The only significant external ornaments to the façade are the string course between the first and second floor and the brick quoins that mark the left edge of the composition. Presumably quoins were to give these simple buildings a sense of architectural dignity.

An anomaly here is that pier widths between windows differ slightly on some of the houses. This gives us an insight into the way spaces were divided internally, with wide piers marking the location of party walls or of significant internal partitions. This is an important clue because the plans of the houses have been altered – they were subdivided in the eighteenth century – so the original arrangement is uncertain beyond the fact that they all have centrally placed chimney-stacks and staircases, both usual for the time.

Numbers 25 and 26 date from 1784–5, built by a local carpenter named Alexander Campbell. Number 25 retains the remains of a good late-eighteenth-century shop front, with a fascia breaking forward over what would have been a pair of shallow bays.

Number 27 retains parts of a bow-fronted shop front of about 1800.

Number 18, at the east end of the court, was built in 1684 and rebuilt in 1778.

Number 19 looks late-seventeenth-century. Indeed, it bears the date 1685 on its parapet and although this seems a relatively recent addition it is probably correct. Both 18 and 19 are now rendered and have modern shop fronts. In the summer of 2019 number 19 continues to function in a traditional Soho mixed-use manner – a shop on the ground floor and 'massage' offered in the rooms above.

Number 20 was built in 1685 on a lease from Barbon to Henry Webb but rebuilt in 1772.

Newport Place

The form of this irregular space evolved in an ad hoc manner. The narrow south portion was part of a path leading to a gate into the Military Ground, eventually developed in the 1670s to form Gerrard Street. The upper, wider portion of the space was 'waste ground' between the wall of the Military Ground and the garden wall of Newport House. Nicholas Barbon, who in 1677 acquired the lease of the ground, evidently entertained ambitions for the site, probably intending to create a square here if he could sweep away Devonshire House to the west, but this did not happen. Little early fabric now survives beyond some much-altered eighteenth-century buildings at the south end of the west side.

Numbers 4–8, with adjoining Newport Court houses, date from 1784. The remains of an elegant shop front survive.

Number 7 is a much-mutilated mid-eighteenth-century house that was topped by a pediment. The narrow windows flanking wide central ones make it clear that this was originally a subtle Palladian design that possessed a miniature monumentality. The pediment was a good example of Georgian builders' intuitive grasp of the art of townscape. This façade closed the vista west along the narrow Newport Court.

Number 9 was built in 1729 by John Meard under a building lease granted by John Jeffreys. It is plain but assured, with flat-topped windows (an early example of the return to this form at a time when segmental window arches were usual) and stone window cills. The façade, now painted white and with a modern shop front, is much damaged, with original details obscured.

Lisle Street

This street has a curious history. The west half was laid out in 1682–3 on part of the garden of Leicester House,[14] while in 1791–2 the east half was laid out on the site of Leicester House itself, then recently demolished. The man behind this 1790s initiative was Thomas Wright, a Covent Garden-based banker, who might have been investing clients' money; it is possible that the east half of Lisle Street was developed using the wages of sin (see p. 37).

Between 1792 and 1795 Wright granted twenty-one building leases, on terms ranging from ninety-six and ninety-nine years, for ground on each side of the street. There were at least eight speculating builders involved, almost all local or London-based building tradesmen. But, as the surviving houses reveal, Wright was able to impose a fair degree of uniformity. Indeed, he even achieved a small urban flourish, suggesting that the composition of the north side was conceived – as far as circumstances would permit – as a palace front, with a pediment contrived to close the view north, along Leicester Place, from Leicester Square. All houses were to be twenty feet wide and have shops on the ground floor with accommodation above, so this was, from the start, to be primarily a commercial street.

Numbers 2, 3 and 4, and 6 and 7 at the west end of the street all date from the early nineteenth century and replace late-seventeenth-century houses that were generally larger and grander than their successors. By the early nineteenth century the west end of Lisle Street had gone down in the world, no doubt in large part due to the commercial nature of the buildings erected to the east during the 1790s.

Number 5, set between these two groups, is a splendid building with a tall stepped gable in Flemish style. It was designed in 1897 by F.T. Verity as a hospital. It is now a pub, which seems a use far more appropriate to its flamboyant design.

Numbers 14–27 (consecutive) survive on the north side and form a handsome uniform terrace that, towards its centre, bends slightly in a concave manner to follow the curve in the street. Immediately to the west of the curve three houses – 17, 18 and 19 – which face south down Leicester Place are designed to form a unified composition that closes the vista from Leicester Square. The central house in the group is topped by the pediment that faces south down Leicester Place. The pediment rises from a mutuled cornice that continues through the terrace as a whole. The house had architraves framing its first-floor windows. Sadly, these were omitted in a mid-twentieth-century reconstruction. Also, within the pediment is a tablet inscribed 'New Lisle Street' and its date, MDCCXCI. The street does not, however, appear to have got under way until 1792.

The houses flanking the pedimented house each had a balustrade at parapet level (plate 15). This has been replaced by plain parapet walls which reduce the palatial grandeur of the original conception There are only fragmentary remains of early shop fronts, except on the two 1790s houses that have survived on the south side of the street – numbers 34 and 35 – which retain most of their original bow-fronted shop fronts. Number 34 still has a particularly good front door, with raised and fielded panels. Set within the shop front, this door originally served the accommodation in the rooms above.

Little Newport Street

Lisle Street is continued to the south-east by Little Newport Street. This probably marks the course of the 'military road' leading into the Military Ground to the west and was developed during the 1680s. By 1691 the street was, according to parish rate books, known by its current name.

Number 7 Formerly the Crown and Grapes public house. It dates from 1784–5 and has an odd faceted corner. It was built by the local speculator Alexander Campbell.

Numbers 8, 9 and 10 (consecutive) form a uniform group that probably dates from the 1770s. The Tuscan pilasters which ornament and visually unite the first floors of the houses were presumably added slightly later.

Numbers 11, 12 and 13 are also of the 1770s.

Number 14 has a late-eighteenth-century front but could, essentially, be largely the original house built on the site in 1685.

Number 15 is also of the 1770s and also built by Alexander Campbell.

Shaftesbury Avenue

The completion of Regent Street in 1825 re-emphasised the need for improved and interconnected 'communications' in adjacent parts of the West End, notably between Piccadilly and Bloomsbury and between Charing Cross via Tottenham Court Road to the Euston Road – a situation that became more pressing after Euston station opened in 1837. The Metropolitan Board of Works (MBW), created in 1855, was the agency responsible for strategic road construction and infrastructure (such as major sewers) in the capital, and in 1877 it secured the Metropolitan Street Improvements Act that authorised the construction of what are now Charing Cross Road and Shaftesbury Avenue. The Act also permitted the widening of Coventry Street. The lines of these proposed streets had been drawn up by the MBW's superintendent architect, George Vulliamy, and the engineer Sir Joseph Bazalgette.

The process was most complex, not least because money became the overriding issue. The MBW had powers and funds for road construction but not for slum clearance or to build along the roads it created. But, despite this limitation, slum clearance and rehousing became one of the MBW's constant concerns. The result was that the routes it chose for the roads it undertook to construct tended to pass through slum areas, thus providing the means for their destruction as long as this was compatible with its money-saving aim of utilising and widening existing roads. Indeed, the socially improving aspect of Shaftesbury Avenue is suggested by the name chosen for it. The 7th Earl of Shaftesbury was one of the wonders of mid-Victorian Britain: an Evangelical Christian and avid philanthropist and social reformer, he was the reference point for all with similar convictions and represented the moralising heart of the nation. Naming the new road after him was a statement of intent.

Using road-building legislation and funds to clear slums, and when possible utilising the existing street pattern, were of course no bad thing, but could cause more problems than they solved. The absence of readily available funds to build new homes for the displaced slum dwellers was combined with an obligation to rehouse them near the sites of their lost homes. So money-strapped industrial dwellings companies were usually brought in, and potentially commercially valuable frontages along the new roads were used for the construction of philanthropic housing. So where one might expect celebratory architecture on these new, wide London boulevards, there are instead often multi-storey blocks of artisans' tenements over humble shops, humdrum commercial buildings and even warehousing. A typical example is the socially admirable but gaunt, looming and far from beautiful Sandringham Buildings on Charing Cross Road. The Buildings were constructed at minimal expense in 1883–5 by the Improved Industrial Dwellings Company, with George Borer as architect. Other types of new buildings next to the road also had to be funded independently of the MBW, which merely acted as landlord of plots of land surplus to road construction.

The powers granted to the MBW, combined with the financial oddness of the enterprise, were largely responsible for the corruption that became endemic. This included the MBW employees expecting commissions

from the businesses to which 'surplus land' was sold or
who in other ways benefited from the Board's decisions
and activities. As the *Survey of London* puts it: 'the history of Shaftesbury Avenue and Charing Cross Road is
a story of lost opportunity', because when the streets
finally opened in the late 1880s, 'the general standard of
the design of the buildings ... erected was deplorable',
compounded by the fact that 'in 1888 a Royal Commission was appointed to investigate the dishonest conduct
of certain of the Board's officers'. But in mitigation, the
Survey points out that 'in face of this depressing record
it should also be remembered that the final achievement
was not merely the formation of over a mile of main
thoroughfare sixty feet wide, but also the abolition of
some of the worst slums in London and the rehousing
of over three thousand of the labouring classes'.[15]

The *Survey* is correct: by conventional criteria, the
architectural standard of the buildings erected along
Shaftesbury Avenue is 'deplorable'. As was typical of the
time, nearly all are designed as expressions of an historical
style, with Flemish Renaissance – a sort of free-form classicism – being particularly favoured. This is all well and
good, but the problem is that most of these evocations
of architectural history are woefully debased and often
cruelly curtailed. But, it must be said, debased architecture is not without its visual pleasures, even delights – and
at its best hovers on the decadent, which of course was
very much the flavour of the late 1880s and 1890s, when
many of the buildings in Shaftesbury Avenue were completed. Indeed, it seems as if the corruption underlying
the construction of this avenue is manifest in its etiolated
architecture. But it's not just the stringy neo-Renaissance

blocks, straining for the sky along the avenue's south side, that appear unhealthy. Some buildings go to the other extreme. Take, for example, the bloated pomposity of the London Pavilion – a vast 'music hall deluxe', designed in 1885 in pretentious evocation of the Roman classical style, or the grandiloquent and gigantic bare-breasted muses in flowing gowns that cavort atop the Apollo Theatre, which opened in 1901 with a flop entitled *The Belle of Bohemia*.

All the important buildings on Shaftesbury Avenue are theatres or pubs, so it was from the start London's new promenade of pleasure. It must be one of the few places in the world where there are significant theatres set side by side – not once but twice. Immediately west of the double-domed Apollo with its muses is the Lyric, a much more staid affair in a generally indeterminate, but most certainly debased, hybrid classical style. The architect was the generally admirable C.J. Phipps and the theatre opened in 1888. Across Rupert Street from the Apollo is the Gielgud, opened in 1906 as Hicks Theatre and until 1994 known as the Globe; it was designed in a weird and wonderful reworking of the English Baroque style by the most able theatre architect W.G.R. Sprague. Adjoining the Gielgud is the Queens's Theatre – so that's four theatres in a row, with only Rupert Street in between. The Queen's now looks most odd – modernist and minimalist in the extreme – but was designed by Sprague to be a twin with the Gielgud and opened later in the same year. However, there was a calamity. The theatre's façade and front of house were very badly damaged in the war, and rather than recreate its Baroque splendour the front was built in the late 1950s in a most economical manner to designs by Bryan Westwood and Sir Hugh Casson. Happily, the lavish auditorium was retained and, it must be said, the stark modern foyer and the auditorium make odd but not unpleasing bedfellows.

The final theatre in the portion of Shaftesbury Avenue within Soho is at its east end, at the junction with Charing Cross and looking onto a rather impoverished version of a Parisian *place* – Cambridge Circus. East of the circus is the Shaftesbury Theatre, built in 1911 to the designs of Bertie Crewe, but although it is on Shaftesbury Avenue this theatre is well beyond the boundary of Soho. Cambridge Circus, created by the MBW as the potentially heroic intersection of Shaftesbury Avenue and Charing Cross Road, is, sadly, a rather pathetic design. Too many roads enter it and most are too wide, so there is no feeling of enclosure and little sense of urban presence, let alone grandeur. This circus, into which ancient Moor Street leaks from Old Compton Street, marks one of the eastern boundaries of Soho. The most dominant building by far on the circus is the Palace Theatre – and this really is quite a piece of work. The style – realised in brick and terracotta – is an inventive evocation of French six-teenth-century Loire château architecture, but vigorous and glorious. And in its construction the theatre, started in 1888, is pioneering, with upper levels supported on vast steel cantilevers – built into the back outer wall – so that the stage can be seen without the obstruction of supporting piers or columns. And, along with terracotta and steel, much concrete was used in the structure to make it as fireproof as possible. But it must be admitted that this vast peninsula of a building, as it noses its way into Soho by way of Romilly Street, is monstrously big. However, after all these years it has rather made itself at home in this part of town — or perhaps, more to the point, Soho has become accustomed to it.

The man behind the Palace Theatre was the brilliant impresario and producer Richard D'Oyly Carte, who commissioned Thomas Edward Collcutt as architect. It opened in 1891 as the Royal English Opera House with a production of Arthur Sullivan's *Ivanhoe*. The opera did fairly well, but D'Oyly Carte failed to follow it up with another solid production and the enterprise started to falter. He quickly leased the theatre to Sarah Bernhardt for a season and within a year sold it at a loss. It was renamed the Palace Theatre of Varieties and reopened as a grand music hall. This move downmarket worked and audiences were regularly pulled in to fill the theatre's huge 1,400-seat auditorium. And that's where it's stayed – the popular and successful home of big-budget musicals.

There are, besides theatres, things well worth looking at in Shaftesbury Avenue – and it greatly helps if you peer above the usually dismal and tatty ground-floor shops. The best pub is, perhaps, the St James's Tavern at the west end, on the corner with Great Windmill Street. Dated 1896, it's a fine and playful piece of seventeenth-century Renaissance-style design; but look closely at the top and you will see, in a blank window, a wheel carved in stone. Why? It's because the previous tavern on this site, dating from the 1730s, had been called the Catherine Wheel. This homage to history – to memory – is a charming touch. You might have to destroy but you don't have to forget.

The frontage on the north side of Shaftesbury Avenue – between Wardour Street and Dean Street – is most revealing. The west half is occupied by a stripped classical brick-built industrial building, utilitarian and functional, while on the east half stands a florid neo-Renaissance creation. The juxtaposition remains startling, and says a lot about the uncertain origin of the avenue. It became a promenade of pleasure and London's new theatreland more by chance than design. It could almost as easily have become a street of industry and commerce with warehouses, manufactories and shops, or a run-of-the-mill residential street with blocks of tenements. It all depended, I suppose, on whom the MBW could find to lease their 'surplus land' to alongside the new road, and this – no doubt – to a degree depended on who could cut a deal with whom. A very odd way to build a city, but I suppose time-honoured.

The eastern portion of the north side of Shaftesbury Avenue between Dean Street and Greek Street, including the Curzon cinema, is now threatened by demolition for Crossrail 2 (see p. 11).

Wardour Street (south)

This southern part of Wardour Street was, as we have noted, traditionally known as Colman Hedge Lane, then from the late 1670s as Princes Street. To the north, the central part of Wardour Street was named Old Soho (as on Rocque's map of 1746), with only the north end known as Wardour Street (as on Richard Horwood's map of 1819). This commemorated the fact that the adjoining Colman Hedge Close came into the possession of Sir Edward Wardour in 1630 (see p. 81). It was only in 1878 that the name Wardour Street was applied to the whole length of ancient Colman Hedge Lane from Oxford Street to Coventry Street. The length of the lane south of Coventry Street is still called Whitcomb Street.

When the parish of St Anne's, Soho, was created in 1686 from part of the ancient parish of St Martin-in-the-Fields, Wardour Street / Princes Street was used to mark the western boundary with the parish of St James's, Westminster. The ground – known as the 'Leastall' or Laystall – immediately to the west of the south end of Wardour Street became, in 1676, the freehold property of the Earl of St Albans, with development largely completed by the late 1680s (see p. 54). Rebuilding generally took place during the 1720s and 1730s.

Numbers 7, 9 and 11 Wardour Street date from 1727 and were built on a lease granted in 1725 by George Bourne (who had recently acquired the freehold of the Vesey's Garden portion of the former St Albans estate) to Henry Parsons, a local watchmaker trying his hand at a modest piece of property speculation. Two late-seventeenth-century buildings stood on the site and these were cleared away and the three smaller houses built. This was the typical pattern of Soho redevelopment in the late 1720s – larger seventeenth-century houses being replaced by smaller, new houses aimed at lower-income tenants. Numbers 9 and 7 were built as a pair with a mirrored plan and have a yellow-brick façade and segmental-shaped brick arches over their windows. Number 9 was long occupied by Benjamin Smart and members of his family, goldsmiths and dealers in bullion, which explains the inscription on the façade – 'Exchange and Bullion Office'. Number 11 is more altered.

Number 25 is a house of c.1800.

Numbers 27–31 form a very picturesque group because

27 and 29 incorporate a memorable two-storey-high entrance arch to Rupert (originally George) Court, which leads to Rupert Street. The houses were built in 1728 on a fifty-one-year building lease granted to the bricklayer John Whetten by George Bourne. The façades of the Wardour Street houses have been altered and stuccoed, but it's worth trying to get inside because number 27 retains 1720s panelling in its main first-floor room and the upper portion of its original staircase. Numbers 29 and 31 also have significant amounts of their 1720s internal detailing, including panelling and staircases. Numbers 22–28 Rupert Street were part of the same Bourne development and built at the same time (see p. 216).

Numbers 41 and 42 are a single composition built in 1904–5 for Willy Clarkson, a once-famed theatrical wig maker and costumier. His fame is emblazoned in bronze on each side of the front door where panels state that the foundation stone was laid in 1904 by the great actress Sarah Bernhardt, and the following year the coping stone was laid by the equally illustrious actor Sir Henry Irving. Clarkson's business occupied the building until 1940. Its cavernous ground floor is now a rather anonymous Chinese restaurant. The building, designed by H.M. Wakeley, is perhaps the most flamboyant Edwardian building in Soho, combining Baroque and Art Nouveau elements in an almost wayward manner, all given extra gusto by the rich mix of materials – red brick, varied stones and blue/green glazed tiles. The composition is striking: in the centre of the ground floor is the main door topped by a large mask and scrolls, with full-height canted bays rising on each side. In the centre, above the door, is a large clock supported by delicate wrought-iron brackets, which proclaims above and below the clock face 'Costumier' and 'Perruquier'. It really is all most splendid.

Excursion into Rupert Street and Rupert Court

Rupert Street

Rupert Street has a curious history. It stands on land acquired by Henry VIII after the Reformation. Until that time it had been owned by the Hospital of Burton St Lazar and so was former monastic land (see p. 80). A parliamentary survey of the land, made in 1650, described it as 'commonly called the Leastall'.[16] 'Leastall' presumably meant laystall, a term for an area along a drovers' route where cattle were held on the way to market and, by extension, a place where dung and other detritus (including human waste from cesspits) was deposited.

After the Restoration this land formed a portion of the Crown-owned Soho Fields estate leased by Henrietta Maria to the Earl of St Albans. In 1676 her son, Charles II, granted the freehold of this portion of Soho Fields to St Albans in exchange for the freehold of Nell Gwynne's house in Pall Mall. The king was, presumably, looking after the interests of his favoured mistress and no doubt reckoned a dung heap in Soho Fields a fair exchange for securing Nell peace of mind. At the time the three and a half acres were divided into three parts, known as 'the lay soyle', Vesey's Garden and Watts Close. St Albans immediately let the ground for building to a group of speculating builders, including Nicholas Barbon. The layout of the long and narrow estate was simplicity itself – just one straight street connected originally to the parallel south end of Colman Hedge Lane by two very narrow streets or courts. No attempt was made to forge connections with Colonel Panton's developments to the west, notably the small and enclosed Panton Square (now lost without trace – see p. 217), or with Sir William Pulteney's estate to the north. The new street came to an abrupt end at its north end just short of Knaves' Acre (now the east end of Brewer Street) on Pulteney land, and was merely connected at right angles to Colman Hedge Lane via the narrow Edmunds Court. The footpath connection to Brewer Street was created only in the 1870s.

To the south the new street made its only significant connection with an existing thoroughfare – Coventry Street, which is the eastward extension of Piccadilly. Ogilby and Morgan's map of 1681–2 shows most of Rupert Street lined with houses, except for a small portion of its north end, still indicated on the map as open ground.

The name given to this new street reveals much about the prevailing spirit of the times, at least among London's landowners who, like St Albans, had profited mightily from the Stuart Restoration. According to rate books, as early as 1677 the new thoroughfare was called Rupert Street. Prince Rupert of the Rhine was one of the tarnished Royalist cavalier heroes of the Civil War who had been regilded at the Restoration. At the beginning of the Civil War, when aged only twenty-three and a rising star, he had been appointed commander of the Royalist Cavalry. Initially he was successful, but after he surrendered the strategically important port of Bristol to Parliament in September 1645 Charles I, bitterly disappointed, dismissed him from his service. The two were eventually reconciled and Rupert was put in command of the defence of Oxford after the king left the city for the north. Once again Rupert was obliged to surrender, but by the time he did, in June 1646, the key first phase of the Civil War and the Royalist cause lay in near-ruin. Parliament did no more to Rupert than banish him, and this proved not only a magnanimous act but also somewhat foolish because after the end of the war Rupert took to the sea to harass Commonwealth shipping, particularly in the Caribbean.

After the Restoration Prince Rupert returned to Britain and once again became a senior military commander, this time focusing on naval rather than cavalry warfare. Despite the poor English performance during the Second Anglo-Dutch War of 1665–7, Rupert's stock remained high in 1677, so not only was this new street named in his honour by St Albans, but also Colman Hedge Lane was renamed Princes Street; so, read together, two of the main streets in this portion of Soho conjured up a Royalist figurehead. The association with this once-dashing cavalier was not absurd because John Strype, in his *Survey of the Cities of London and Westminster*, published in 1720, describes the street as 'pretty handsome [and] well built'[17] – an apt description of Prince Rupert himself.

The street's long and enclosed cul-de-sac character must have made it memorable, in a sense more a narrow square than a conventional thoroughfare.

Nothing survives of late-seventeenth-century Rupert Street – certainly nothing above ground and recognisable – with the very few extant early fragments dating from the 1720s and 1730s when it was largely rebuilt. The slicing of Shaftesbury Avenue though the centre of the street during the 1870s and 1880s not only destroyed much but – naturally – did much to change its visual and urban character, transforming it from one long, continuous street into two short ones.

The north part of the street is now dominated by the side elevations of theatres that front onto Shaftesbury Avenue, on the west corner the Apollo and on the east the Gielgud (see p. 207).

Number 4 possesses the narrow façade of a house of *c*.1730.

Numbers 22–28 were part of the same Bourne development and built at the same time as 27–31 Wardour Street (see p. 212), and have been much altered. Numbers 22 and 24 now have façades of *c*.1800 but retain elements of panelling and staircases from the 1720s; number 26 has been refaced in early-eighteenth-century style and number 28, the Blue Posts public house, was rebuilt in larger scale in the nineteenth century.

The houses in **Rupert Court** appear to have been rebuilt. Elevations are now white tiled and most contain large, wide, late-nineteenth- or early-twentieth-century windows. All have shop fronts at ground level.

Coventry Street

Coventry Street is shown on the 1585 survey as a short lane connecting what is now the Haymarket to the junction of Wardour Street with Whitcomb Street. The street takes its name from Henry Coventry, who from 1673 to 1686 lived in what became known as Piccadilly Hall, located near the junction with the Haymarket. Ogilby and Morgan's London map of 1681–2 shows both sides of the street lined with buildings.

The ground to the north of Coventry Street, roughly between what are now Great Windmill Street and Rupert Street, had been acquired by Colonel Panton. Here Panton had, in 1673, started to build Panton Square – a grand name for what was in effect a large court or yard, connected to smaller yards, used for stabling. In 1720 John Strype described the square as 'a very large Place for Stabling and Coach-houses, there being one large Yard within another'.[18]

The prospects of Panton's square improved during the eighteenth century. He died in 1685 and in 1691 his daughter Elizabeth married the 5th Baron Arundell of Wardour. They seem to have worked to elevate the estate, so that by the early eighteenth century it included some aristocrats among it tenants. And in 1763 Panton Square was even home to a leading diplomat, the Ambassador of Morocco. However, this allegedly had an unfortunate consequence, as explained in the *Survey of London*. One of the ambassador's 'attendants happened to displease him [so] he had him brought up to the garret, and there sliced his head off'. It was reported that a violent crowd subsequently gathered before the house, 'broke into it, demolished the furniture, threw everything they could lay their hands on out of the window, and thrashed and beat the grand Moor and his retinue down the Haymarket'. The *Survey* admits that 'It is not known whether this story is true,' but points out that 'the State Papers contain numerous references to the irregular behaviour of the ambassador and his staff at about this time'.[19]

The Arundell family retained ownership of the land until 1919 when they sold it to J. Lyons & Co., who in the early 1920s obtained an Act of Parliament to close Panton

Square and demolished it for the extension of its existing 'Corner House' in Coventry Street.

Lyons' tea shops, which started in 1898, became a much-loved institution, particularly during the years of the First World War, when they were places of meeting and of retreat, where spirits could be rekindled in simple but hygienic surroundings and with a cheap but decent cup of tea, with a slice of cake. They were 'tea-total' of course, the food being simple and good value for money; and although the tea shops started as workers' institutions Lyons managed, to a degree, to cross class boundaries. Lyons' 'Corner Houses' opened throughout London and beyond, and was one of the first food retail chains. Interiors grew more ornate in the late 1920s and 1930s after the company hired the architect Oliver Bernard, an English pioneer of Art Deco, as consultant. And the chain's owners – Joseph Lyons and his brothers-in-law Isidore and Montague Gluckstein – thought big. They manufactured their own cakes and groceries, which were sold around the world, and in 1913 built the huge and stylish Regent Palace Hotel (see p. 313). But times change. Lyons' customers abandoned the tea rooms as competition grew intense. They became dowdy, the favoured resort of the desperate, and the last 'Corner House' closed in 1977.

The Coventry Street and Rupert Street Lyons' Corner House was designed by W.J. Ancell in 1907, and has a white façade of moulded blocks of glazed terracotta, presumably intended to be self-cleaning in the rain. The style of architecture is lively eclectic English Baroque. The block is now in rather grim mixed use, mostly aimed at the tourist market, and proclaims itself the Trocadero, once an upmarket restaurant owned by J. Lyons & Co.

The west extension of the 'Corner House', on the site of Panton Square, was built in 1921–3 to the designs of F.J. Wills.

Numbers 3–4 were built in 1912 to 1913 to house the Rialto cinema and a large, double-height basement restaurant. Designed in the Beaux-Arts style by Hippolyte J. Bland, the auditorium for the cinema is oval in form with a gallery, and was originally decorated in cream and gold with neo-Greek ornament. Externally the façade to Coventry Street is dominated by a tall arch with, above it, a balustrade and pedimented belvedere. All very handsome. The cinema now houses a casino. In 1924 the basement restaurant became the Café de Paris nightclub. In 1941 two German bombs exploded in the nightclub and many were killed (see p. 119). But it soon reopened and remains in operation. As with the cinema, it is oval in plan, with a gallery and neo-Greek detailing, and a pair of staircases sweeping each side of the small stage.

Old Compton Street

The building of the houses on Compton Street, as it was initially called, was under way by the mid 1670s and the street was fully lined with houses by the mid 1680s. It was developed by Richard Frith and his associates and was, in effect, the south termination of the mini new town they, with the Earl of St Albans, had created south of Oxford Street, with Soho Square as its focus, on what in 1698 became the Portland estate. The street appears to have been named to flatter Henry Compton, Bishop of London (see p. 276), who at the time was involved with Frith in a land-swap that allowed St Anne's Church to be well sited to the south of the west end of Compton Street.

Something of the appearance and early character
of the street is hinted at by John Strype in his *Survey*.
Strype is fairly dismissive because, after noting that the
houses were 'well built', he suggests that the street is 'of
no great Account for its Inhabitants, which are chiefly
French'.[20] This is a puzzling, if ambiguous, statement.
Since the 1680s at least, south Soho had been the home
and workplace for Huguenot workers in precious metal
who were wealthy, educated, admired, mostly highly
successful and, of course, Protestant. Indeed, they were
at the time the model citizens of Soho, as they were
elsewhere in London and as Strype made clear when he
praised them as 'Patterns of Thrift, Honesty, Industry,
and Sobriety' (see p. 35).

There is a possible explanation for Strype's gentle
condemnation of Compton Street, and this is implied
by the elevations of both sides of the street included in
Tallis's London Street Views of 1838–40. By this time many
of the houses Strype knew in 1720 had been rebuilt, but
probably enough of the early houses survived in the 1830s
to give a sense of the original appearance of Compton
Street. If this is the case then, to judge from Tallis, it was
not a street calculated to impress those seeking noble
urban prospects. It is long and wide but there are no
architectural accents – no pediments closing vistas, no
columns or pilasters defining united compositions, and
no ennobling uniformity of elevations. Houses vary from
two to three windows in width, and most seem to be
no more than individual compositions slotted into the
street without any great concern for artistic possibilities
or consequences. In the 1680s Compton Street was one of

the major new thoroughfares of Soho, as long as Frith or Greek Street and Soho Square combined; it was, indeed, the southern anchor to Soho Square. But evidently its architectural potential was not realised. It was humdrum, partly commercial, perhaps with numerous shop fronts from the start. This could have been the reason for Strype's dismissive description.

The commercial character of the street increased during the eighteenth century. According to a Portland estate survey of 1792, only seven or eight of the seventy-eight buildings did not have shop fronts.[21] The survey is fascinating, showing detailed ground-floor plans of the buildings in Old Compton Street and neighbouring streets along with names of occupants, their trades or their type of shop. By this date Compton Street was not only one of Soho's most important shopping thoroughfares, but it also played its role in the area's still-discreet sex industry. The 1788 edition of *Harris's List of Covent Garden Ladies* records at least one prostitute living and working in Old Compton Street: a Miss Burn, based at number 18 (the site of what is now number 47 – see p. 96), and it was at a corner in New Compton Street in 1780 that Henry Angelo, a fencing master to the fashionable, had met 'a starving and destitute waif named Emma Lyon'. A few years later, in Rathbone Place, he encountered her again, but this time she was plump, well groomed and beautiful, the kept courtesan of Charles Grenville, who in 1786 passed her to his uncle, Sir William Hamilton. Against all the odds Sir William married Emma, and so was forged Lady Hamilton – the seasoned harlot, one-time denizen of Old Compton Street, who passed into history as the unlikely muse of the hero Admiral Lord Nelson.

Numbers 2, 4 and 6 were built in 1734 by John Price, a local bricklayer. Number 2 faces onto Charing Cross Road and forms a very good group with numbers 101 and 103 Charing Cross Road (see p. 226). Number 2 now contains a public house called the Compton Cross, which in 2017 replaced Molly Moggs, a well-known gay bar that terminated the promenade along Old Compton Street, a most vibrant thoroughfare that is now the heart of gay Soho.

Number 8, the adjoining house to the west, is taller, with architraves to first-floor windows. It probably dates from the very early nineteenth century.

Numbers 5 and 9 are eighteenth-century in origin.

Numbers 11–23 form a mixed group of eighteenth-century buildings. Several were destroyed or damaged in a large fire in 1785 but a number evidently survived – notably 13, 15 and 17 – because their elevations look early-eighteenth-century, with the half-windows between 15 and 17 being a late-seventeenth- and very early eighteenth-century detail. There is also a good early-eighteenth-century staircase in 17. Numbers 19 and 21 appear to be entirely late-eighteenth-century in date. The fronts of all these houses have been rendered or painted and now have modern shop and café frontages at ground level. The entire group has recently been painted a rather unpleasant pale green because all are in the same ownership – the Soho House private members' club, which occupies a warren of rooms within the uppers floors of most of these houses.

Number 27 Four storeys high above ground floor and with a three-window-wide brick elevation. Very plain, built c.1781.

Number 29 Built in 1728 by William Bignell, a Soho glazier, on a lease from the Portland estate. Inside there is a good early staircase and a substantial amount of panelling.

Numbers 31 and 33 Built in 1724 by William Bignell as a mirror-plan pair. The string courses on both houses probably had the same detail but it was omitted on a later re-fronting. Inside, good staircases with deeply carved tread ends, and panelling.

Number 35 Until recently an early-eighteenth-century house, with some original interior details. Now it has a recent, and very poorly detailed, brick façade.

Number 37 Built in 1728 by William Bignell, with an interior similar to numbers 29, 31 and 33. Retains elements of early-eighteenth-century interiors, but the exterior has been altered.

Numbers 36–38 Early-nineteenth-century. In 1846 number 38 was altered for a firm of linen drapers by David Mocatta, a pupil of Sir John Soane's from 1821 to 1827 who in 1839 designed Brighton railway station in an erudite Italianate style. It is now stuccoed with pediments to the second floor. Number 36 has a good plain brick front.

Numbers 40–42 have ornate mid-nineteenth-century Greek Revival façades of unified design: panelled piers between the first-floor windows, and pediments and circular wreaths above the second-floor windows. All rather impressive. The house is probably slightly earlier.

Number 61 Part of a uniform group that appears to have been rebuilt in the twentieth century. But it is of interest because it houses Camisa & Son, a 'Continental' family-run delicatessen that is the most characterful and authentic survival of Soho's nineteenth-century Italian community, now famed for its fresh pasta and sauces.

Number 63 dates from *c.*1732, but was re-fronted in a nineteenth-century elevation, except for the arch to the first-floor central window, which is original, along with the window jambs below. Nicely wrought and a most satisfying detail.

New Compton Street was the eastward extension of Compton Street and Little Compton Street (now united as Old Compton Street), leading to the St Giles Rookery. It was partly destroyed and separated from Soho by the construction of Charing Cross Road.

Excursions into Moor Street and Charing Cross Road

Moor Street

This small street branches diagonally, to the south, off the east end of Old Compton street. It was laid out on the south-east edge of the Earl of St Albans's Soho Fields estate and first appears in parish rate books in 1683, when the building of the houses in the street was probably complete. Its diagonal axis is almost certainly dictated by a path that led to West Street via an ancient 'field-opening', and then on to St Martin's Lane. If this is the case, it suggests that Moor Street commemorates a path through the fields of Soho, in existence before the area was built upon from the 1670s.

In 1734 the south side of the street was rebuilt by William Dunn, a carpenter, and William Lloyd, a Soho bricklayer, on a sixty-five-year building lease from the Portland estate, as the earl's former estate was then known. Two years later they rebuilt much of the north side of the street.

Numbers 10 and 11 A modest pair on the south side of the street with what appear to be late-eighteenth-century plain brick elevations. They are probably survivors, partly rebuilt, of the Dunn and Lloyd speculation.

Number 13 On the north side, four storeys high and three windows wide, it was built in 1738 by William Bignell. Its brick façade, with well-wrought window arches of yellow brick set in plum-coloured brick walling with rudimentary red-brick window jambs, could date from Bignell's time. At ground level is a curious shop front. *The Survey of London* described it in 1966 as a 'well restored shop front . . . elegant in design, and of early nineteenth century character' incorporating 'a six panelled door of early eighteenth century character'.[22] The shop front – with its three marvellous lunettes above windows and central door – most fortunately survives, but in the summer of 2019 is in a sad condition, painted dark blue with details picked out in bright white in a most unsubtle manner. When I started writing this book, the early-eighteenth-century door survived. On recent inspection it appears to have been replaced by a poor replica.

Number 14 Built in 1736 by Dunn and Lloyd, and the original brick façade might survive below layers of later paint.

Number 12 Built with numbers 1–3 Old Compton Street in a garish Edwardian Baroque manner in 1904 to the designs of Charles H. Worley. It was conceived as a commercial building, with shops at ground-floor level and offices or workshops on the first floor lit by wide, arched windows. The building has great presence on its key corner site and – although boisterous – is certainly not without a certain charm. Particularly notable are the dark-green glazed bricks facing much of its façade – a fashion at the time because, as well as being visually striking, such glazed bricks were seen to offer the possibility of 'self-washing' façades. But this was an empty hope, since the rain in Edwardian London carried as much soot as water and, rather than being cleaned by a downpour, such façades were merely streaked with rivulets of oily soot.

Charing Cross Road

Number 101 A small house of *c.*1734 that suggests the modest character of the buildings that stood on Hog Lane/Crown Street before the widening and reconstruction from the late 1870s as Charing Cross Road. It is only two storeys high, with box sashes set flush with the brick façade and within windows topped by segmental arches. The brick arches are crude and simple, revealing the economy of the building's construction. It was seemingly built with 2–6 Old Compton Street (see p. 222).

Number 103 Built as a pair of houses, probably early in the eighteenth century. It was a public house called the Bull's Head from at least 1759, but the name changed in 1894 to Tam O'Shanter; some alterations of that time are visible. The pub closed in 1960.

Numbers 4–6 A strange survival. The tall, narrow building dates from the 1890s but its ground-floor interior was remodelled and extended to the rear in 1937, when it was in the possession of the Italian Fascist government. It was created to give the regime a showcase and rallying point, of a fitting sort, in central London. So the style is the stripped classical that had evolved during the late 1930s as the house style for totalitarian regimes, although here with references to the earlier Rationalist Modernism that Italian Fascists had preferred in the late 1920s and early 1930s. The interior is notable for its curving gallery supported on simple square-section piers and its minuscule entrance colonnade that springs into action as soon as you enter the street door. Originally it was home to the Italian Benevolent Society and several other organisations including Fascio di Londra and L'Italia Nostra. After Italy declared war on Great Britain and France in June 1940 the building was seized by the Custodian of Enemy Property and never returned to the Italian government. During the war it served as a club for New Zealand forces and is now a most useful little library and reading room operated by Westminster City Council.

The building is a reminder of how difficult the early war years were for the Italian community in Soho, when its restaurants and shops were occasionally attacked during anti-Fascist riots and Italian-born males interned as 'enemy aliens'.

Frith Street

The first documentary reference to this street is in June 1678, when Richard Frith and William Pym took a lease on a site on its west side for building. It was then known simply as a new street. Ogilby and Morgan's map of 1681–2 shows the street as fully built and named Frith Street. However, this is a mistake because not all the plots had been developed by the early 1680s.[23]

Numbers 5, 6 and 7 These form a small but memorable

group. Number 5 was built in 1731 and is, with its simple and classically correct stone doorcase and flat-arched windows, a most advanced design for its date. The client was William Duncombe, who, having won a large lottery prize in 1725, retired from his job at the Navy Office and set himself up as a playwright and – apparently – amateur property developer. The builder he used was a Marylebone bricklayer named Joel Johnson. The first occupant in 1731 was Mary Newdigate, who in that year had as a lodger the 'untutored' poet and friend of Jonathan Swift, Mary Barber (plate 16).

Numbers 6 and 7 Among the architecturally most interesting houses in Soho. The pair – originally part of a roughly uniform group of five houses – were built c.1718 on land that had been part of the Monmouth House site. In 1716 Sir James Bateman had acquired Monmouth House, in 1717 employed Thomas Archer to alter it, and released land on Frith Street for speculative development. The builder seems to have been William Thomas, who was instructed to construct the houses in accordance with recent London Buildings Acts, aimed at achieving robust and fire-resistant structures. Thomas was also required to follow a design for the elevation and, remarkably, this design survives. It shows the pair much as built but – more important – it suggests that the client did not wish to leave the appearance of the houses up to the discretion of the speculating builder; he wanted them constructed to an agreed design of some considerable architectural sophistication. Presumably an architect produced the design, and this was quite possibly Thomas Archer. There is no documentary evidence to confirm this but the design – a mix of Palladian restraint and classical authority and Baroque articulation – makes Archer a strong contender. The houses possess a strong Palladian sense of proportion, with a first-floor piano nobile and squat attic windows placed – Roman triumphal-arch-style – above a bold cornice. But, as built, the houses deviate significantly from the design, and this gives them a solemn Baroque theatricality. In the design the houses are divided into two pairs by giant pilaster strips. The house to the south was left in isolation. In typical and inventive Baroque manner, the pilaster strips have 'capitals' that are in fact sections of cornice that break forward. But in execution the piers between the windows also break forward slightly, so the whole elevation has a strong and rhythmical sense of movement. This façade treatment was not unprecedented within the English Baroque school. Nicholas Hawksmoor experimented with this type of articulation and layering – for example in the Clarendon Building of 1711–15 in Oxford. But more intriguing is a pair of terraces of c.1708 in Albury Street, Deptford. These terraces have elevations articulated by pilaster strips that – as in Frith Street – are formed by the piers between windows breaking forward slightly. The terraces in Deptford were almost certainly built by Thomas Lucas, a bricklayer who was part of Hawksmoor's building world and who worked on Hawksmoor's Christ Church, Spitalfields, of 1714–29.

Perhaps over more intriguing is the fact that construction of the Albury Street terraces started just before work commenced, on an adjoining site, on St Paul's Church. The church was designed by Thomas Archer in 1712 following an Act of 1711 promoting the building of fifty new Anglican churches in London. Interestingly, the Frith Street houses – like those in Deptford – vary in width. The visual discipline of the pilaster strips was a brilliant way in which to disguise the variations and give the design a visual unity.

So this pair of houses in Frith Street are part of a larger architectural world than that defined by early-eighteenth-century Soho. And if they were in fact designed by Thomas Archer they are a rare surviving example of early Georgian Baroque street architecture created by one of the leading architects of the age. The façades of both houses were reconstructed – in reasonably authentic manner – in 1909, but the pilastered Doric paired doorcase is original and their panelled interiors generally survive.

The plan-form of these houses is typical of Soho houses of the period. They are each one room wide and two main rooms deep, with shallow rear closets off the back rooms and compact dog-leg staircases set at the end of entrance halls.

Numbers 5, 6 and 7 are now an hotel named Hazlitt's (William Hazlitt lodged and died in number 6 in 1830), so there is limited public access to some rooms (plate 17).

Number 15 Built in 1733–4 and now notable for its amazing early-nineteenth-century 'Gothick' shop front. It's a flamboyant affair, not archaeologically authentic in its forms or details but highly decorative and engaging. It was created c.1816, when Gothic was still regarded as no more than a native and antique picturesque style. The earnest Gothic Revival, when the style was seen as Christian and morally and structurally righteous, was still a decade or so away. Above the door is a fine Regency fanlight of the then standard, rather abstract, design with nothing particularly Gothic about it. The shop is thought to have been created for Charles Clarke, a bookseller.

Numbers 16, 17 and 18 form a group of *c.*1735, built on a Portland estate lease by William Bignell, a Soho glazier. The houses have segmental arched windows. Number 18 is well preserved internally. In the entrance hall is a Doric box-cornice elaborated with a course of dentils, and a pair of fluted Doric pilasters that lead to an original dog-leg staircase, with carved tread ends to its lower portion.

Number 20 A dull twentieth-century building, but it stands on the site of the house in which Wolfgang Amadeus Mozart and his family set up home in September 1764, and it was from here that in January 1765 he dedicated his Opus 3 (K.10–15) to Queen Charlotte. Also from here Leopold Mozart touted his son's talents. An advertisement in *The Public Advertiser* of 11 March 1765 invited ladies and gentlemen to take a ticket to 'gratify their curiosity, and not only hear this young Music Master and his sister perform in private; but likewise try his surprising Musical Capacity, by giving him anything to Play at Sight, or any Music without Bass, which he will Write upon the spot, without recurring to his Harpsicord'. The Mozarts left London in July 1765.

Number 22 A building of little architectural but great social interest. It was in an attic laboratory here that, in January 1926, J.L. Baird first gave a demonstration of his new invention – television. It now houses Bar Italia (see p. 146).

Number 26 Built *c.*1735 by Francis Tredgold, carpenter. A modest house with an altered and stuccoed front. But its interior is well preserved, with panelling and a good original staircase.

Numbers 29 and 30 Built *c.*1735, altered, but the façades are partly original. Both are threatened with demolition for Crossrail 2.

There is a very good group on the north-west corner of Frith Street with Romilly Street (plate 18). In Frith Street it comprises numbers 37 and 38 and numbers 39, 40 and 41.

Numbers 37 and 38 Built in 1781, seemingly with 24 Romilly Street, which adjoins them to the west. They have plain, four-storey brick elevations with shops on the ground floor. Number 37 has an elevation to Romilly Street composed almost entirely of blind windows.

Numbers 39, 40 and 41 Built in 1743 by John Blagrave, a carpenter, on a building lease granted by a Soho lawyer who was an assignee of an earlier Portland estate lease. The windows are linked with horizontal cill bands – most effective. The interiors are much patched and mended, especially number 41; and it is surprising to see sash boxes still being fully exposed and set flush as late as the early 1740s. In theory such details had been banned in central London in the first decade of the eighteenth century as a potential fire hazard. This detail confirms what a backwater Soho was in the mid eighteenth century – and presumably John Blagrave was a very conservative type of carpenter. The interiors were very plain, but some good details survive, for example the entrance hall and first-floor panelled rooms in number 40.

Numbers 44, 45, 47 and 48 Built in 1804–7, after a fire destroyed the previous houses on the site. A uniform, noble and standard design for the date, with first-floor windows set within arched recesses.

Number 49 Also built *c.*1805, but as a separate development.

Numbers 58–64 One of the best and most characterful late-seventeenth- to nineteenth-century groups in Soho.

It starts, at its south end, with the Dog and Duck public house, built in 1897 to the designs of Francis Chambers for the Cannon Brewery. Located on the corner with Bateman Street, it is numbered 18 Bateman Street. The interior is an exceptionally fine survival, with tiles, mirrors and excellent joinery, a front and back bar (presumably originally a saloon bar and a public bar) being fitted onto a long, narrow site. Between the bars is a staircase, probably leading originally to dining rooms.

Number 58 Of *c*.1800, with huge first-floor windows, which were dropped in depth *c*.1820. There are no quarter bricks – called queen closers – to the bottom courses of window jambs, as was conventional at that date. This reveals that the lower portions of the windows are alterations. There is a good lamp above the door.

Number 59 Also of *c*.1800 and built as a pair with 58, but it is narrow in width so there is only room for a single window per floor; however, all the windows are very wide and of tripartite form.

Number 60 Probably built with adjoining number 61 *c*.1688 by the carpenter Richard Campion. The exterior and the interior, with fine bolection panelling, are both well detailed and preserved and reveal what standard houses in Soho's main streets would have looked like when the area was first developed in the late seventeenth century. The handsome Ionic doorcase, with its array of favoured neoclassical details including paterae and acanthus leaves in the frieze, is an addition of *c*.1778 (plate 19).

Early occupants of this house were aristocratic or socially ambitious, as was the case with much of late-seventeenth- and early-eighteenth-century Soho. These included Elizabeth Price in 1688, a high-class courtesan, who claimed clandestine, if contested, marriage to the Earl of Banbury and styled herself countess. In 1691 the house was occupied by Lady Butler and from 1692 to 1698 by Colonel John Beaumont, who threw in his lot with William of Orange in 1688, campaigned in Ireland and in 1690 fought at the Battle of the Boyne. As well as being an experienced soldier Beaumont was also a 'lethal duellist'.[24] Later inhabitants of the house, or parts of the house, included the painter Nathaniel Hone during the 1750s and the journalist, travel writer and author Stephen Graham. His best-known work is, perhaps, the autobiographical *A Private in the Guards*, published in 1919. It tells of Graham's experience, as a gentleman ranker of relatively advanced years (he was thirty-three), training with the Guards and fighting in France through 1918. It is a gripping and penetrating tale in which Graham reflects on the degrading, depersonalising brutality of the training – and the need for such training to endure the appalling experience of war. Graham was living in the first floor with his wife at the time of his death in 1975.

On one of my early Soho incursions I wandered into the house and was confronted by Mrs Graham. In those days – I suppose it must have been the late 1970s – the entrance halls and staircases of Soho houses that were in multi-occupation were almost part of the public street. Front doors were left open – or at least unlocked – for tenants and their friends to come and go and so it was easy to explore. But being caught inside could be embarrassing if you had no practical reason for being there. Mrs Graham challenged me. I simply said I was there for the architecture. She fully understood and invited me into her first-floor apartment for a look around and a cup of tea. I suppose she must have been in her eighties, so this really was very decent behaviour. I remember her wonderful panelled walls – particularly the bulging and sinuous curves of their bolection mouldings, the neoclassical frieze in the front room (I imagine the same date as the doorcase), and the delightful and sensible plan. A large, three-window-wide front room – full of light – served as the bedroom; there was a smaller rear room, where we sat at her tea table, and then a small and mysterious closet off to the rear. These three rooms were like a private apartment in a contemporary country house – a bedchamber and a drawing room, with a closet or cabinet for the intimate reception of special guests and for intrigue. I hasten to say that Mrs Graham did not show me her closet. We spent an hour or so together, spoke about the house and her husband, I left, and never saw her again. It was a strange and magical meeting. The next time I called – some months later – she was gone. Dead, I assumed. The house was then occupied by a rich young man, the son of an eminent architect, who blanketed bright white paint all over Mrs Graham's mellow and ancient-looking olive-green panelling.

Number 61 Built at the same time as 60, it has been much altered. Its façade dates from 1950 and little survives inside.

Numbers 63–64 date probably from c.1690. They are, however, much altered, probably in 1734 by a carpenter named John Clarkson. The rear of these houses can be glimpsed from Royalty Mews, entered from Dean Street. On the east side of the mews are two-storey nineteenth-century industrial buildings which replaced stabling that must originally have served the Frith Street houses. In addition, the splendid rear elevations and closet wings of 26–28 Dean Street, built in 1734, rise over the west side of the mews.

Carlisle Street

The street was named after the mansion, built in the mid 1680s, that stood at its west end. Occupied originally by the Countess of Carlisle, it was destroyed by bombs during the Second World War. Its loss still hurts – not only because it was a fine example of late-seventeenth-century domestic architecture that was beautifully fitted to its site, which closed the vista west from Soho Square with tremendous presence, but also because it was part of the myth of London. It was a mansion, complete with crowning pediment, fitted into one end of a narrow street that seemed to serve – in Parisian fashion – as its courtyard.

Indeed, on Rocque's map of 1746 the west portion of Carlisle Street, beyond Dean Street, is called King's Square Court, suggesting that from early on this little court was conceived as a small square forming a dignified setting for the mansion. This sense of seclusion was rare in London and evidently attracted the attention of Charles Dickens, who threaded the house into the narrative of *A Tale of Two Cities*. It served as the model for the lodgings of the traumatised and occasionally profoundly disturbed Dr Manette, whose home was in a building that formed 'a quiet street corner not far from Soho Square'. Dickens continues: 'A quainter corner than the corner where the Doctor lived, was not to be found in London. There was no way through it, and the front windows of the Doctor's house commanded a pleasant little vista of street that had a congenial air of retirement on it ... It was a cool spot ... a wonderful place for echoes, and a very harbour from the raging streets.'[25]

Numbers 4, 5 and 6 Much-altered houses dating from when the street was laid out in 1685. The façades were mostly rebuilt in the late eighteenth century, with numbers 5 and 6 now looking like a pair built *c*.1780. Number 6 was the home of John Christopher Smith, G.F. Handel's secretary and friend. Many original details survive inside the houses, with 5 being particularly good; it retains panelling and a Doric box-cornice in the entrance hall, with an arch supported by panelled pilasters (a standard late-seventeenth-century detail) framing the staircase compartment, which retains the original staircase with a stout, square-section newel.

Number 16, of 1773, was rebuilt with narrow piers.

Number 17 is the best surviving house in the street. It dates from 1765 and was built by George Smith Bradshaw, an upholsterer and tapestry maker. The pedimented doorcase with carved brackets is finely detailed, and inside there are some good fireplaces and joinery.

Number 19 Built in 1735 by John Sanger, carpenter. Now the Toucan Bar.

Dean Street

Dean Street, like several other streets in Soho, is still numbered in the eighteenth-century manner. The numbers start on one side (the north-east corner) then run consecutively down the east side of the street to Old Compton Street and then back up the west side. Therefore, naturally, there are odd and even numbers on each side of the street. But in these notes geographical order is ignored and houses are described in numerical sequence.

Number 6 The rear elevation of John Trotter's former Soho Bazaar of 1801–4 at 4–6 Soho Square (see p. 9). The elevation is austere and functional with wide windows. The broad fanlight over the door is particularly fine.

Number 8 is an oddity for Soho – a Gothic Revival house of 1878 by Eales and Sons, faced with red brick and designed in a Victorian permutation of an Italian medieval style. Goodness knows why – it has nothing to do with its location, of course, and only a broad connection to the Gothic Revival theories of the day. But it's rather good.

Numbers 11 and 12 A much-altered eighteenth-century pair, with façades rebuilt in appalling manner from first-floor-window level upwards. What remains suggests an original building date perhaps as early as the mid 1730s. The front door of number 11 is on Carlisle Street; it is embellished with a somewhat mutilated but not unattractive doorcase, incorporating a delicate pediment with mutules perched on blocks of plain frieze and a moulded architrave over Doric pilasters. An unusual design.

Numbers 26, 27 and 28 form a group, erected *c*.1734 by John Nolloth, a carpenter of St James's, on a sixty-five-year building lease from the Portland estate. The houses have uniform and handsome elevations, simple but with Baroque details – notably the brick aprons below the windows of 26 and 28, and the large brick cornice above the second-floor windows that makes the top storey read as an attic. The ground and first floors are, sadly, altered. The block (with 29 to the south) now houses the Quo Vadis restaurant, but from January or February 1851 to

1856 two small rooms at the top of 28 were the home of Karl Marx and his family. Marx had arrived in England in August 1849.

The principal occupant of the houses (and ratepayer) was an Italian-born cook named John Marengo. Another sub-lessee was Morgan Kavanagh, an Irish 'teacher of languages' from whom Marx evidently rented his two rooms. Marx started writing *Das Kapital* while living here and researching in the British Library. The life of the Marx family within this *altes Loch* (old hovel), as Marx was later to call it, was grim, haunted by poverty and sickness. While living here three of the Marx children died. The Marx family's chaotic way of life in Dean Street is suggested by the report of a Prussian agent which, even if something of an exaggeration from a hostile source, presumably captures the essence of the Marx home. The family, stated the agent, lived

in one of the worst, therefore also the cheapest, quarters in London ... [Marx] occupies two rooms ... in the whole apartment there is not one clean and good piece of furniture to be found; all is broken, tattered and torn, everywhere clings thick dust, everywhere is the greatest disorder; ... his manuscripts, books and newspapers lie beside the children's toys, bits and pieces from his wife's work-basket, tea-cups with broken rims, dirty spoons, knives, forks, lamps, an inkwell, tumblers, Dutch clay-pipes, tobacco ash ... sitting down is really a hazardous business ... But all this gives Marx and his wife not the slightest embarrassment; one is received in the friendliest way.[26]

The census return for 1851 for 28 Dean Street throws
additional light on the Marx household and places it in
the context of its immediate neighbours and, to a degree,
that of mid-nineteenth-century Soho. The first person
mentioned in the census is John Marengo. He is listed
as 'head' of his household, aged thirty-seven. His wife
Ann was forty-six and born in Hatfield, Kent. They had
one servant, Catherine Brown, aged nineteen and born
in Ireland. The second household consisted only of Morgan Kavanagh, aged fifty-one, born in Dublin. The third
household also consisted of one person, Peter Pepigni,
thirty-eight and married (but his wife was absent on the
day of the census), a confectioner, born in Italy. Then
there is the Marx household. 'Charles Mark' is listed as the
'head', aged thirty-two, a 'Doctor (philosophical author)'
by occupation and born in Prussia. His wife, 'Jenny Mark',
was thirty and born in Prussia, but the birthplaces of the
children reveal very directly the peripatetic nature of the
family's life. The eldest daughter, 'Jenny C', aged six, a
'scholar', was born in France; 'Henry E', aged four and
also a scholar, was born in Belgium, as was 'Jenny L',
aged five, a 'scholar', while the nine-month-old 'Jenny E'
had been born in Soho. The family had lived briefly at
the now demolished 64 Dean Street before moving into
number 28. Despite their poverty, and perhaps reflecting
the elevated social origins of Mrs Marx, the family had
a 'servant' living with them – a twenty-seven-year-old
woman born in Prussia named Helena – and a forty-seven-
year-old married nurse named Elizabeth Moss from
Bethnal Green. Although very poor in 1851, it was, it
seems – notwithstanding the barbed comments of the
Prussian agent – something of a genteel poverty. Jenny

von Westphalen – the future Mrs Marx – was born into
Prussian aristocracy, and on her maternal side was related
to the Dukes of Argyll and the royal house of Stuart.
She met Marx when a child, through her brother, who
was a school friend, and they married in 1838 and went
to live in Paris. When Marx became politically active and
revolutionary the couple were exiled from France and
Prussia, spending spells in Brussels and Cologne until
seeking refuge in London in 1849.

Quite how the eight people in the Marx household lived
in the space available is hard to imagine. The apartment
is generally described as consisting of two rooms, which
is no doubt broadly correct. But, being at the top of the
house, the family would have had sole use of the staircase
landing, a most useful space. The houses do have small
rear closet wings, but these rise only to second-floor level.

It is interesting to consider to what degree this household was a microcosm of mid-nineteenth-century Soho.
The house could contain about fifteen or sixteen rooms
– including basement and closets, although some were
barely habitable – and contained four separate households
and thirteen people on the day of the census. So it was
crowded, like mid-nineteenth-century Soho; and also like
Soho its inhabitants were cosmopolitan – Italian, Irish,
English and Prussian – with a wide mix of occupations. In
fact, the Italian component is perhaps the most interesting
and a reminder that as early as 1851 Soho was acquiring a
sizeable Italian population.

Karl and Jenny Marx eventually had seven children, and
it is poignant and illuminating to reflect on the differing
fates of the four Marx children listed in the 1851 census.

'Jenny C' – Jenny Caroline, known as 'Jennychen' –

was born on 1 May 1844. She became a politically active socialist/Marxist. Her French birth seems to have given her life a French orientation. She wrote for the French socialist press, and exposed and vilified British ill-treatment of Irish Fenians, especially after the execution of the 'Manchester Martyrs' in 1867. She married Charles Longuet in 1872, a 'veteran' of the Paris Commune of the previous year – when the city was ruled briefly by a radical socialist government – and died in Paris on 11 January 1883 from cancer of the bladder. Her father died two months later.

'Henry E', Charles Louis Henri Edgar, was born on 3 February 1847 and died on 6 May 1855. He was never to leave 28 Dean Street. His funeral would have centred around this house after his small body had, perhaps, lain in state in one of the upper rooms. Henri Edgar's slightly younger brother, Henry Edward Guy, 'Guido', had already died. He was born in London in September 1849 and died just over a year later, while the family lived in Soho but before they moved into 28 Dean Street.

'Jenny L', Jenny Laura, was born in Brussels on 26 September 1845. In 1868 she married Paul Lafargue. The two committed suicide together on 26 November 1911. Paul Lafargue was a young French socialist who came to London in 1866 to work for the First International. There he became a friend of Karl Marx and got to know Marx's family, especially Jenny Laura, who fell in love with him. The Lafargues began several decades of political work together, translating Marx's writings into French and spreading Marxism in France and Spain. During most of their lives Laura and Paul Lafargue were financially supported by Friedrich Engels. They also inherited a large amount of Engels's money when he died in 1895. The couple committed suicide together because they believed they had nothing left to give to the movement to which they had devoted their lives. Laura was sixty-six and Paul sixty-nine. He left a suicide note saying:

Healthy in body and mind, I end my life before pitiless old age which has taken from me my pleasures and joys one after another; and which has been stripping me of my physical and mental powers, can paralyze my energy and break my will, making me a burden to myself and to others. For some years I had promised myself not to live beyond 70; and I fixed the exact year for my departure from life. I prepared the method for the execution of our resolution, it was a hypodermic of cyanide acid. I die with the supreme joy of knowing that at some future time, the cause to which I have been devoted for forty-five years will triumph. Long live Communism! Long Live the Second International.

Lenin spoke at their funeral in Paris. Nadya Krupskaya said that Lenin – her husband – had told her, 'If one cannot work for the Party any longer, one must be able to look truth in the face and die like the Lafargues.'

'Jenny E', Jenny Evelyn Frances, was born on 28 March 1851 and died on 14 April 1852. She is stated in the census to have been nine months old, which indicates it was conducted in December 1851.

Karl and Jenny Marx were to have two more children after 1851. One, an unnamed child, was born and died on 6 July 1857, so after the family's departure from 28 Dean Street. But another, Jenny Julia Eleanor, was born in Dean Street on 15 January 1855. She became very active in Marxist politics and lived with a fellow Marxist, Edward Aveling. Unfortunately he proved unfaithful and she committed suicide on 31 March 1898 at Jew's Walk, Sydenham. She had been the first to translate Gustave Flaubert's *Madame Bovary* into English, and the means and circumstances of Eleanor's death (she took prussic acid and dressed herself in white for her pact with death) to a degree mirrored those of Flaubert's tragic, lovelorn heroine. The novel had, evidently, been most suggestive.

Number 29 dates from *c.*1692, and is relatively little altered externally, with the exception of the ground- and first-floor elevations. In 1739 a half-interest in a leasehold title to the site, held of the Duke of Portland, was assigned to the architect Sir John Vanbrugh's sister, Robina. It is possible Sir John knew the house although it is probable his sister did not live in it, but viewed it merely as an investment. In 1737 all or part of the house was occupied by the painter Joseph Francis Nollekens and his son Joseph, the famed sculptor, who was born there in August that year. Nollekens senior lived in the house until his death in January 1748 and his widow until 1752. From 1770 to 1773 the house was occupied by François-Hippolite Barthélémon, the composer and leading violinist at Vauxhall Gardens, and in 1811 was the home of the caricaturist Robert Cruikshank, brother of George.

Number 31 The Crown public house, a corner structure apparently inspired by the Art Deco style, so presumably remodelled in the mid to late 1920s. But it probably incorporates elements of late-seventeenth or early-eighteenth-century buildings on the site.

Numbers 33 and 33a Built in 1734 by the speculating

builder William Bignell, under a sixty-five-year lease from the Portland estate. Number 33 appears to have been largely rebuilt, or re-fronted, in recent years. Certainly the rubbed-brick arches are modern and lack the finesse of genuine eighteenth-century ones. But 33a is much better preserved, and although its ground floor is altered it possesses a handsome mid-nineteenth-century shop front. From 1748 to 1775 the pair housed Jack's Coffee House and from 1813 to 1849 Walker's Hotel.

Numbers 39 and 40 Built c.1732 but much altered, with façades now rendered or refaced.

Number 41 Built in 1731, probably re-fronted in the 1770s, and in the mid nineteenth century Gothic-style drip moulds were added to the upper windows. It was home to the Colony Room (see p. 131).

Number 48 The building might include fabric from the first building on the site, constructed on the Portland estate in 1691, but this house was probably substantially reconstructed in 1734 by Charles Paulentine, a local joiner. He seems to have built the house – only two windows wide – to live in rather than as a speculation. This would appear to be the house that, with front stuccoed and shop front added, survives – or at least survived into the 1970s. I photographed it then and it had about it a splendid atmosphere of decayed authenticity: the upper portion of the façade was restrained by a large, vertical wrought-iron strap set between the second-floor windows, and the sash boxes in the windows were heavy and well aged. The genuine Soho character of the house was captured by *Picture Post* in 1956, in an article entitled 'I am in the Queen of Soho'. The piece includes photographs by Thurston Hopkins showing smiling girls – evidently prostitutes – posing at both of its first-floor windows, much as harlots displayed themselves in the windows of eighteenth-century London brothels. But the façade has now lost its air of charming antiquity and, needless to say, the girls have gone, replaced by office workers and the ubiquitous Thai restaurant on the ground floor. The façade, spick and span with tie bar gone, is, I fear, a modern reconstruction.

Number 49 is what now calls itself the French House but until recent times was the York Minster public house. The building dates from the early twentieth century and, designed in weak neo-Georgian style, is not of great quality but – importantly – is far from being offensive, and the ground-floor pub is good. It has a central bar with small, intimate sitting and drinking spaces around it. No doubt the bar space was originally divided into public bar, saloon bar and private bars and snugs, as was usual from the early 1880s. There was a restaurant on the first floor and, although it regularly changes its nature, there remains a restaurant there still. This pub was run by a German landlord until the outbreak of the First World War and then – with things becoming a trifle hot for German businesses in London – the licence was acquired by a Belgian named Victor Berlemont; and oddly, although no doubt out of a sense of patriotism, it became known informally as the French House. During the 1950s and 1960s the pub became a favourite drinking place for Soho outsiders, artistic characters and – presumably – for the girls from next door. So it acquired, and retains, a reputation as being one of London's last bohemian haunts. The current licence holders remain faithful to the Berlemont creation and now hawk the pub's history and its 'Frenchness' with determination. They have changed its name officially to the French House and sell Normandy cider as a house speciality. What this means is that it is packed with tourists, usually gullible and forgiving beings, with little room left for Soho's few genuine residents. But this is no bad thing – at least the pub survives and thrives – and a visit is well worth the effort. Saturday mornings or early Monday evenings are best, and the wine on offer is far more drinkable than in the average London pub.

Number 51 The Golden Lion public house, neo-Tudor, loud, large and showy, dated 1929. During the Second World War it became well known as a meeting place for homosexual servicemen. Its reputation as a gay pub lingered into the 1950s and beyond. It is now under threat of demolition for the construction of Crossrail 2.

Excursion into St Anne's Court

The court is a long alley running between Dean Street and Wardour Street, and marks the boundary between three estates (see p. 54). The west portion of the alley was laid out in the Pulteney estate and was in existence by 1681, while the east part was laid out in the Portland estate and had been lined with buildings by 1690. To the south was the Pitt estate. The two portions of the alley do not run straight east–west: midway between the two main streets is a set-back. This is where the Pulteney and the Portland estates met.

Numbers 27 and 28 St Anne's Court and numbers 86 and 87 Dean Street form one group. They were built in 1735–6 by the Soho glazier and builder William Big-nell, who also speculated on Old Compton Street. The designs of the houses in the court are very simple and rise only three storeys above ground level, while those on Dean Street tend to be four storeys. Number 28 is reasonably well preserved, apart from the ground floor and the architraves added to the windows. Number 27 has been re-fronted. Number 86 Dean Street, on the corner with the court, is of the same scale as the houses in the court, but it has pediments and architraves to its centre windows on the first and second floors. This, of course, adds a bit of grandeur and raises the house's pretensions to match those of Dean Street. But the pediments are an odd ornament for the 1730s and the profile of the first-floor architrave – if original – suggests that all was in fact added in the early nineteenth century. A good amount of panelling survives inside. Number 87 has been re-fronted in poor manner.

Beyond these corner buildings the court is now an architecturally bleak place, although it hosts a good mix of convivial uses. In the 1960s and 1970s there were sound-recording studios along its north side, now replaced by editing suites related to the film industry. In number 17 was located the Trinity Studios where in 1969 David Bowie recorded his single 'Space Oddity' and in 1972 his album *The Rise and Fall of Ziggy Stardust and the Spiders from Mars*. The Beatles and the Rolling Stones also used the studio, which closed in 1981.

Return to Dean Street

Numbers 69–70, dating from 1731–1, are much altered but retain some early panelling and one 1730s staircase. Their upper level housed the Gargoyle Club (see p. 126).

Number 76 Until recently this was, arguably, the finest Georgian house surviving in Soho. It was built in 1732–5 in high style by Thomas Richmond on a lease from the Pitt estate. It is larger than most in the street – not just in width but also in volume – and was decorated in outstanding manner, with rich and fine panelling and a staircase with sumptuous painted walls that depict a romantic seascape and numerous ships viewed through a trompe-l'oeil loggia (plate 21). The house was a very precious survival until 2009, when tragedy struck: it was engulfed by fire and terrible damage was done. However, what survived the flames – and the rebirth of the house – is more or less miraculous (plate 20).

As built, number 76 was two rooms wide and two rooms deep and had a small rear closet; the front volume included a large room and the wide staircase hall and compartment. This arrangement is reflected in the four-window-wide façade, where one of the first-floor windows is arched while the others are flat-topped. Externally this design gives the house an asymmetry that would have seemed awkward in the 1730s. But internally it makes perfect sense because the arched window forms the centre feature of the three-window-wide first-floor front room. To express externally the internal hierarchy of the house, all first-floor windows are ornamented with rustic blocks, to make it clear that the first floor – with its handsome reception rooms – is the most important one. The *Survey of London*[27] suggests these rustic blocks are a later addition, but this is not certain and is indeed unlikely, since number 75 had a similar arrangement at first-floor level.

I knew the house pretty well before the fire. It was

occupied by a film company and the front door was
generally unlocked during the day. It was possible to pop
in to look at the painted staircase and not too difficult to
see the main panelled rooms on ground- and first-floor
levels. It was superb. The paintings on the upper walls of
the staircase compartment were wonderfully solemn and
somewhat mysterious and the panelling was massive in
detail. All was stately and assured. I arrived on site the
morning after the fire. I wanted to speak to the owners,
I wanted to meet local conservation officers, some of
whom I knew well and, most of all, I wanted to see the
extent of the damage and – if possible – persuade myself
that something positive could be done. I went back several
times during the following days, talking to firemen who
had fought the blaze, to occupants of the building, to
members of a salvage squad sent in by Westminster City
Council. The house was grade-II*-listed and all fittings
that could be saved from the ruins were to be quickly
put in secure storage.

The story that emerged was extraordinary. From
previous experiences I knew that fires can behave oddly
and that damage can be unpredictable – but few fires
were odder than this one, and few less predictable. As it
was explained to me at the time, the fire started at the
back of the house, in an extension beyond the rear wall,
thus building up energy and ferocity out of sight. It then
spread along an air-conditioning or ventilation duct into
the rear portion of the house. Smoke and smell gave it
away, not flames. People realised there was a fire some-
where – but where, and how serious was it? Evacuation
started in a sedate and orderly manner, the fire brigade
were called – but their arrival was delayed by another fire

or false alarms elsewhere. When they did arrive the fire had taken hold more seriously and, even if slow-moving, proved tenacious and initially unquenchable. It spread and slowly devoured the back portion of the house, panelled room after panelled room, spreading up the secondary staircase, the well acting like a chimney. A vast amount of water was pumped into the house from a high level, which created a lake in the top-floor room. This growing pool of water, massive in weight, broke the floor joists and beams and cascaded down to do the same thing to successive levels below, one after another, until the basement was reached.

When I first got inside the ravaged house for a proper exploration a day or so after the fire, I was stunned. I'd seen photographs of the house at the height of the blaze – burning like a furnace – but, to my amazement, the staircase and painted hall survived almost intact. The water pumped into the house had literally broken its back but had also prevented the fire from spreading from the rear of the house into the main front rooms. The brick wall between the back and front rooms had done its job of acting as a firebreak, kept cool by the cascading water. The only serious damage to the painted wall (beyond some smoke staining) was a little scorching to the painting on the wall between the staircase gallery and the first-floor front room. The timber studs behind the painting had started to burn but – thank goodness – this finger of flame was quickly extinguished.

I looked into the ground-floor front room. It was an incredible scene: I could see up to the sky and down into the basement, full of rubble and salvage men picking around for details and packaging them for storage in steel containers placed on the street in front of the house. Details included the ground-floor marble fireplace that had toppled from the wall, but most of its parts seemed little the worse for the experience. And, most extraordinary of all, the panelling on the walls of the front rooms remained in place, looking little damaged, although it now lined the walls of a vast, floorless cavern. With the staircase and its painted walls intact, the panelling of the main rooms safe and the façade not even touched by the flames, it was clear that this catastrophe was not terminal, that much could be salvaged and that a well-repaired and restored house could retain a high degree of authenticity – or at least the front portion could. The rear rooms, wonderfully panelled, where the fire raged uncontrolled for too long had gone entirely. Oddly, the secondary staircase, up which the fire had leaped, was not entirely destroyed. The heat must have been intense for a long time, but the portion of the secondary staircase from ground floor to basement survived in good condition, hardly singed and its paint not melted. How, I can't imagine – nor could the fireman I spoke to. But, as he reminded me, fires are strange things.

Repair of the house was complex, not just technically but also financially, with issues arising over insurance money. But all agreed that it was too good to lose and too much survived to make demolition an option. Ownership of the house changed hands and by 2016 repair and restoration were complete; it is now a clubhouse for the Soho House group.

I went to the opening. I was impressed. The staircase looked much as it ever did, with the painting cleaned and the small fire-damaged section repaired in an honest manner – which means, following the accepted theory about historic repair, that the new work is plainly new, so as not to confuse or compromise the authentic old, but executed in a self-effacing and sympathetic manner. The panelling in the front rooms had been repaired, and the original fireplaces reinstated. But it was the rear that came as a shock. The theory that repairs should be honest and not ape the original work had not been applied. To my amazement, the rear rooms had been recreated as if the fire had never happened. They could have been made minimal and modern but they were not, thank goodness. This house was so glorious before the fire, so entrancingly complete, that repair, restoration and recreation were the only civilised options. So, due to a collective act of will, the house has not been lost but lives again to delight and entertain. It offers a most interesting and relevant lesson for other Soho buildings. Not only must we keep what we have got, but a little bit of enlightened recreation, when opportunities arise, might not be a bad idea. Interestingly, Soho Estates was involved in this project. It owns much of Soho (see p. 294) and it should be encouraged to apply the lessons learned here to other historic buildings and sites in the area.

As repaired and recreated, number 76 Dean Street is the sole survivor of a group of four, generally similar, large houses (numbers 74, 75, 76 and 77), all built on leases taken by Thomas Richmond in the early to mid 1730s.

Number 75 was, internally, even more spectacular than 76, with a very fine staircase hall – painted in illusionary manner, with life-size figures set within a painted trompe-l'oeil arcade – that in the late nineteenth century was attributed to Sir James Thornhill or his son-in-law, William

Hogarth. This attribution had no authority whatsoever but it delayed proposed demolition and in 1913 prompted the Commissioners of Works to serve a Preservation Order under the then new Ancient Monuments Act. This order required parliamentary confirmation and unfortunately the First World War intervened, so the house remained in limbo, empty and decaying. But there was great public concern about its fate, mostly because of the Hogarth attribution. For example *The Sphere* on 14 January 1914 argued that this 'handsome Georgian mansion ... might well be devoted to the public as an eighteenth-century museum', and while conceding that 'it is not in the least certain who painted the ... Venetian style ... paintings on the walls', noted that it is 'generally assumed that Thornhill lived here and that Hogarth made love within its walls' – presumably referring to Hogarth's courtship of Thornhill's daughter. *The Sphere* also mentioned the campaign to save the house headed by the *Daily Mail* and an appeal publicised in *The Times*, and concluded that 'we cannot have too many of these mementos to add to the interest and fascination of London'.[28] How very true, but the delay and the decay caused by the war years, the owner's appeal against the confirmation of the Preservation Order and the absence of evidence to connect Thornhill or Hogarth to the mural told heavily and bitterly against the house. Despite an almost decade-long battle to save it, and much public interest, the house was demolished in 1923. Attempts had been made to rescue its fittings, the murals were removed in sections from the walls and its staircase and staircase hall were salvaged and eventually purchased by the Art Institute of Chicago for re-erection as a museum display. The murals proved too damaged to re-erect and were lost. The staircase has since been deaccessioned by the Institute but purchased by the Spitalfields Trust that plans to bring it home. The replacement building is dull neo-Georgian. (plates 22, 23 and 24)

Number 77 Also built around 1733 and similar in scale to numbers 75 and 76, and its painted staircase walls were said to be finer than those at 76.[29] It was gutted after the First World War. All that survives is its façade, which shares a cornice with 76. The triangular and segmental pediments to the first-floor windows were added in the mid nineteenth century.

Number 74 The smallest and simplest of this group, altered in the early twentieth century and subsequently demolished. In its place is a large pastiche-Georgian office building of 1954 that also occupies the site of number 72, which dated from the mid 1750s. This is called Royalty House, in memory of the Royalty Theatre which from 1834 until 1955 occupied the ground behind 72, 73 and 74 Dean Street. The theatre had been started by the actress Frances Maria Kelly, who lived in number 73, and it functioned until 1938. She enjoyed the patronage of the 6th Duke of Devonshire, a highly artistic individual. The architect was Samuel Beazley, one of England's leading theatre designers in the early nineteenth century, and it was here in 1875 that Richard D'Oyly Carte staged the first ever Gilbert and Sullivan comic opera, *Trial by Jury*. It proved to be a hit. The yard behind number 72 had been, from the late eighteenth century, the location of the anatomy school operated by Joseph Constantine Carpue. He pioneered reconstructive rhinoplastic surgery and experimented enthusiastically with galvanism and electric medical treatment. He vacated the school in 1833.

This parade of urban palaces, all, except 74, with glorious Baroque-style painted staircase halls, must have been astonishing, and in its way a peculiar evocation of the palazzi that Grand Tourists would have known from their forays along the Grand Canal in Venice.

The questions begged by the scale and quality of these buildings are how on earth were they financed, and if Thornhill and Hogarth did not paint their interiors, who did? Who was this ambitious development aimed at and who initially occupied these palatial houses? Some of these questions can't be answered, but what is clear is that Thomas Richmond, the speculative builder behind this grandiose project, had access to money because the initial construction costs of these four large houses must have been huge. Perhaps he mortgaged the sites and so effectively borrowed the money. Certainly, he must have worked in close and creative collaboration with his landlords, the Pitt estate, and it is clear they had great architectural and social ambitions for the central portion of the west side of Dean Street controlled by the estate. Evidently, they believed there was still a market for grandeur in 1730s Soho and were willing to gamble to attract profitable tenants. This belief ran counter to the prevailing trend in the late 1720s and early 1730s to replace the large, late-seventeenth-century houses with smaller ones aimed at merchants, craftsmen and tradesmen, as exemplified by the story of Meard Street (see p. 265). One can't help but wonder at Richmond's audacity. But, of course, in the 1730s Soho's future was less certain. It is only with the power of hindsight that we see the early-eighteenth-century move towards craft manufacturing, light industry and increasingly cramped housing as irreversible.

After all, Great Marlborough Street, started in 1704, rapidly attracted aristocratic occupants and retained many in the 1730s; and numerous houses in Poland Street, built during the first decade of the eighteenth century, and in Great Pulteney Street, built in 1719 and 1720, were large, ambitious and well occupied by prosperous tenants until late in the century. So in the mid 1730s Richmond's gamble seemed, perhaps, a justified risk.

There is much that is not known about this story; however, what can be established is that Richmond was a carpenter, but was also described in his will as a citizen and a wax chandler. This suggests he was a man of some status, probably associated with the ancient City livery companies representing carpenters and wax chandlers.

Richmond's first involvement in Soho was in 1716 with the Pulteney estate; in the 1720s he was involved in speculative building in Grosvenor Square, the great new London housing enterprise, and by 1726 was living in the parish of St Anne's, Soho, being made a church-warden in 1727. Soon after this he started his long and productive relationship with the Pitt estate and it is reasonable to assume that, having built large aristocratic houses successfully around Grosvenor Square, Richmond persuaded the estate that the same exercise could be profitably undertaken in Dean Street. The connection between Grosvenor Square and these Dean Street houses is underpinned by the fact that 44 Grosvenor Square, built in 1727 by Richmond, had a painted hall very similar to that in 75 Dean Street. (Number 44 Grosvenor Square was demolished in 1967 and part of the staircase mural,

showing figures within a trompe-l'oeil arcade, is now in
the Victoria and Albert Museum.)

Richmond died in 1739 and his will reveals that he did
not leave a vast estate. He seems to have built expensive
houses but failed to amass a fortune for himself, so we
can only conclude that his gamble with his palatial Dean
Street houses did not pay off.[30]

The biggest mystery, in a way, is whether Richmond
designed these four houses. At the time it was usual for
builders to act as their own architects, generally sticking
to prevailing traditions and perhaps taking inspiration
for details from recently completed architect-designed
buildings of fashion or from the architectural pattern
books that started to appear in large numbers after
1730 as printing became cheaper. If Richmond was the
architect, he was evidently a man of considerable architectural ability, with an eye for fashion and a desire to
give the group of houses, of varied width, a sense of
unity without trying to impose a rigid uniformity.

The result was admirably subtle, with elevations of
generally similar design punctuated by pilaster strips
and united below a common cornice. The rusticated
first-floor windows on 75 and 76 were, assuming they
were original, a grand touch, presumably inspired by
the designs of James Gibbs and by some of Palladio's
north Italian buildings. And the plans of both 75 and 76
seem to have been influenced by Palladian theories of
design, most popular in 1730s Britain, which promoted
'ideal' proportions that were permutations of the square
or cube, such as square and a third (3:4), square and a
half (2:3), and double square (2:1). Both houses were
conceived as roughly 3:4 in plan area and incorporated

square-plan rooms at ground- and first-floor levels. Equally, the design of the panelled rooms was magnificent, with much use made of pilasters, particularly to frame fireplaces, and cornices enriched by carved detail or dentils. And the joinery of the staircases in both 75 and 76 was executed to the highest standard. Richmond might have delegated much of this detail design to the tradesmen he used, or – as was often the case – it could have been bespoken by the first occupants of the houses.

The practical details about the four houses do not reveal much. Richmond was granted leases for 75, 76 and 77 in February 1732, all with a one-year 'peppercorn' or rent-free period. The lease for 74 was granted in March 1733, also on one-year 'peppercorn' terms. The fact that the smallest house came last might suggest that all was not going well and ambitions were downsized, but there are many other possible readings.

The initial occupants of 74–77 Dean Street are more revealing. Number 75 was first occupied by Bulstrode Peachey Knight, who negotiated for the lease before the house was finished, so it is reasonable to assume its fine interior and painted hall were completed for him, perhaps even commissioned by him. Knight was a wealthy landowner in Sussex and Hampshire and an MP who had made a good marriage to the widow and heiress of William Knight. He took his new wife's surname and her maternal estate of West Dean in Sussex. Sadly, the *Survey of London* confirms that 'nothing is known of the identity of the craftsmen employed to decorate the house or of the painter of the staircase hall'. All that can be said is that the composition, with figures promenading and lingering within a trompe-l'oeil arcade, seems inspired by the murals of 1724, painted by William Kent and decorating the King's Staircase at Kensington Palace. Perhaps, in the same way that carpenters such as Richmond might be influenced by newly completed fashionable buildings when designing their speculations, skilled painters of decoration based their compositions on recently completed designs for royalty or the aristocracy. It makes sense. Peachey Knight did not long enjoy his own palace: he was dead by 1736 and his widow died two years later.[31]

Number 76's first occupant was James Hamilton, the 7th Earl of Abercorn, who was a Fellow of the Royal Society. His second son was the Honourable John Hamilton, an officer in the Royal Navy who was promoted lieutenant in March 1735 and who distinguished himself later that year at the wreck of the *Princess Louisa*. If the mural in the staircase hall was painted slightly after the house was completed, then John Hamilton's Royal Navy connections might well explain its maritime theme and, as the *Survey of London* points out, 'the presence of an eighteenth-century battleship among the fantastic seascapes painted in the walls'.[32]

Number 77 was first occupied by Sir Kenrick Clayton, a Buckinghamshire landowner and MP who remained in residence until 1750.

The pattern of occupation of 75, 76 and 77 during the eighteenth century offers answers to the question of whether or not Richmond and the estate were wise to build such large and aristocratic houses in Soho at a time when London's aristocracy were favouring homes to the north of Oxford Street and to the west, in the newly developed Cavendish-Harley and Grosvenor estates.*

After Peachey Knight's death in 1736 number 75 Dean Street was occupied until 1750 by various members of his family. Then it was taken by the Earl of Seafield and remained well occupied until 1800. Then things started to change, no doubt reflecting social shifts taking place in Soho generally as commerce and trade increased and surviving high-class residential enclaves dwindled. From 1801 the lease of number 75 was acquired by Philip Rundell, a partner in a firm of silver- and goldsmiths, and from this time the house was always at least partially in commercial use.

In 1742 Lord Abercorn left 76 Dean Street for Cavendish Square, which of course suggests that Richmond and the Pitt estate had failed in their aim to make Dean Street a place of fashion. But the house remained pretty well occupied, as a single habitation, until the end of the century, including among its tenants the 2nd Earl Bathurst and the 2nd Earl of Aldborough – so Richmond was perhaps to a degree vindicated. But the house then fell empty for a few years and in 1800 the remaining lease was taken by the parishes of St Giles in the Fields and St George, Bloomsbury. They used the house to accommodate pauper children removed from the workhouse, so it became an annex for the poorhouse of two of the

---

* There could be confusion here because from 1734 the Cavendish-Harley estate, just to the north-west of Soho, across Oxford Street, also became known as the Portland estate. This was because Lady Margaret Cavendish-Harley married William Bentinck, 2nd Duke of Portland and Marquis of Titchfield, in 1734. Lady Margaret did not die until 1785, but from the time of this marriage the Cavendish-Harley estate became known as the Portland estate. It is now the Howard de Walden estate.

most troubled parishes in London, which included within their boundaries one of the worst slum areas in London, the fearful St Giles Rookery. It then became a school of industry until 1810, when it was taken for commercial use by goldsmiths and then leather cutters. So ultimately Richmond's hopes for the house and Dean Street were most cruelly dashed.

After Sir Kenrick Clayton left number 77 in 1750 the house remained in the occupation of gentry and aristocracy. Tenants included the 4th Earl of Peterborough (1708–79) and his countess until 1788, and, until 1798, Sir Charles Cottrell-Dormer. Then, as with numbers 75 and 76, a dramatic change took place that confirmed the shifting pattern of life in Soho. When Sir Charles moved out the piano maker Thomas Tomkison moved in and by 1833 all the rooms in the house were in use as workshops. From 1854 until 1921 it was occupied by the food manufacturers Crosse & Blackwell, its painted interior being recorded in 1914 as still intact.

Number 78 Constructed by Thomas Richmond *c.*1732 on the Pitt estate, a good and relatively well-preserved example of the more modest houses erected during the early Georgian rebuilding of the late-seventeenth-century streets south of Soho Square. The windows have segmental arches, there are red-brick dressings to the window jambs, a rubbed-brick string course, and a bold timber doorcase with fluted Doric pilasters supporting a triglyph frieze. The interior retains its panelling, there is a good authentic staircase, and the plan – front room, rear room, closet and dog-leg staircase set against the rear façade – is standard for the time, date and status of the building. As with most Soho houses of this type, the closets are well panelled, revealing that they were treated as cabinets, serving and equal in standing to the rooms they adjoined and not merely utilitarian service rooms for close stools or storage. This particular house is notable because during most of the 1740s it was occupied by Peg Woffington, a well-known Irish actress who cut a dash in the society of mid-Georgian London and was, for a while, the mistress of the actor David Garrick. The affair appears to have been conducted in this house.

Numbers 79 and 80 Also of 1732 and also by Richmond, but the ground floor of 79 is modern and nineteenth-century and 80 has been rebuilt.

Number 88 This house and shop front dates from 1791, according to the *Survey of London*.[33] The first occupant of the existing house was Thomas Norman, whose trade is unknown. In fact, the shop front is more puzzling than the *Survey*'s simple description suggests. Even a rudimentary inspection reveals that either it is formed by the fusion of two shop fronts to form a single design, or it is a shop front designed at a certain time but which embodies two distinctly different phases of mid- to late-eighteenth-century taste. The most obvious phase is the Rococo, fashionable from the 1740s into the early 1770s, and best expressed here by the mildly asymmetrical, delicate and swirling wreaths in the shop's fascia or frieze. Then there are the reeded, geometrical neoclassical details of the pilasters framing the doors – and indeed the splendid house door, with its incised bead mouldings and flutes – and the fluting and scrolls below the fascia. This is all typical of the 1790s, but the twisted rope moulding in among the reeding suggests an early-nineteenth-century date. This is a splendid piece – certainly one of the half-dozen best Georgian shop fronts to survive in situ in London, and perhaps one of the earliest. A nice touch is that it still serves as a shop selling useful things and is not a mere ornament on the tourist track flogging useless trash.

Number 89 Now the Nellie Dean public house, seemingly created in the late nineteenth century within a house of about 1800.

Number 90 A most splendid corner house of 1756–67 presenting its tall, main, three-window-wide elevation to Dean Street, with its side elevation and long wing to Carlisle Street. A noble rusticated ground floor wraps around the entire building, evoking the quality of a Roman temple plinth. The rustication is probably an early-nineteenth-century embellishment. The front elevation is given additional architectural presence by the framing of all first-floor windows with architraves, with a pediment added to the centre window. It is probable that these too are later additions. There is also a cornice above the second-floor window, so the top storey, with its square windows, reads as an attic. All is inspired by Renaissance palazzi and Roman triumphal arches. The side elevation of the main house has blank windows while the wing, as tall as the main house, is two windows wide. There is also a fine pedimented doorcase to Dean Street, with a mezzanine window above to light the hall – a most unusual detail.

The area north of number 90 is, in the summer of 2019, a large building site, although works are nearly complete. Courts and buildings – including the handsome late-nineteenth-century Bath House public house – have recently been cleared away for the construction of Crossrail and related commercial buildings. A tall and windowless stunted tower now rises on the north side

16. Detail of the front elevation of 5 Frith Street, built 1731.

17. Number 5 Frith Street, far left, with numbers 6 and 7, built c.1718 but with façades rebuilt in authentic manner.

18. Numbers 37–41 Frith Street, built 1743–81 – on the corner with Romilly Street. A fine and diverse 18th century group.

19. Numbers 58–61 Frith Street, built from c.1688 to c.1800.

20. Number 76 Dean Street, right, a Soho palace built 1732–5. To the left is number 75, rebuilt in the mid 1920s.

21. The upper level painted staircase hall in 76 Dean Street, dating from 1732–5. Photographed in 1945.

22. The upper level painted staircase hall in 75 Dean Street, dating from 1732–5, in 1912. Demolished in 1923.

23. First floor front room in 75 Dean Street, 1732–5, in 1912. Demolished in 1923.

24. Entrance hall and staircase of 75 Dean Street, 1732–5, in 1912. After demolition in 1923 the joinery was reassembled and displayed in the Art Institute of Chicago.

25. Stone-wrought Doric doorcase on 68 Dean Street, built 1732 by John Meard.

26. The west end of St Anne's Church, built 1677–86 with tower altered and steeple added in 1803 to the designs of Samuel Pepys Cockerel. This view dates from 1828.

27. Number 52 Berwick Street, constructed in the 1730s but probably altered in the later 18th century.

28. Number 78 Brewer Street, a delicately and harmoniously proportioned design of great simplicity, sophistication and beauty. It probably dates from the late 18th century.

29. The west side of Lexington Street, dating from *c.*1719, looking towards Broadwick Street.

30. Number 46 Broadwick Street, right, dating from 1706 but altered, and 48–58, dating from 1722–3.

31. The west side of Golden Square showing, from left to right, a portion of 19a–20, 21, 22 of 1915, 23 and 24.

32. Numbers 2–8 Ganton Street and, right, part of 37 Marshall Street, all dating from c.1821–5.

of the recently re-established Diadem Court, which links Dean Street to Great Chapel Street. This grotesque tower is, presumably, a ventilation shaft and engine room for the Crossrail tunnel beneath.

Great Chapel Street

Here a few early buildings survive on the west side – notably 20 and 21, which are an early-nineteenth-century pair with shop fronts. And number 22, on the corner with Hollen Street, is a late-Victorian pub, the Star at Night, which currently advertises itself as the London Gin Club.

Meard Street

Meard Street, with the pair of early 1730s houses on Dean Street – numbers 67 and 68 – that adjoin its east end, is one of the most moving and atmospheric early Georgian enclaves in London. All the surviving houses were constructed between 1720 and 1732 by the speculating builder and carpenter John Meard the younger. The street was built partly on the sites of two late-seventeenth-century courts that opened off Wardour Street and Dean Street but which did not communicate with each other, and partly on those of late-seventeenth-century houses and their gardens.

The western portion was started in 1720 on the Pulteney estate and the eastern portion a decade or so later on the Pitt estate. The junction between the two estates and the two building campaigns is marked by a slight set-back in the line of the houses in Meard Street, most notably on the south side.

The houses of 1720 to 1722 were built on leases granted to Meard by William and John Pulteney. The leases for the houses on the south side of the street were for a term of sixty-one years. The houses are uniform but not organised to form a unified composition. They are generally typical of their date, although a trifle old-fashioned because they still have square-headed windows, with handsome rubbed-brick arches and jambs ornamented with red-brick dressings. The doorcases, where they survive, are all uniform, and formed by simple Doric pilasters supporting entablatures. The house plans are standard for Soho of the time, with each of the main floors consisting of a front and back room and a small rear closet. Most retain their original staircases with carved tread ends, and pine panelling of a rather grand raised and fielded type in the lower front rooms. Sadly, only the south side of the 1720s street survives, comprising houses numbered 13, 15, 17, 19 and 21. These are all three windows wide and four full storeys high including basements, with fifth floors being attic rooms created within the roof spaces.

This first phase of the development was initially known as Meard's Court, but in the early 1730s Meard continued the court to the east towards Dean Street in a most ambitious manner. He extended the 1720s terraces off Wardour Street by the addition of houses to their east ends. At the same time he widened the court on which the new houses faced to create a small square that connected to Dean Street. This transformed the cul-de-sac court into a through street.

The houses framing this widened court were larger and substantially grander than those of the first phase of the development. These later houses are all five full storeys high, three windows wide and uniform, with wooden doorcases formed by brackets, embellished with carved acanthus leaves, and supporting cornices. A pair of small houses were added in the early 1730s to the east end of the south terrace and are now numbered 9 and 11, and the larger houses on the south side of the street are numbered 1, 3, 5 and 7 and form an intact terrace. Three large houses survive on the north side – numbers 2, 4 and 6 – set to the west of the large and much-altered 69 Dean Street, which also dates from the 1730s. The houses on the north side are mutilated, all with later shop fronts inserted. The pair of houses on Dean Street – numbers 67 and 68 – built by Meard in 1732 as part of the development are larger than the Meard Street houses, each with handsome stone-made Doric doorcases (plates 5 and 25).

When the second phase was completed in 1732 Meard fixed a stone with this date – and the name 'Meards Street' – on the side wall of 68 Dean Street. Like only a handful of the most successful and ambitious early-eighteenth-century speculative builders, Meard had built himself into the fabric and history of London by creating an entire street and naming it after himself. This piece of pride was a reflection of the status he had achieved by the 1730s. He had advanced from 'carpenter' – as described in the early leases – to 'Esquire'. He had made money and reputation supervising work on a number of the 'Fifty Churches' being completed throughout London during the 1720s to the designs of Nicholas Hawksmoor, John James and James Gibbs, had probably worked on St Paul's Cathedral, and was a justice of the peace and a Freeman of the City of London.[34]

Something of the early social history of Mead Street can, to a degree, be reconstructed using parish rate books. The houses seem to have been reasonably well occupied, by single tenants who tended to be craftsmen or members of the artistic professions, and so were typical of Soho's population in the 1720s and 1730s as it changed from an aristocratic to a merchants' and tradesmen's quarter.

For example, number 1 was occupied from 1738 to 1742 by Burkhardt Tschudi, a harpsichord maker, and number 9 from 1739 to the mid 1740s by Batty Langley, an architect and from the late 1720s to the late 1740s the author of many influential pattern books. Batty's brother Thomas was also in occupation and seems to have run a drawing academy from the house.

By 1758 Elizabeth Flint occupied furnished rooms in part of number 9, for which she paid five shillings a week, a considerable sum at a time when a London working man earned around £1 a week in wages. Bet was described by Dr Samuel Johnson as 'generally a slut and drunkard; occasionally whore and thief', and since her main occupation appears to have been prostitution it would appear that – in the manner of Mrs Goadby (see p. 38) – Bet operated from her Soho rooms in a discreet and even stylish manner. Johnson became acquainted with Bet Flint because she had literary aspirations. As he explained to Mrs Piozzi, 'Bet Flint wrote her own life, and called herself *Cassandra*, and it was in verse. It began: "When nature first ordained my birth, A diminutive I was born on earth, And then I came from a dark abode, Into a gay and gaudy world." Johnson explained that Bet brought me her verses to correct; but I gave her half-a-crown, and she liked it as well.'[35] Johnson also recalled that Bet's lodgings – no doubt those in Meard Street – were 'genteel' and that she had 'a spinet on which she played, and a boy that walked before her chair'.[36]

One possible reason for Bet's failure to complete her autobiographical poem is that in 1758 she was arrested for stealing a quilt from her Meard Street landlady. This arrest led to a sequence of events that delighted Johnson. Bet had, he said, 'a spirit not to be subdued', so when she was obliged to go to jail to await her trial 'she ordered a sedan chair, and bid her footboy walk before her. However, the boy proved refractory, for he was ashamed, though his mistress was not.'

The story of the trial is outlined in the *Proceedings of the Old Bailey*. On 13 September 1758 Bet was indicted for stealing 'one dimity counterpane, value 5s. two linen napkins, value 1s. one silver spoon, value 10s. one pillow, value 2s. one linen pillow case, value 6d. the goods of Mary Walthow, spinster, out of her ready furnish'd lodgings'. Mary Walthow was examined and stated that she kept 'a house in Mares-court, Dean-street, Soho', where 'the prisoner took a room of me ready furnished, at 5s. a week'. In the process of the examination spinster Walthow revealed that she did not own the house or have legal title to its contents. It was in fact owned by a Captain Baldwin, who was then abroad, with whom Walthow had lived as his servant for seven years. When asked if she had any written power to confirm her rights of possession over the house and its contents, Walthow had to admit that she had none, only the captain's 'honour and word'. This was enough to liberate Bet: since the accuser could not prove ownership of the 'stolen' items there was no charge to answer.[37] After Bet was acquitted Johnson recalled her saying, '"so now the quilt is my own, and now I'll make a petticoat of it." Oh! I loved Bet Flint.'[38]

Other early residents of Meard Street included – at number 11 from 1755 – Abraham Browne, 'one of his Majesty's and of the Queen's Band, and First Violin at Ranelagh'; at number 17 from 1722 was Edmund Paine, a watchmaker; at number 6 in the 1780s the painters James Jefferys and Thomas Hearne, and in the 1720s, in the long-lost number 18 on the north side, Handel's friend Johann Christoph Schmidt, father of the musician Christopher Smith who also became Handel's amanuensis.[39]

By the time the philanthropist and social reformer Charles Booth and his secretary George Herbert Duckworth explored Meard Street in October 1898 its social character had greatly changed. Its houses were multi-occupied by a rich mix of working people, mostly in humble trades and diverse in their origins and ethnic backgrounds. In intensity of occupation and variety of residents Meard Street was an accurate reflection of the character of much of late-Victorian Soho.

Booth stated that Meard Street had become a 'Jew's Haunt',[40] but that this change in the street's residential character had only taken place in the last '4 or 5 years', with many Jews coming 'here from Whitechapel & some from abroad'. So the early 1890s appear to have been another period of dramatic and speedy change in Soho as it absorbed an immigrant population seeking accommodation, safety and employment in the ever-growing metropolis. Booth also offered a portrait of life in the street. There were a 'great many children ... well fed, dirty, well clothed', and that these were Jewish children is made clear by Booth's 'General Remarks' about the district: 'Many Jew children few of other nations.' He colour-coded the street purple and light blue in 1898, whereas it had all been purple on the 1880s poverty map. So he thought the street had seen a slight decline. Booth's assertions can be tested by reference to the two census returns that define the critical period – those of 1891 and 1901.

According to the 1891 census number 1 Meard Street, one of the surviving 1730s houses on the south side of the street, was occupied by twenty-four people, organised as seven separate family groups. There were fifteen adults and nine children, and types of employment listed included boot cleaner, dressmaker, house painter, French polisher, waiter, tailoress and shop dresser. All the occupants had been born in England, most in and around London. The husbands of two of the married women were not listed, perhaps because they were away from home on the night of the census, and one person was a visitor, so it's reasonable to assume that twenty-five people lived in the house.[41]

Number 1 Meard Street contains a small closet wing, and has three rooms on the ground and first floors and perhaps four on the second. It is five storeys high including the basement, and so in 1891 it could – if all the floors were inhabited – have contained about sixteen or seventeen rooms available for its twenty-five occupants. This would not have been exceptional – and was certainly possible – with husbands, wives and younger children and children of the same sex sharing the same room. However, the division of the space must have been awkward because with seven households and only five floors some families clearly had to share the same floor, suggesting that some of the families all had to live in one room.

To put the occupation of number 1 Meard Street in context, it's worth looking at a couple of other neighbouring houses of the same size. In 1891 number 4 was occupied by a staggering thirty-eight people in seven family groups. All had been born in England except for the seven-strong Treftz family of bakers, who had all been born in Germany.[42]

Number 5 contained twenty-two people in five family groups, all of whom had been born in England or Scotland with the exception of Mrs Panorimo, who had been born in India.[43] Number 6 contained thirteen people in three family groups, two families – the Probeks and the Hamburgs – having come from Germany, where all four parents and a niece had been born, while two children had been born in London.[44]

The houses at the west end of Meard Street, significantly smaller in volume if not in number of floors, were nevertheless packed with occupants. For example, the 1891 census return for 13 Meard Street reveals that it contained seventeen people organised in five households. Types of employment included window cleaner, carpenter, 'General Handyman', and hairdresser's assistant. All had been born in England, most in London.[45]

Number 14 housed twenty-three people in four family groups, with one family, the Franklins, of German origin but all seven of their children born in London.[46] Number 17 contained twenty-seven people in four family groups, all British-born with the exception of the Opas family, in which the father Abraham, a forty-year-old tailor, his wife Bella, their two eldest children and a servant named Mary Jacobs had been born in Poland. The remaining five

Opas children had been born in London.[47]

The families in the remaining houses on the north side of Meard Street were, according to the 1891 census, British-born, so to judge by the names of the residents and their places of birth there was only a small Jewish population in Meard Street at the time, seemingly sustaining Booth's observation that the Jewish community was a new arrival in 1898.

In the 1901 census number 1 Meard Street had twenty-five people in residence organised in five family groups. All the families present in the house ten years earlier had moved. There were ten adults and fifteen children and their jobs included plumber, police constable – one Samuel Bastard aged fifty – tailoress, bricklayer's labourer and 'Cardboard Roller'. All had been born in England, nineteen of them in London.[48]

Number 5 Meard Street contained nineteen people in four household groups, all born in England except for Arthur White, a forty-eight-year-old tailor, who had been born in Dublin. Number 7 housed twenty people in eight separate households, again all of whom had been born in London with the exception of Ermenius Agosti, a twenty-nine-year-old cook, who had been born in Italy, as had his twenty-four-year-old wife Maria and his brother Albino, a waiter. The 1901 census also lists four other young Italian men – all single – who were waiters or cooks in restaurants. They were described as 'heads' of their own household, which means they rented directly from the landlord and were not lodgers of another occupant.[49]

In 1901 number 13 Meard Street contained twenty-two people in four households. The members of the families had been born in England, except for sixty-year-old John

Slack, who had been born in Ireland and worked from home as a tailor.[50] In number 17 there were nineteen people in four family groups. All had been born in England with the exception of one man born in Scotland.[51]

So, to judge from these households, Booth appears to have been wrong to suggest that all of Meard Street had become a 'Jew's Haunt' by 1898. But things are not that simple. As the census moved west along the north side of Meard Street the picture changed. Numbers 6–20 Meard Street contained the mix of people implied by Booth, revealing that the Jewish community – coming either direct from Poland and Russia or from Whitechapel, Aldgate and Spitalfields – congregated for reasons now unknown in the west part of Meard Street, mostly on the north side. Presumably the families chose to settle in the same or in adjoining houses for reasons of security but also because of a shared cultural and religious identity. With the hindsight provided by the 1901 census it is possible to see the trend of Russian/German/Jewish occupation under way in the earlier census. Sadly, with the exception of 6 Meard Street, the early-eighteenth-century houses on the north side of Meard Street occupied by this Jewish community have long been demolished.

In 6 Meard Street in 1901 there were twenty-six people in occupation in four family groups, ten of whom had been born in Russia or Poland, with thirteen of their children born in Soho or in the East End of London – particularly in Commercial Street, Spitalfields. Most of the households who had occupations were tailors, working from home.[52] The remaining seven houses – numbers 8–20 – contained nearly 160 people, of whom over seventy were born in Poland, Russia, Austria and the Netherlands.[53]

Number 23 Meard Street – a late nineteenth-century building with a shop adjoining the south-west corner with Wardour Street – possessed an exclusively Eastern European community, almost certainly all Jews. There were seventeen people in occupation, in three family groups, of whom eight had been born in Poland or Russia, while the remaining nine – the children of the families – had been born in London. The occupations of four of the men are listed: one was a 'General Provisioner', presumably running the shop, while the others were tailors, mostly working from home.[54]

Wardour Street (north)

Number 74 House, with shop, of *c*.1825.

Number 77 The Duke of Wellington public house, on the corner with Winnett Street (originally Edmunds Court) laid out in the 1670s. The pub is interesting. Tall, stucco-clad with simple neo-Greek detail and a radial corner, it looks *c*.1820–30. But the adjoining house, now stuccoed, could be considerably earlier.

St Anne's churchyard and tower These are the melancholic memorials to one of Soho's most important early buildings, St Anne's Parish Church. Construction of the church started in 1677 and its foundation, so soon after construction had started on the new and nearby church of St James's, Piccadilly (1672–84), is a reflection of the rapid growth of west Soho in the 1670s. Both these new parishes had been carved out of the ancient, large and rambling parish of St Martin-in-the Fields.

Sir Christopher Wren designed St James's Church and was probably intimately involved with the design of St Anne's, although his precise role remains unclear; however, it is documented that, in some capacity, he worked on the design of St Anne's with the architect William Talman. The dominance of Wren is suggested by a document of 1685 that appoints twelve commissioners to bring St Anne's to completion. The only commissioner mentioned by name is Wren, while Talman is referred to as 'surveyor of buildings'.[55] But what is certain is that both churches were created under the patronage of Henry Compton, the Bishop of London who steered them to completion and consecrated St James's in July 1684 and St Anne's in March 1686.

Compton is famed as being one of the 'Immortal Seven' – along with the Earl of Devonshire – who invited William of Orange and his wife Mary Stuart to 'invade' Britain in 1688 and promised local support in a campaign to remove Mary's father, the wilful and scheming Roman Catholic James II, from the throne. The plot went extraordinarily well for William, Mary and the 'Immortal Seven', and within a few weeks James's regime had utterly collapsed and he had fled, leaving the throne secure in Protestant hands, with William and Mary being crowned in 1689 by Bishop Compton. The ousting of James II was subsequently described by the victors as the Glorious Revolution. But, of course, James's supporters perceived the event as a lawless tragedy aided and abetted – to their contempt and dismay – by the monarch's own daughter, evidently a Godless woman who, by her treachery, broke God's fourth Commandment to honour her father and mother. The Glorious Revolution led rapidly to the passing of a Bill of Rights that confirmed the deposition of James and the Protestant succession to the throne, limited royal power by stipulating particular parliamentary controls over the monarchy, and guaranteed 'liberties' and rights of law to loyal subjects. But the Glorious Revolution also led to sixty years of Jacobite intrigue, in league with foreign Roman Catholic powers, against the British throne, and to actual or potential military action.

It is within this religious and political context that the foundation of these two churches must be seen. Both were to serve rapidly expanding areas of London – St James's a largely aristocratic population and St Anne's an increasingly artisan or merchant one – and it was through new Anglican churches such as these, architecturally dominant and within easy reach of their potential congregations, that the Anglican faith and the principles of the Protestant monarchy were to be promoted and the population policed. St Anne's had an additional task. As Huguenots arrived within its parish, it had to contend with a powerful group that, although Protestant, did not regularly worship in Anglican churches but in its own Calvinist 'temples'.

Both these churches were subtle but, nevertheless, determined essays in political architecture, intended to remind all – Protestants, Dissenters or Catholics – that in England Church and State were united and that the Anglican Church was the Church of the State and the source of temporal as well as spiritual power.

Given the political aspect of St Anne's origin, it is intriguing to see the architectural strategy that Wren, Talman and Compton hit upon. The site on which the church was to be built was acquired by the parish of St Martin-in-the Fields from the speculating builders Richard Frith and Joseph Girle, who had obtained the Earl of St

Albans's leasehold interest on this Crown-owned land. From the start of the project Compton was actively engaged, offering £5,000 in 1676 towards construction of the new church. Clearly, for him this was a most important building and there was some urgency about its completion. The church that arose was impressive in its size and general design but the materials of construction and the restrained elegance of its minimalist form and details make it clear that money was an issue. The church sat slightly above the level of, and set back from, Wardour Street, with its east elevation aligned with the axis of what is now Romilly Street. This street was almost certainly laid out in the year the church was started on the site – 1677 – so it seems to have been aligned to offer a prospect of the east end of Soho's new and major public building.

The design of this east elevation was impressive and must have made a handsome terminal feature when viewed from Romilly Street. The body of the church was roughly of 3:4 proportion, one favoured by Andrea Palladio. This meant that the church was relatively wide – about sixty-four feet – in relation to its length of eighty feet, with a hall-like interior organised as a basilica with a central nave flanked by narrower aisles. The box-like body of the church was covered by a mighty pitched roof that presented wide gable-pediments at the east and west ends of the building. This rational arrangement gave the church a noble simplicity and an almost barn-like appearance that recalls Inigo Jones's St Paul's, Covent Garden, of nearly fifty years earlier and that was, in the 1670s, regarded as an exemplary church design.

East elevation of St Anne's Church looking along Romilly Street, *c.*1820.

The two pediment-topped elevations of St Anne's were treated differently. At the east end the centre of the façade broke forward to create a small chancel for the altar. This chancel contained a large, semicircular headed east window and was topped by a smaller pediment that nestled neatly within the raking sides and apex of the larger gable-pediment. This arrangement of a smaller pediment set within, or overlapping, a larger pediment was no doubt inspired by the west elevations of Palladio's basilica-plan churches in Venice – notably San Giorgio Maggiore of 1566–1610 – where smaller pediments are set within and rise above lower, wider pediments.

Palladio seems to have hit upon this particular solution after studying the ruins in Rome of the early-fourth-century Basilica of Maxentius. This antique basilica has a plan of 3:2 proportion and in his reconstruction, published in his *quattro libri* of 1570, Palladio shows a long elevation of the basilica with a narrow central pediment rising through a lower, wider pediment. In Palladio's own buildings these interlocking pediments are invariably supported by a screen of pilasters or engaged columns. The central, nave pediment at the east end of St Anne's was not furnished with pilasters – no doubt these were viewed as too expensive an ornament – but the corners of the break-front were dressed with stone quoins, as were the east corners of the main building. Pale stone quoins set against red-brick walls – as at St Anne's before its walls were rendered – were a favoured Wren device and would have given this church a similar appearance to St James's, Piccadilly, and, indeed, to other of Wren's public buildings where economy of construction was essential, such as the Royal Hospital at Chelsea. This use of brick, and St Anne's east elevation with its overlaid pediments, were echoed in more modest manner in 1702 in St Thomas's

Church on Kingly Street, another Soho project associated with Wren (see p. 363).

Interestingly, a preliminary design for the east front of St Anne's shows the nave pediment absent and in its place a huge semicircular lunette, placed within the centre of the main pediment. This would have been a most striking external motif, even outlandish, with the curve of the lunette following the form of the barrel-vaulted nave ceiling within the church. Such an odd detail, its curved sides crammed hard up against the raking sides of the pediment, is unlikely to have originated with Wren. So a picture emerges of a somewhat vernacular church, designed initially by a surveyor or local builder, and then civilised by Talman and Wren.

St Anne's west elevation also displayed an all-embracing gable-pediment but its central feature was not a pedimented bay but a west tower, breaking forward to contain an entrance vestibule. This was reached via a west door, although the usual way of entrance to the church was through doors at the west end of the aisles. The original tower was a simple affair with a square plan and robust corner buttresses – almost medieval in feel – topped by a bell-shaped dome supporting an open lantern. This was not completed until 1718.

Inside the church eight Doric piers divided the two aisles from the barrel-vaulted central nave. These piers supported galleries on three sides from which rose Ionic columns supporting an entablature that in turn helped support the roof. From this entablature sprang the central barrel vault, while aisle ceilings also rested upon it. So, as with St James's, Piccadilly, piers, gallery fronts and Ionic columns were integrated elegantly into a single and unified architectural composition. A giant order of columns, rising from floor to ceiling height, would have given the interior Baroque monumentality, but this was a solution Wren tended to reject in favour of the more delicate integrated system. One reason Wren favoured this approach is that, for him, galleries were integral to the design. He, no doubt like Compton, viewed the churches he designed as primarily preaching boxes that should contain the maximum number of people and offer most a good view of, and proximity to, the pulpit so that the word of God could be clearly heard. This was a direct reflection of the Protestant faith that professed to value the sermon proclaimed in rational manner above the Roman Catholic mysteries of the Mass. So the focus of Wren's Protestant church interiors was the pulpit, not the altar, and a key part of this strategy was the galleries that increased the capacity of the church and ensured that a large proportion of the congregation were relatively near the pulpit. This aim explains St Anne's almost square plan.

This interpretation is not mere speculation because Wren himself confirmed his aims when describing St Anne's sister church and near-contemporary, St James's, Piccadilly: 'it should seem vain ... in our reformed Religion ... to make a Parish-church larger, than that all who are present can both hear and see'. For the 'Romanists', argued Wren, 'it is enough if they hear the Murmer of the Mass, and see the Elevation of the Host, but ours are to be fitted for Auditories'. To achieve a church that could contain 2,000 people who could 'both ... hear distinctly and see the Preacher' became a mission for Wren that was realised 'in building the Parish Church of St. James's, Westminster, which, I presume, is the most capacious ...

that hath yet been built'. Wren then described the key internal characteristics of the church – ones shared with St Anne's. It is, he noted, 'very broad ... the middle Nave arched up ... and the whole Roof rests upon the Pillars, as do also the Galleries'. Wren concluded by suggesting that St James's 'may be found beautiful and convenient, and ... the cheapest of any Form I could invent'.[56]

St Anne's endured through the eighteenth century little altered, but in 1801 the stability of the tower was called into question and by 1803 it had been rebuilt to the designs of Samuel Pepys Cockerell (plate 26). This is the structure that survives today and it is decidedly an oddball piece of work. It would appear to commemorate the late-eighteenth-century fashion for experimentation with classical design. The object was, in general, to reinvigorate and reinvent classicism and to make an ancient architectural language appropriate for the new age. In many ways this became a quest for the essence and origin of classicism. The usual approach was to reduce detail, to favour abstraction, to aim for a sculptural simplicity and to prefer the use of powerful primary forms such as cubes, cylinders and spheres. The great and inspired British champion of this approach was Sir John Soane, whose works on occasion achieve a sublime severity and poetic power. Cockerell does not quite manage this with his Soho tower and steeple, but his design is striking in its strange originality and, without doubt, captures one's interest – if only because one can't look at the design without feeling compelled to work out what's going on.

It's like a puzzle. The lower square-plan portion of the tower seems to have been rebuilt, in broad terms, to the late-seventeenth-century design. There are the corner

piers and the tower is brick-built. But the upper portion
is slightly recessed and divided from the lower portion by
most queer stone details, including a bold, projecting string
course upon which squat shallow segmental arches cut out
of deep stone copings, while below the string course are
aprons of stone of step-profile. Quite what point Cockerell
is trying to make is uncertain, but presumably these details
are derived from the Roman or neoclassical language of
death – a most popular source of inspiration around 1800
and clearly appropriate for a church tower overlooking
a burial ground. Presumably Cockerell derived much
of this detail by contemplating catafalques, sarcophagi
and cenotaphs. It has long been observed that he was
inspired by French neoclassical funerary architecture
and, no doubt, antique memorials.[57] On top of this brick
tower Cockerel placed a tall, stone-faced pedestal with
chamfered corners that rise, via a podium formed by steps
(as on the Mausoleum of Halicarnassus), to support a
lead cylinder which, via another podium formed by steps,
supports a sphere embellished with four clock faces. On
top of this sphere is a wind vane. The combination of
rectangular and cylindrical forms – perhaps inspired by a
similarly composed Roman monument at Saint-Rémy-de-
Provence – is certainly not elegant but it is characterful
and continues to hold its own within Soho's ever more
architecturally disparate and challenging skyline.

The churchyard over which the tower now presides is,
with Soho Square, the only significant and grassy public
open space in Soho. It is a pleasant place but, sadly, furnished with few memorials on which to ponder. The only
two of any significance are to Theodore, King of Corsica,
and to the essayist William Hazlitt.

Theodore is remembered on a tablet fixed to the west face of the tower. Born Theodore Freiherr von Neuhoff, he was a German adventurer who in 1736, with Tunisian assistance, helped free Corsica from Genoese domination. What he wanted in return was to be made king of the island. He had his wish but nothing went smoothly. There was in-fighting and perpetual conflict with Genoese and French forces. Theodore went abroad to seek money and assistance but fell into debt in Amsterdam and London, where he was confined to a debtors' jail until 1755. He was released, declared himself bankrupt, made over his alienated kingdom and worthless title to his creditors, enthralled Horace Walpole who liked nothing better than a picturesque incompetent, died in 1756 and was interred in St Anne's churchyard. Walpole wrote the epitaph for his headstone. It reads in part: 'Fate poured its lessons on his living head, / Bestowed a kingdom but denied him bread.'

On the north side of the churchyard is a headstone marking Hazlitt's burial place. He was a perpetual revolutionary, committed political irritant and painfully honest self- and social observer who died in 1830, having passed his last days in a desperate fashion – in constant pain and drugged on laudanum – in his lodgings in 6 Frith Street.

St Anne's was badly damaged by bombing in 1940 and the ruins stood until 1953, when the walls of the gutted church were partially demolished. In 1965 the site was fully cleared, excluding the tower and spire but including the damaged rector's house of 1706 on Dean Street, part of the site being sold for commercial development. This craven and heartless act on the part of the London

Diocesan Fund (in whom the ruins and site were vested) displayed the extreme moral turpitude of the times. The church should of course have been repaired, but instead the ruins – the physical memorial to much of Soho's early life – were simply swept away.

Numbers 157–165 A good and characterful Georgian group. Numbers 157–159 have early-nineteenth-century façades, numbers 161–165 date from the mid 1730s. Numbers 159–163 were leased to John Perry, carpenter, in 1735, and 165 was built as a speculation by a carpenter named John Gunter. The furniture maker Thomas Sheraton lived in number 163 for a while in the mid 1790s.

Number 187, on the corner with Noel Street, has a handsome yellow-brick front of *c*.1790, but its ground floor has been altered and the building is now in a poor state.

Wardour Mews south of D'Arblay Street is long and narrow and has some very good nineteenth-century workshops with loading bays.

D'Arblay Street

Laid out in 1735 on Doghouse Close by the Portland family, it was called Portland Street until 1909, and then renamed to commemorate Madame D'Arblay (Fanny Burney), who lived in Poland Street (see p. 322). The street's first houses were occupied by 1737.

Numbers 2, 3 and 4 Built under leases of 1736 and 1737 granted by the Portland estate to John Phillips, plasterer. Until recent years number 2 retained its original brick façade, with segmental window arches, well wrought in rubbed brick, and timber box sashes set flush with the façade. Numbers 3 and 4 had undistinguished mid-nineteenth-century façades, not very well crafted. When I photographed the group in the early 1970s number 2 sported a large vertical hoarding proclaiming 'Non-stop Striptease', and just in case you didn't get it, added, at the bottom of the hoarding, 'continuous'. And on the ground-floor fascia it promised its customers 'Quartetts [*sic*] & Triple Acts', with admission fixed at 50p. Number 3 contained, on its ground floor, the Pergola coffee bar, and number 4 housed businesses in the fabric industry, including a belt maker. Now the façades of 2 and 3 have been rebuilt in matching early-eighteenth-century manner. It's not badly done, and works as pleasant urban wallpaper; but, naturally, all authenticity and historic interest has been lost. The Victorian elevation of number 4 has been suffered to remain. The uses in mid 2019 are, from east to west: hairdresser, tanner and waxer, and tailor and clothes shop. They all appear to be independents, so not bad for Soho.

Number 13 A very good house of the late 1730s, built under a lease granted by the Portland estate in 1734–5 to Edward Prestidge and Peter Vandercom, masons. It was part of a small, uniform group with 10 and 11, but sadly these were demolished in the 1960s. The façade is now stuccoed and lined out with false ashlar joints. This is almost certainly a later alteration, but original are the splendid stone door surround, with bold brackets, the stone quoins and the stone cornice. The use of so much stone on a modest London house of the early eighteenth century is very rare. Cheaper timber was the usual material of choice, but the generous use of stone here is, no doubt, due to the fact that the pair of speculators who built this group were stonemasons. There is a good staircase inside.

Numbers 24 and 25 A good pair of *c.*1736 built by Thomas Seaton and Samuel Austin, carpenters, on a Portland lease. There are substantial remains of an early-nineteenth-century shop front on number 25. The adjoining houses to the west, numbers 22 and 23, are almost certainly of the same date and build, but their fronts were stuccoed in the mid nineteenth century and altered. Numbers 20 and 21 probably also date from the 1730s, but are stuccoed.

Number 25 makes an interesting case study. When I first photographed it in about 1972 the shop was occupied by 'M. Klein', who sold 'trimmings wholesale and retail', a good, traditional Soho business. When I photographed the house in 2015 the shop contained 'BM Soho Beat Control', a 'DJ store' selling vinyl, which had been ensconced here for twenty-five years until it suddenly closed. A subsequent notice put out by BM Stores to its customers announced that it had been forced to vacate D'Arblay Street and regretted that its long-time home 'will join the massive gentrification of Soho [that] regrettably we could no longer afford to fight'. The shop is now occupied by a hairdresser.

Numbers 32 and 33 Built in the 1730s, but much altered at ground level and their façades look slightly later-eighteenth-century. Number 33 is a wide house that bridges over the entrance to Wardour Mews.

Numbers 34 and 35 A little later in date, built as a pair and furnished with wide workshop windows at the first and second floors, with one window per floor. These were built as modest houses, with simple details. The façades were in a slightly decaying state until a few years ago. They have now been rather crudely repaired.

Excursion into Portland Mews

South of D'Arblay Street, with a good collection of mid-nineteenth-century stable buildings and workshops.

Berwick Street

The south part of the street was laid out *c*.1687 on Colman Hedge Close, and extended north onto Doghouse Close from *c*.1707. The original houses were rebuilt from 1731 to 1741, when the land was under the control of the Duke and Duchess of Portland.[58]

The street is still numbered in late-eighteenth-century manner: the numbers start at the south end of the east side and continue along the east side (odds and evens – not alternating) to the north end of the street where it meets Oxford Street, then go along the west side from north to south, so the highest numbers on the west side of the street face the lowest numbers on the east side.

Numbers 10 (now the Islamic Centre) and 11 Both two windows wide, with plain brick façades that appear to date from *c*.1800. Number 11 is more altered.

Number 15 Modest, with a good brick façade, probably late-eighteenth-century.

Numbers 20 and 21 Perhaps eighteenth-century, both façades rebuilt in brick in the nineteenth century. Number 21 now houses the splendid My Place café, popular with local residents.

Number 24 A handsome three-window-wide façade of

*c.*1825, with first-floor windows set in relieving arches, as was the fashion at the time. There is a crowning cornice above the second-floor windows, with a raised central tablet. Presumably it once contained a name or a date, but is now blank. This was probably built as a tavern.

Numbers 25 and 26 Rebuilt in the late eighteenth century as a modest pair, with the façade of 25 being an economically wrought affair dating from the mid to late nineteenth century. The façade of 26 is modern (and executed without regard to tradition) as is, no doubt, the whole of its structure. I photographed this pair in 1972, when 26 was intact, with a façade of late-eighteenth-century appearance but desperately derelict. It was then being offered at auction as an 'available freehold commercial site'. The building, in its gloomy and mouldering state, was incredibly atmospheric, but subsequently rebuilt in lame fashion.

Number 30 has architraves to its windows, and cornices supported by brackets above the first-floor windows. This decoration must date from the mid nineteenth century, but originally the house probably dates from the 1730s.

Number 31 Probably built as a pair with 32 in the 1730s, but now faced with render or Roman cement, scored to simulate ashlar.

Number 32 Built in the 1730s by Robert Hutchinson, a carpenter,[59] it has well-made cut-brick arches and probably the original brick façade, although repointed in a somewhat insensitive manner. There is a modern shop at ground level.

Number 33 The façade is rendered, marked out with false ashlar joints, and probably dates from the 1730s with early-nineteenth-century alterations.

Number 39 A small house with one wide workshop window per floor, c.1810.

Number 40 Eighteenth-century, presumably dating from the 1730s but re-fronted.

Number 42 Eighteenth-century, re-fronted.

Numbers 46, 47 and 48 A 1730s group, all re-fronted except 47, which was a speculation by Benjamin Lovett, a painter. Number 48, which until 2018 housed W. Sitch and Co., a long-established Soho purveyor of antique lighting fittings (see the brass candelabra still hanging outside as a trade sign), was leased by the Portland estate to George Gillingham, bricklayer.[60]

(There are four good cast-iron bollards on the corners of D'Arblay Street and Berwick Street marked 'St James's, Westminster', of c.1820.)

Number 51 Built by Thomas Bilcliffe, carpenter, but has been rebuilt.

Number 52 A little house with great aspirations. Its first floor contains just a single, large Venetian window, with spare and most sophisticated decoration, topped by a wide, tripartite window. After 1750 or so the Venetian window seems to have become something of a favoured Soho vernacular classical detail, no doubt inspired by the many – and now mostly lost – examples that once ornamented Soho Square (see p. 154). *The Survey of London* suggests this house dates from the 1730s,[61] but, as existing, it does not look this early. It may well have been built then, but with its façade and interior altered in the late eighteenth or early nineteenth centuries (plate 27).

Number 56 Berwick Street and 145 Oxford Street On the corner with Oxford Street, a fine and large early-nineteenth-century pair of houses, now one, no doubt originally with shops on the ground floor. On the opposite corner stands Berwick House, dated 1886 – a playful turreted composition with much debased classical decoration.

Number 57 The Green Man public house, a fine building of c.1835 with first-floor windows set in a blind arcade formed by relieving arches and no doubt a purpose-built tavern, like the similar number 24. The pub claims there has been a licensed premises on this site since 1736 – so from the time this part of Berwick Street was being rebuilt – and that the existing pub dates from 1895. This presumably is the date of the ground-floor frontage and bar.

Numbers 58–60 The remains of a much-altered and once-uniform 1730s group.

Number 67 On the corner with Noel Street, a good, large house of c.1800.

Numbers 71 and 72 Both date from the eighteenth century, but both have been mutilated.

Number 77 Built about 1735, but much mutilated.

Number 79 A house of c.1735–6, rendered.

Numbers 80 and 81 A pair of 1735–6 on the corner with Livonia Street with, on the Livonia Street elevation, a plaque, crowned with a ducal coronet, stating that this was Bentinck Street (the family name of the Dukes of Portland) and dated 1736. Livonia Street was never a grand enclave, merely a wide court from which an alley led north to a mews. Another matching plaque survives within the street. Some good interiors survive.

Looking at the 1901 census returns for Berwick Street, it's possible to discover a little more about the ethnic origins of its population and to see how its character changed from north to south. For example, number 52 at its north end near Oxford Street – the charming house with the Venetian window lighting its first-floor front room – had six occupants on the night of the census, organised as two-family households composed of five adults and one child. One of the adults was an eighteen-year-old female servant working for the family of Matthew Shields and his wife Ida, who had a four-year-old daughter. All had been born in London, with the exception of Matthew Shields, who had been born in Manchester, and his wife who had been born in Milan.

But the census return for number 79, 450 or so yards to the south, suggests that the nature of the community in the street was starting to change. This larger, mid-1730s house – of five storeys and with perhaps sixteen rooms – contained twenty-eight people, in five family groups. Fifteen of the occupants had been born in Russia or Russian-controlled Poland, while nine of the children had been born in London of Russian- or Polish-born parents. In addition, there was one family of German origin, three of whose children had been born in Belgium. The names and trades of the 'heads' of the families, as well as their places of origin, suggest that this was probably an entirely Jewish household. These included thirty-four-year-old William Lazarus, a hairdresser who worked from home; thirty-six-year-old tailor Joseph Sacolsky, who also worked from home; thirty-two-year-old David Zide, and twenty-five-year-old Reuben Franks, both of whom were also tailors.

The census shows that numbers 80 and 81 Berwick Street had more mixed communities, with English-born families sharing houses with families of Russian, Polish and German origin.[62] But it would seem that the Jewish population of Berwick Street was gathered at its centre and south end, where the street market was located, while the north end functioned as an overspill from Oxford Street. The 1891 census for 10 Berwick Street, a house of c.1800 that survives at the south end, seems to confirm this trend: it contained eleven people on the night of the census, organised in three family groups, with one family of six people – the Brutlachs – being of German origin.[63]

(There is a very good pair of cast-iron bollards of c.1820 on the corner of Livonia Street and Berwick Street.)

Excursion into Walker's Court

Currently undergoing a large rebuilding project. The existing buildings were much damaged and of little architectural interest, but those in the court possessed a fascinating social history because the gaunt buildings on the west side had long played an important role in Soho's post-Second-World-War sex industry, having housed Paul Raymond's titillating Revue Bar at number 11 from 1958 to 2004, and more recently – in the same location – the far smarter and more artfully and ironically decadent late-night venue called The Box.

The scheme, being undertaken by the Raymond family's Soho Estates, is described by the developers in breathless terms: '[It] will create a vibrant mix of uses in one of the most exciting areas in Soho', with 'key elements' including 'the revival of the famous Boulevard Theatre, new high-quality shops and restaurants, improved public realm and a new headquarters for Soho Estates.' It all sounds highly commercial and probably another step towards the replacement of Soho's distinct and special character with the bland and placeless. The architecture has started to emerge from its scaffolding and does look pleasingly more idiosyneratic than usual. Let us wait and see. Perhaps the development will be a pleasant surprise, or perhaps just one more nail in the coffin, as Soho – sanitised, 'gentrified' and exploited – loses what is left of its soul.

But there is a 'hold-out'. In the centre of Walker's Court is a small building not owned by Soho Estates and here, in stoic fashion, a traditional Soho shop remains in operation, selling saucy books and sex toys.

This is not the only large site in Soho that's being rebuilt. There is the big hole behind Portland House, Greek Street (see p. 175), and Soho Estates is also building on a large adjoining site created by the demolition of the famed Foyles bookshop, just east of Greek Street, on the corner of Manette Street and Charing Cross Road. As with Walker's Court, Soho Estates has demolished this building for the creation of a 'vibrant' new mixed-use development that, in mid 2020 towers seven storeys high.

Soho Estates, built up over years by Paul Raymond (who died in 2008) and his son-in-law John James, now owns more than sixty acres of Soho and is worth an esti-mated £370 million. Its declared aim is to replace sleaze and decay with edgy, upmarket bars, shops and restaur-ants. So naturally Madame Jojo's – which hosted some of Soho's more bizarre cabaret and sex adventures for nearly fifty years from a ramshackle building on Brewer Street next to Walker's Court – has been expunged by this scheme, at least in its authentic incarnation. If it makes a comeback you can be sure it will not be quite the same.

Perhaps it will return as its less challenging previous incarnation, the Jack of Clubs music venue, where in 1964 David Bowie – the then hapless and unsuccessful Davie Jones – made an early appearance with his soon discarded group the King Bees.

Soho Estates' schemes might reflect contemporary wisdom and the international vision of urban life, from Mumbai to LA; but is it Soho? 'Oh no dear,' as Muriel Belcher of the Colony Room might have said, but in no doubt more pungent words.[64]

Brewer Street

The street's origin is as a field boundary between different, ancient parcels of agricultural land that had traditionally been in the ownership, or under the control, of different estates. During the second half of the seventeenth century this land and ownership boundary, which had long served as an east–west route through the fields, was exploited by different estates who turned it into a new street by granting building leases along its north and south sides.

Most of the entire south side of what became Brewer Street, together with the centre of the north side, were in the possession of the Pulteney estate, and building work started at the east end of this estate's portion of the street in the early 1660s. By 1670 the west end of Brewer Street was called the 'New Way', referring to the route laid out by the estate. In the early 1680s construction started on the Pulteney estate land on the north side of the new street.

The land forming the north side of Brewer Street between Bridle Lane and Warwick Street was part of the south edge of Gelding Close, and in the 1680s this southern portion of Gelding Close was under the control of Martha Axtell and her associates (see p. 344). In 1684 she granted fifty-one-year building leases on most of this land to a group of speculating builders, including John Taylor, Abraham Bridle and William Partridge, who worked elsewhere on the Axtell estate, notably around Golden Square. However, Isaac Symball had an interest in part of the land between Bridle Lane and Lower John Street and he also granted building leases.

On Ogilby and Morgan's London map of 1681–2, Brewer Street is shown half built up, but is not named – although its east portion is called 'Poultney' Street. The first recorded mention of it as Brewer Street is in the rate books of 1675, and it seems to have been given this name for a most practical reason because, from the mid 1660s, two major breweries were located on its north side.[65] The east end of Brewer Street (east of the junction with Great Windmill Street) was, as we have noted, originally called Knaves' Acre, then Little Pulteney Street, and it was not until 1937 that this portion of the street was renamed Brewer Street. The numbering starts at the east end.

Numbers 7–37, St James's Residences represent an attempt in the early 1880s by the freeholders – the Crown – to replace the long-decaying houses, alleys and courts of Knaves' Acre with robust and hygienic new dwellings and shops. The building – incorporating the entire block between Great Windmill Street and Rupert Street (down which it extends a short way) – is not without architectural ambition. It is six storeys high (including the dormer-lit roof space), built of mellow red brick and with a sprinkling of classical ornament. The architect was

Robert Sawyer. The ends are treated as pavilions with areas of rusticated wall and stone trim, while the centre had some additional ornament to help give the long composition a focus. The effect has been somewhat diminished since a large portion of the centre of the Residences has been rebuilt in most economical manner – no doubt following war damage.

In the early 1880s the St James's vestry persuaded the Crown that the building should contain homes, work-shops in an internal court, and shops for the area's more able working population, and this is what it continues to do. There's a pub – the Duke of Argyll – on the corner with Great Windmill Street, and a variety of shops at ground level, including a few serving Soho's sex industry, because this part of Brewer Street is within the boundary where it still ticks over. Since 1973 the Residences have been run by the Soho Housing Association and provide affordable homes for working people, and in the court behind the sex shops is a nursery. Off Rupert Street an arch and covered way lead to a former stable-yard that now functions most successfully as a restaurant. So the block contains a characterful mix of uses – indeed, it is quite a little urban village of the sort only found in Soho. It is such odd amalgamations that still make Soho special.

Numbers 10 and 12 Late-eighteenth-century, but re-fronted in a most workmanlike and generally authen-tic manner, probably sometime in the late nineteenth century. They now house one of Soho's few surviving 'licensed' sex shops, essentially a bookshop with an 'adult' department downstairs. This shop, with Walker's Court which it adjoins, forms what is essentially the epicentre of Soho's now much-reduced and dwindling sex-trade area.

Number 18 On the corner with Green's Court, a late-nineteenth-century rebuild that contains Lina Stores, an Italian delicatessen and café founded in 1944 by a lady from Genoa called Lina. The shop promotes itself for its sale of 'authentic' Italian fare, specialising in cured meats and fresh pasta. It seems fine, and certainly generally little changed in all the years I've known Soho.

Numbers 26 and 28 Much altered, but probably an eighteenth-century pair.

Numbers 45 and 47 A handsome pair dating from the late eighteenth century. Number 45 incorporates a nineteenth-century pedimented arch leading to a rear yard and workshops.

Number 54 On the corner with Bridle Lane, essentially a building dating from c.1685, and so a precious survival of the early days of Soho's urban development. Its relatively small size – it's only three storeys high and three windows wide – reveals the modest ambitions of the initial speculating builders working in this portion of Brewer Street. The building is now clad with stucco, presumably seen in the nineteenth century as the cheap and quick solution to problems presented by crumbling bricks and decaying lime-mortar pointing. The bold string course above the first-floor windows is a typical early detail. The shop front is modern and the house's interior much altered.

Number 57 A mid-to-late-eighteenth-century elevation with a passage below. This leads to Smith's Court, oblong in plan with nineteenth-century stabling and workshops on three sides, the fourth being modern. In the nineteenth century this court was a workplace for farriers, but is now a quiet enclave with a café and a specialist bookshop. On the south side an opening leads to a narrow lane – also known as Smith's Court – that runs into Great Windmill Street (see p. 304).

Number 58 A four-storey house with a plain brick front which must date from *c*.1800.

Numbers 63–64 (originally 41) The site of the once-famed 'Hickford's Rooms', located behind a rather grand and wide house built in 1718 by the French Huguenot architect Nicholas Dubois. John Hickford acquired the lease of the house in 1738 and his 'Rooms' flourished from 1740 into the early 1760s, when it was the only West End concert room of significance, its subscription concerts being an important part of the London winter season. It was here, on 13 May 1765, that the nine-year-old W.A. Mozart and his sister gave a recital. It was announced in the *Public Advertiser* of 11 March as a performance 'For the Benefit of Miss Mozart of Thirteen, and Master Mozart of Eight [*sic*] Years of Age. Prodigies of Nature ... with all the OVERTURES of this little Boy's own Composition'. Tickets were for sale at half a guinea each – a relatively large amount – but seemingly sales did not go too well, because a few days before the concert they were halved to five shillings each. The work the brother and sister played was probably the Sonata K.19d.

Hickford's Rooms faced tougher competition from the mid 1760s but survived, in various guises (as a dancing school and fencing school as well as concert hall), until 1937, when it was acquired by the neighbouring Regent Palace Hotel and – in heartless and most stupid manner – demolished for the construction of a staff annex. Just imagine if this room, where the child prodigy gave an early performance, had survived! It would be a place of pilgrimage from around the globe.

Number 64 On the corner with Lower James Street is the Crown public house. A splendid mid-nineteenth-century building three storeys high, it was seemingly purpose-designed as a pub because its upper façade to Lower James Street is occupied by one wide first-floor window topped by a large blank arch within which is incised 'The Crown Tavern'. This was a time when modest inns and taverns tended to be designed along domestic lines, with the days of the sparkling and ornate nineteenth-century 'gin-palace' still to come (see p. 366). Although domestic in design, the façade to Brewer Street is a trifle more ornate than those of its neighbours, with cornice-topped architraves to first-floor windows linked by stucco panels to architraves around the second-floor windows. And above all is a crowning eaves cornice that sits over the fluted friezes of the second-floor window architraves. All very competent as a piece of classical design, and most satisfying.

Number 71 Now a modest building of little interest, but the house that stood here in the eighteenth century – then numbered 38 – was the home for thirty-three years of a most extraordinary person. The Chevalier d'Éon moved to London in 1762 to serve as a diplomat in the French embassy. Previously he had worked under cover for the French court in St Petersburg and then served briefly as a captain of dragoons during the final stage of the Seven Years' War. Among the qualities that distinguished the Chevalier while working at the embassy were his plump but delicate figure, softly spoken voice and a complete indifference to women. It was rumoured that d'Éon – who often preferred to dress as a woman – was, in fact, a woman. There can be little doubt that he promoted – indeed, made a virtue of – his androgynous status. He became a feature of the sexually orientated but essentially political Hellfire Clubs mobilised by such figures as Sir Francis Dashwood, and through these clubs, and his ambiguous position at the embassy, made useful contacts and gleaned valuable information – no doubt much of it about prominent figures who would do any-thing to keep d'Éon's secrets secret. D'Éon was evidently a master of intrigue but he was unable to survive the collapse of his world. The French Revolution, when it came in 1789, had no use for Royalists or émigrés and in 1810 he died in London, impoverished and an exile. When being prepared for burial his body was checked by those still curious about his sexuality and many were surprised to discover that 'Madame' d'Éon was in fact a man.

Number 78 This is one of the most pleasing buildings in the street. It's a corner house, dating from the late eighteenth century, which presents a plain and very pre-cisely proportioned main elevation to Brewer Street. The first-floor windows are double-square in proportion, those of the second floor 2:3 (square-and-a-half) and the third-floor windows are square. The widths of wall between the vertical jambs of the windows are the same width as the windows themselves. This harmonic relationship between window sizes and proportions was not just to create visual harmony: it was also a rational expression of function. The first-floor windows are deepest because the first-floor rooms are the highest and would have contained the main entertaining/reception rooms, with lower rooms above for lesser uses. The side elevation to Lower John Street is entirely without window openings; but it does have blank Venetian windows at the first and second floors (formed by arched recesses each flanked by narrower, flat-topped recesses) and a blank lunette at attic level. Who designed this miniature masterpiece? Sadly, we have no idea, but surely not one of the usual speculating builders operating in late-eighteenth-century Soho (plate 28).

Numbers 80, 82 and 84 are a most remarkable survival. All three houses date from c.1690 – numbers 80 and 82 obviously so, but also probably 84, which is stucco-clad and a storey higher. It is perhaps considerably rebuilt behind its altered and heightened façade. Both 80 and 82 retain their original three-storey-high brick façades; number 80 is three windows wide and 82 is two windows wide. The façades are simple and uniform. All windows have flat lintels formed of cut brick and are fitted with sash boxes set flush with the façade. The shop fronts are modern and the condition of both houses poor, number 80 having been very badly re-pointed in relatively recent times. However, as surviving original window shutters suggest, its interior is at least partly intact. As the *Survey of London* records of 80 in 1963: 'The stair, which has moulded closed strings, simply turned balusters, Doric column newels, and a slender moulded handrail, is complete from the first floor to the garret', with some box-cornices and plain panelling also surviving. Number 82 had 'a dog-legged staircase … complete above the first-floor level, and some ovolo-moulded panelling … in the first-floor rooms'.[66] These houses have survived many tribulations over the centuries, not least the cutting-through of Regent Street not far to their west. They are a very rare and valuable survival and must be properly protected.

Number 36 Bridle Lane, forming part of a group with 54 Brewer Street, probably dates from the late seventeenth century, although it is much altered and its elevation now stuccoed.

Excursions into Great Windmill Street, Archer Street, Sherwood Street and Denman Street

Great Windmill Street

The east side of what became known as Great Windmill Street appears on the 1585 map of the area and is marked as being in the possession of Widow Golightly. The map also shows a windmill that stood on what is now Ham Yard, which until the mid eighteenth century was known as Windmill Yard. In 1612 Robert Baker acquired the Golightly estate, on part of which he built Piccadilly Hall. The west side of the future Great Windmill Street had been owned by the Mercers' Company until acquired by Henry VIII in 1536. During Elizabeth I's reign the land was granted to, or purchased by, various individuals who were generally humble, and included a brewer. So by the early seventeenth century the uses of this Soho enclave were decidedly mixed but dominated by stabling and brewing, later joined by merchants' houses, offices, store rooms and manufactories. It is typical that the eminent Huguenot gold- and silversmith Paul de Lamerie had a house and office in Great Windmill Street from 1712 until 1737.

The form of the street appears to have been resolved by the 1670s, largely as a result of speculations and appeals to the Privy Council (which acted as a sort of planning authority for certain types of development on certain parcels of land) undertaken by Colonel Thomas Panton. By the time of Ogilby and Morgan's map of 1681–2 'Windmill Street' is shown with continuous lines of buildings on both its sides.

Nothing whatsoever survives of the street's original buildings, and there is very little that is early. But there are some things of interest.

Number 16 One of the oddest and most atmospheric architectural fragments in Soho. The house was built in 1767 for the Scottish physician and anatomist Dr William Hunter to serve as his home and – as its large size suggests – as an anatomical museum, theatre and lecture hall. It was filled with bizarre, preserved body parts that were intended to inform the medical profession and astonish the public. The building was designed by fellow Scot Robert Mylne, an architect and engineer of considerable talent who in the late 1760s designed the sublime Blackfriars Bridge. Alas, virtually nothing of this fascinating establishment survives beyond the much-mutilated elevation to Great Windmill Street. Hunter occupied this building until his death in 1783, when the business was taken over by a succession of Scottish medical men. Clearly, it was a lucrative exercise, catering to a popular interest in the rapidly evolving scientific and medical discoveries of the age. But by the 1830s public tastes and interests had changed, medical speculations were less exotic and novel, and the enterprise closed; Hunter's specimens were removed to Glasgow University, where they remain. The building became a print works, a 'French dining room' called the Hôtel de l'Étoile and in 1887 was sold to the proprietor of the Lyric Theatre;

its interior was soon devoured during the creation of the theatre on Shaftesbury Avenue. Presumably the sad and abused main elevation was permitted to survive because preservation was cheaper than destruction. But although only a fragment, this battered façade does offer a reminder of one of the medical wonders of Georgian London.

The Lyric Tavern stands on the opposite side of Great Windmill Street, on the corner with Ham Yard. The existing building dates from 1892, and is a pleasant example of late-Victorian pub architecture. But its origins are far older. There was a tavern on the site by the late 1730s, when it was called the Ham and in 1756 the Ham and Windmill. So in its history, if not in its fabric, this is among Soho's oldest pubs.

The Windmill Theatre stands to the north of Dr Hunter's house. It is one of London's more notorious theatres. Erected in 1897, it became the Palais de Luxe cinema in 1910 and in 1930 was gutted to form a 'modern' theatre; from 1932 it launched its 'non-stop' revues, commencing around midday. This move away from showing American talkies to 'flesh-and-blood vaudeville' was touted as a patriotic response to the difficult days of the Depression. As *The Times* explained on 4 February 1932, 'The Windmill Theatre turned last night from talking films to variety and *revue* turns ... Mrs. Laura Henderson hopes in this way to give employment to British artists and to put into British pockets money that would otherwise go to Hollywood. It is a deserving enterprise, and last night's audience heartily applauded its gallantry.' Laura Henderson – the sixty-nine-year-old wife of a wealthy jute merchant – was proprietor of the Windmill and her manager was Vivian Van Damm.

The Times, although supportive of the sentiment behind the revue, was critical of its artistic quality. It suggested that the producer should 'try to fashion a variety programme with a character of its own. The entertainment now depends on ... tricks, and on the dancing girls' who achieved 'some pretty effects'.[67] The owner and her manager perhaps took *The Times*'s advice to heart – but not in the way intended. Rather than coming up with something original, they merely increased the tricks and the girls so that the revues increasingly featured scantily attired young women who – to satisfy the Lord Chamberlain – had to stand stock-still, especially when stark naked. This gently titillating pantomime continued into the 1960s, when the world – and the law – changed, making such innocent and constrained displays of female flesh redundant. The Windmill's famous slogan – 'We never closed' – refers to its finest hours during the war, when, almost alone among West End theatres, it didn't close, except during the second week of September 1939 when all London theatres were compulsorily but briefly shut by a jittery government. The Windmill Theatre survives in operation, but its profile is now much lower than in the past.

Number 23 A curious piece of architecture: squeezed onto the narrow plot of a small Georgian house is a most ambitious neo-Gothic design incorporating a ground-floor arcade with appropriate Gothic detailing, a first floor with a slightly projecting oriel including an image of the keys of St Peter, and a third floor, including a Romanesque-style arched window, topped by a gable-pediment. In the centre of this lively composition, set within a circular recess, is a bust of 'Edward Geoffrey 14th Earl of Derby', a generous benefactor to the parish. This is the main entrance to St James's and St Peter's Church of England Primary School, built in 1870. St Peter's Church had been opened in Great Windmill Street in 1861 but was demolished in 1954. In 1877 the school was extended into adjacent Archer Street, where it seems to have adapted and lightly Gothicised – rather than replaced – a late Georgian house. The primary school is still going, and still under the aegis of the Church of England.

Numbers 29–30 A group of three modest houses, each two windows wide, that appears to date from 1790 to 1810. Adjoining them is Smith's Court (formerly Angel Court), now with nineteenth-century stabling, workshops and warehousing.

Number 21 was a house of similar late-Georgian date and scale, with particularly good brickwork, mostly in its original condition. In mid 2019 it was still in productive use, but the tenants had departed by August because consent for the building's demolition was granted by Westminster City Council in May 2018. Demolition started in December 2019 (plate 3).

Number 40 A modest house of c.1735.

Archer Street

Archer Street first appears in the parish rate books in 1675, when it is called Arch Street, but in Rocque's map of 1746 it is named Archer Street. It was part of Colonel Panton's building enterprise, and in his building petition of 1671 is referred to as the 'short street leading from out of Windmill Street over against Windmill Yard towards St Giles'. Until the 1830s Archer Street was only connected to Rupert Street by a narrow, right-angled passage.

Number 6 has a curious, and not displeasing, tripartite elevation. It dates from the mid eightteenth century.

Number 7 has a façade of *c*.1800. It now houses a more or less traditional Italian café and gelateria called Gelupo.

Number 12 The Bocco di Lupo restaurant, as proclaimed in terracotta lettering above its ground-floor windows. The building dates from the late nineteenth century.

Numbers 13–14 A quietly fascinating building. Neo-Georgian and unassuming, it was designed in 1912 for the Orchestral Association by H.P. Adam and C.H. Holden, who were among the leading designers of their day, forging a modern British architecture – often realising demanding new building types – based on the inspiration of history. Like Edwin Lutyens, they emerged from the late-Gothic, Arts and Crafts tradition and in the 1920s and 1930s tended towards a sculptural, almost abstract rendering of the British classical tradition. Holden (who teamed up with Adam in 1907) was responsible for some of the most powerful cemeteries created in northern France and Belgium in the early 1920s for the Imperial War Graves Commission, and was architect in 1926 for the high-rise London Transport headquarters at 55 Broadway, St James's, and for numerous stations on the Northern and Piccadilly Underground lines, notably the Rotunda at Arnos Grove.

In Archer Street this team went for a building inspired by the early Georgian brick-built domestic architecture of Soho, but they did not produce an imitative pastiche. Two sites have been united to form a single building that, with its central emphasis and wide, squarish windows, does not look like a slavish reproduction of Georgian domestic design. It's a gentle reinvention of a tradition that is appropriate and presumably intended to blend with the then still largely early Georgian character of the area. Holden also liked to integrate sculpture with his architecture – as in 1906 he did in collaboration with Jacob Epstein for the British Medical Association Building (now Zimbabwe House) off the Strand, and at the London Transport headquarters. In Archer Street the centre of the building sports Charles K. Pibworth's relief carving of Euterpe, in Greek mythology the muse presiding over music and lyric poetry – the 'giver of delight'.

Number 16 A modest house with a façade of c.1800.

Sherwood Street

In 1670 Sir William Pulteney assigned the land on which this street stands in trust to Francis Sherard, the younger brother of the 2nd Baron Sherard of Leitrim. By the late 1680s Sherard, bitten by the bug for building, had 'erected and caused to be erected' houses on both sides of a new street that almost immediately became known popularly as Sherwood rather than Sherard Street.[68]

All early buildings are long gone, the only significant and interesting structures being the fragmentary remains of the Regent Palace Hotel, which also fronts onto Glasshouse Street, and the Piccadilly Theatre. The theatre dates from 1928 and was designed by Bertie Crewe and Edward Stone in a somewhat reduced Art Deco manner, with little detail. It has the feel of being a most economical project. The design of the theatre embraces the adjoining Queen's Heart public house, on the corner with Denman Street. It claims to have been founded in 1788 and, thank goodness, still appears to be thriving.

The Regent Palace Hotel was opened in May 1915, designed in a majestic Beaux-Arts manner by Henry Tanner, F.J. Wills and W.J. Ancell. When new it was the largest hotel in the world, with its tall, terracotta-clad English Baroque-style elevations dominating the surrounding Georgian fabric. But this mighty beast, developed by J. Lyons & Company, slowly descended into gloom, brought low by changing fashions in hotel accommodation and sad neglect. Most of it was, tragically, demolished in 2010, when its heart was ripped out and its two domed ends retained to 'sandwich' a new building of almost brutally contrasting design. But not all was lost. In fact something rather wonderful has been gained. In the 1930s the hotel commissioned Oliver Bernard – the architect who brought the Art Deco interior to Britain, and father of Jeffrey Bernard (see p. 145) – to create a number of jazzy new public rooms. What Bernard created, in superb Art Deco style, is as good as anything in New York or Paris. But, exuberant and high-quality as they were, these interiors fell into decline along with the rest of the hotel. By the 1990s, known collectively as the Atlantic Bar, they were an odd curiosity and something of a specialist interest. You would descend from Glasshouse Street into a subterranean Art Deco wonderland, in which carpets were stained, seat covers torn, such lighting as worked was low, and the few customers present were clearly intent on negotiating and closing deals – mostly of a worldly and urgent nature. And those loitering in this heady, streamlined 1930s concoction who were not selling or purchasing flesh were goggle-eyed architectural historians who'd gone to look at a few gracious Art Deco curves and found they were getting a lot more than they'd anticipated. Amazingly, much of this has been saved and brilliantly repaired, restored and even extended in a witty and informed Art Deco manner. This 1930s underworld has been reborn a bright and sparkling fairyland. The cocktail bar, stripy and glorious, lives again; there is a small, circular cabaret theatre and the original grill – generously gilded, dating from 1915 and in the Beaux-Arts style, not Art Deco – is now a large and splendid restaurant that succeeds in being genuinely Parisian and stylish in feel. It's now named Brasserie Zédel, entered from Sherwood Street; and, given the close proximity of the tourist tat of Piccadilly Circus, the genuine glamour of this Art Deco and Beaux-Arts fantasy – and the exceptional value for money offered – is a wonder in itself.

Denman Street

This street, originally called Queen Street, was laid out in the early 1670s by the speculator Colonel Thomas Panton. John Strype described it in 1720 as 'pretty neat, clean and ... well inhabited'.[69] In 1862 the Metropolitan Board of Works changed the name to Denman Street, to commemorate Dr Thomas Denman, an eminent physician in his day, who had lived in a long-lost house on the south side of the street.

No early buildings survive in the street, but on number 9 – one of a pair of tall, gabled houses on the south side dating from the late nineteenth century – a handsome doorcase has been fixed, presumably saved from the previous house on the site. The doorcase has elegantly detailed consoles supporting a cornice and evidently dates from c.1740. Why was this relic preserved in the 1890s?

Perhaps the door is from Denman's house. This is the sort of delightful find that makes the exploration of Soho so rewarding. (These buildings were demolished in late 2010, although doorcase is preserved in situ.)

Lexington Street

Until 1885 the north end of Lexington Street was known as Cambridge Street and the section south of Beak Street as Little Windmill Street. It was named in deference to an extinct title of the Sutton family, which was connected with the Pulteney family and eventually inherited much of the Pulteney estate.[70] The street had been laid out and lined with buildings from 1686, but from 1718 the Pulteney estate redeveloped this street as it did, during the next five years or so, much of its Soho land.

The speculating builders who took leases from the estate in the early years of the eighteenth century were mostly carpenters, including Edward Collens, no doubt a relative of Joseph Collens. The Collenses were evidently making the early Georgian rebuilding of Soho into something of a family enterprise. It was usual at the time for London estates to require builders to produce houses that corresponded to a given 'rate' of building, as specified in the 1667 Building Act. This was a rule-of-thumb method by which the estate could ensure that it got decent buildings – reasonably well wrought, and of an agreed scale – so that it inherited something of value when the building lease expired. But in this development only a few of the leases specified that the houses had to be of the 'second rate' (which was a decent scale of house for the estate), most simply requiring that good bricks and mortar were used. This failure to be more

demanding suggests that the estate had difficulty in tempting
speculators to invest in the project. The consequence is that
buildings would have been artistically modest, with just basic
structures run up and, no doubt, corners cut.

Only two small groups of early houses survive, both
at the north end of the street. Perhaps this reflects some
inherent fragility with the early-eighteenth-century speculations (plate 29).

Lexington Street south of Beak Street is formed mostly
of large-scale and undistinguished late-nineteenth- and
twentieth-century industrial or commercial buildings.

Numbers 41–53 form the larger of the two surviving
groups. These houses were built *c*.1719 by a mix of
tradesmen. *The Survey of London*[71] identifies these men, so
typical of the humble speculators who, eager for a quick
profit, created the vast majority of Georgian London.
Numbers 41, 49 and 53 were built by Caleb Waterfield and
Thomas Cook, carpenters; 43 by John Walker, bricklayer;
45 by John Hiron, joiner; 47 by Andrew Andrews, a sash
maker, and 51 by Thomas Whitford, plasterer.

Numbers 47 and 49 retain fine façades of 1719, while
47 also has the substantial remains of a very good late-
eighteenth- or early-nineteenth-century shop front. There
are also the remains of an early shop front on number 49.

Houses in the remainder of the group have façades
that have been rebuilt or altered in various ways at various times, but most retain good interior details. These
houses form an excellent group with the houses they
adjoin, at right angles, in Beak Street. Seen together the
houses in these two streets offer, with Broadwick Street
in the background, one of the liveliest and most complete
Georgian vistas in Soho.

Numbers 44 and 46, the smaller group, are also of 1719. The speculators involved were Mark Dixon and Edward Collens, carpenters. Both houses now have façades of *c*.1810, with internal sash-shutters to the first-floor windows. Today these buildings house Andrew Edmunds's splendid, long-established restaurant, a print shop and the Academy Club, so parts of their interiors can be inspected. The plans are usual for early-eighteenth-century Soho houses. Each house is two windows wide, four storeys high above a basement, and contains a front room, a back room, a narrow and shallow rear closet, and a dog-leg staircase placed in one corner at the back of the house. Much panelling survives, mostly of a simple kind, as do a few early stone fire surrounds, and in number 46 a good open string staircase with shaped tread ends.

The north end of Lexington Street is currently an oasis of good, small independent cafés and restaurants. As well as Andrew Edmunds at number 46, there is Mildred's restaurant in the stucco-fronted number 45. Both are worth going to, not only for their food but also because once inside you can get a good look at surviving panelled rooms.

Excursion into Silver Place and Ingestre Place

Silver Place is a paved court running east off Lexington Street. It's short and narrow but architecturally interesting because it reveals the humble, commercial and industrial nature of west Soho in the nineteenth century.

Numbers 1 and 1b on the south side are small houses that date from the early nineteenth century and, with wide windows or shop fronts, were tailor-made for industrial or commercial use.

Numbers 5 and 7 on the opposite side of the court, which were constructed with 12–15 Ingestre Place, are later, larger and more ambitious, but also places of commerce and industry. They are fitted with uniform shop fronts and have wide workshop windows on all three of their upper floors.

Ingestre Place was created in 1868 by the amalgamation of New Street and Husband Street and named after Lord Ingestre, who helped to fund the industrial dwellings, built in 1853–6, that fronted onto both these streets.

Broadwick Street

Until 1936 Broadwick Street was two streets – Broad Street to the west, and the narrower Edward Street to the east. Broadwick Street now stretches west from Wardour Street to Carnaby Street, although Broad Street's original west termination was Marshall Street.

Broad Street and Edward Street were laid out across four separate estates – an unusual communal enterprise for Soho – with house-building starting in Edward Street in 1686. The estates, largely defined by ancient field boundaries, were – from east to west – Colman Hedge Close and Little Gelding's Close (both at the time under the control of James Pollett), Pawlett's Garden (owned by the Pulteney estate) and Pesthouse Close (owned by Lord Craven). Pollett kicked off development in 1686 when he was on the rise and enjoying the patronage of James II (see p. 8), and immediately after he had obtained a lease on Colman Hedge Close from Edward Wardour. The street proceeded in fits and starts from east to west, with its final portion, on Pesthouse Close, not being completed until 1736.

It was presumably Pollett's ill-fated scheme to create a hay market at the junction with Edward Street and Berwick Street (which was also a Pollett initiative – see p. 82) that led to the unusual width of Broad Street. His ambitious market proposal had crumbled by 1690, but its memory seems to have lived on – in reduced manner – in the width that Broad Street was to achieve.

Broad Street served, as it grew west during the first decades of the eighteenth century, as an informal market area and gathering place, rather like the village green of west Soho. This market tradition is perhaps one of the origins of the Berwick Street market, which by the late nineteenth century had become a major Soho enterprise. The market survives – but barely – with stalls and barrows located at the south end of the street. Most now sell various types of street food, but there is one selling dairy products and another fruit. And look out for the few ancient timber barrows still in use, most made in Neal Street, Covent Garden. These have probably been doing trade on the street for 100 years or so.

This village green and market role probably explains why one of west Soho's main pumps and sources of public water was located in Broad Street. Grander households would have had their own, admittedly somewhat intermittent, water supply provided by private water companies such as the New River Company. The pump on Broad Street gained notoriety – indeed a place in medical history – when the locally based physician Dr John Snow analysed its water and mapped the pattern of the spread of cholera during an epidemic in 1854 among those using it to demonstrate beyond reasonable doubt that cholera was waterborne (see p. 96). Snow's epoch-making study is commemorated in the name of a late-Victorian pub on the corner of Broadwick Street and Lexington Street.

Numbers 46 and 48–58 are the survivors of the street's original buildings and are really its only buildings of significance (plate 30). Number 46 dates from 1706, and although much altered externally it retains its original plan – with a back and front room per floor and a rear closet wing – as well as raised and fielded panelling to the ground-floor entrance passage and first-floor rooms, and its original staircase with twisted balusters and square-plan newels typical of its early date.

Number 46 is now the solitary survivor of an informal group of early houses that remained into the early 1970s. I documented the dereliction, and then destruction, of most of this group. To the east side of 46, forming the corner with Poland Street, was a large, gaunt and impressive pair of houses – numbered 42–44 Broadwick Street – that formed a uniform group, four windows wide and originally three storeys high, but seemingly re-fronted in the late eighteenth century and heightened to five storeys in the nineteenth century. These houses also dated from 1706, and although their exterior was altered the *Survey of London* in 1963 made much of their interiors, especially the surviving staircase: 'the first floor ... retains ... substantial portions of original raised-and-fielded, ovolo moulded panelling, dado rail and box-cornice', the staircase having 'carved tread ends, turned balusters' and a handrail 'ramped up at the landings over newels composed of four clustered balusters'. On the landing between the ground and first floors was a 'plaster semi-dome moulded in the shape of a scallop-shell'. It sounds sensational – and most unusual.[72]

The building had a particularly impressive presence in Poland Street, where its tall elevation was formed mostly by an heroic, largely windowless and generally sublime brick wall. On the ground floor was a shop selling textiles and an arched front door, which meant that the ground floor was numbered as part of Poland Street. Adjoining it was a smaller brick-built house, number 63 Poland Street, of 1823 and only one window wide, and then the Star and Garter public house. I remember noting a hoarding directing to a Mayfair agent all enquires 'regarding developments on this site'. Sinister. Appeals for action were futile. Next time I visited Broadwick Street demolition was under way, with a digger in Poland Street chewing hungrily at the pathetic remains of the once-haughty brick elevation. Once again, those responsible for stewardship of Soho's history had failed.

Numbers 48–58, to the west of 46, form a terrace that in its monumentality, uniformity, length and commanding location is unmatched among Soho's surviving early Georgian domestic architecture. The terrace was built in 1722–3 on the Pulteney-estate-owned Pawlett's Garden, continuing the line already established by Pollett when setting out Poland Street and Berwick Street. The main contractor was John Mist – a paviour – who agreed to build houses of the 'second' rate according to the Building Act of 1667.[73] So this is a 'statute'-controlled speculation which no doubt explains the uniformity and sustained scale of the development. The matching doorcases of the terrace, with carved brackets supporting cornices that frame rectangular blocks instead of keystones, are much like the doorcases on the east end of the south side of Meard Street. Although dating from the early 1730s, this similarity suggests that the builder of Meard Street – John Meard, who was probably responsible for a long-lost house in nearby Great Marlborough Street – had a hand in the construction of this remarkable terrace. Unlike the best houses of similar date in nearby Poland Street and Great Marlborough Street, these Broadwick Street houses were never occupied by people of fashion or members of the aristocracy. Presumably the nearby burial ground, workhouse and the pesthouse that survived into the mid 1730s kept prime tenants away. Instead, early occupants included successful tradesmen such as the landscape gardener Charles Bridgeman, who lived at number 54 from 1723 to 1738.

When I first knew Soho, decades ago, the terrace was magnificent not only for its architecture but also for its noble decay and wonderful mix of workaday Soho uses. This gave it an air of tremendous authenticity and interest, its panelled entrance halls and rooms being little touched – or repaired – since they were constructed. Then a development company, armed with a 'conservation' architect, got interested and soon this fragile and precious terrace was transformed. Simple but honest Victorian sash windows were replaced with new 'early-Georgian-style' sashes, much panelling was heavily repaired and the terrace's atmosphere – once innocent of the attentions of any self-conscious restorer – was lost. The most obvious mark of the heavy hand laid upon these houses is the bland and far from authentic-looking uniform brass fanlights that have been fixed above each front door. True, the terrace was saved, and given the strength to last another few hundred years; but surely this could have been done in a slightly more sensitive manner? Over-restoration can be almost as deadly as demolition, and today, of course, instead of housing a vibrant mix of uses, all the houses are offices.

Excursions into Poland Street and Dufour's Place

Poland Street

Poland Street, which occupies the central portion of a sliver of land, once known as Little Gelding's Close, was laid out in the 1680s by James Pollett. The earliest leases date from the 1690s, but building generally got under way in 1705. The delay was probably due to the financial and political troubles Pollett, a Roman Catholic with James II as his patron, encountered after the Glorious Revolution of 1688 (see p. 83). When construction began it was organised by Pollett's executors: he had died in 1703.

The enterprise was well organised – one of the executors' first actions was to arrange the construction of a communal sewer for the proposed new houses – and Poland Street rapidly became one of Soho's grandest streets. It could not vie in width with the contemporary and adjoining Great Marlborough Street (see p. 366), but it was soon adorned with a number of large and fine houses occupied by members of the aristocracy. Significantly, one of Pollett's executors, the ambitious and successful speculator Joseph Collens, was also deeply involved in the creation of Great Marlborough Street on the adjoining Millfield. Evidently the development of these two fine streets was, to a degree, co-ordinated and intended to be mutually beneficial.

The first seven houses built in Poland Street were completed in 1705 (they stood on the west side between numbers 50 and 63). By the end of the following year fifteen additional houses had been finished on the west side and eighteen on the east side, with the street fully built by 1707. Most of the speculating builders involved were bricklayers by trade.[74]

The street soon became a popular home for architects: in the mid 1740s Giacomo Leoni lived at the now demolished 52, and from 1756 to 1766 Sir William Chambers lived in the also now demolished 58. Artists, too, created something of a community in the street. In 1767 Paul Sandby, the painter and engraver, replaced Chambers at 58, who in turn in 1772 was replaced by Thomas Malton, an architectural draughtsman. Gavin Hamilton is also said to have lived in the street in 1779, and, as we have noted, from 1785 to 1791 William Blake lived in 28 – or at least in part of it. The house has long been demolished but it was here that Blake wrote *Songs of Innocence*, *The Book of Thel*, the narrative poem *Tiriel* and *The Marriage of Heaven and Hell*. Blake's impoverished circumstances suggest that the street had by the late eighteenth century already started its social decline.

A portrait of the street, as it approached the cusp of its social change, is offered by the satirical novelist and diarist Fanny Burney. As a child and teenager she lived from 1760 to 1770 with her father, the musicologist Dr Charles Burney, at the now demolished number 50. In 1832 she remembered in a memoir of her father that Poland Street 'was not then, as it is now, a sort of street that, like the rest of the neighbourhood, appears to be left in the lurch'. In the 1760s London tenants of taste and means were not, she suggests, 'as fastidious as they are become at present, from the endless variety of new habitations'. She also recognised that Poland Street had changed since the 1760s, like London itself: 'Oxford Street ... into which Poland-street terminated, had little on its further side but fields, gardeners' grounds, or uncultivated suburbs. Portman, Manchester, Russell, Belgrave squares, Portland-place, etc. etc., had not yet a single stone or brick laid, in signal of intended erection.' This then semi-rural prospect for Poland Street, the lack of competition in the supply of comfortable homes, meant that in the 1760s it was still attractive. Consequently Dr Burney enjoyed the company of illustrious neighbours. He had 'successively ... the Duke of Chandos, Lady Augusta Bridges, the Hon. John Smith and the Miss Barrys, Sir Willoughby and the Miss Astons; and, well noted by Mr Burney's little family, on the visit of his black majesty to England, sojourned, almost immediately opposite to it, the Cherokee King'.[75] *The Survey of London* notes that 'there is no sign of these titled residents in the Poland Street rate books for the years when Dr Burney lived in the street' but, charitably, suggests that 'it is possible that they occupied furnished houses and did not pay rates'.[76]

In the nineteenth century Poland Street became a favoured habitation of craftsmen, particularly jewellers, engravers and carvers. And so it was part of the Soho transformation from a place of domestic grandeur to trade, manufacturing and commerce, and along with this change came demolition and the replacement of houses by larger utilitarian structures. But some of the original aspirations, despite the sad dilapidations of the intervening years, are still echoed by the large scale and architectural ambition of a few of the street's surviving early buildings.

Number 7, built in 1706, was one of the largest houses in the street. In keeping with the early aristocratic atmosphere of Soho, it was first occupied by the Countess of Sandwich. The façade has been rebuilt, seemingly c.1800, and the door retains a good frame, dating from the rebuild, with lion-head masks and a delicate fanlight. But the entrance hall still has its high-quality raised and fielded panelling from 1706 and there is a very fine staircase in a panelled compartment, with turned and twisted balusters, carved tread ends and newels in the form of Corinthian columns. Well worth a look if you can slip inside.

Number 11 has a far from promising frontage, with heavy cement-made architraves around second-floor windows and a large arched window at first-floor level, so seemingly a commercial building. But look carefully and you can see brick arches behind the architraves. This is in fact a mutilated and obscured eighteenth-century elevation. The *Survey of London* records that, in 1963, this house was similar in plan to number 7, but more modest in scale, with its original dog-leg staircase including twisted balusters and fluted newel columns, and fragments of panelling surviving in the first-floor rooms.

Number 15 Built in 1706 and by 1716 occupied by the Earl of Suffolk. But in the late eighteenth century the original house seems to have been entirely rebuilt and it is this building that now survives in much-altered form. In March 1811 Percy Bysshe Shelley acquired lodgings in the

house after being sent down from Oxford. He moved here
with his friend Thomas Jefferson Hogg, but seems to have
left after only a few months. Now the ground floor and
basement house Vasco and Piero's Pavilion restaurant,
one of the more pleasant and still authentic of Soho's
Italian family-run restaurants, although it has only been
in this house for thirty years or so after being expelled
from its premises on Oxford Street, which had a charming
and playful Festival-of-Britain-style interior. A few of the
pavilion-like fittings designed by Angus McBean in the
early 1950s for the Oxford Street restaurant were installed
in Poland Street and survive.

Number 23 Ye Old King's Arms public house, built
in 1706 and, although altered, not substantially rebuilt.
It's been a public house since at least 1718 and has been
known as the King's Arms since at least 1739, and so
must be one of the oldest continuously occupied pubs
in London. The rate books give the name of the first
innkeeper as Edward Crusdon. The ground-floor frontage
dates from the mid nineteenth century. The first-floor
windows have very shallow segmental arches – quite
an early use of this form – and between them is set a
plaque which states that within the tavern 'The Ancient
Order of Druids was revived on the 28th November 1781'.
Druids had made a comeback in the early eighteenth
century, with their great champion William Stukeley
arguing that they offered evidence of a significant British culture, steeped in ancient wisdom and even with
direct links to the Classical world, long before the arrival
of the Roman conquerors. But the Ancient Order of
Druids was not a pagan or even a religious society. It
was more of a dining club where like-minded men – all

believing in what were held to be the Druidic traditions of justice, benevolence and friendship – could gather to their mutual satisfaction. The order evidently chose to imitate Masonic practice by calling its places of gathering 'lodges', by creating and courting an air of mystery about its origins and purposes and by indulging in some form of initiation. These harmless affectations nearly got it into serious trouble in 1794 when the government – fearing sedition in the wake of the French Revolution – became very suspicious of any 'secret' society, assuming that all could be fronts for incendiaries and revolutionaries keen on liberty, fraternity and equality. Fear of suppression and arrest caused the order to rapidly shrink in size, but Lodge number 1 – at the King's Arms – survived. The order recovered, expanded to the United States and, in one form or another, continues to this day.

Number 24 dates from about 1707, and although re-fronted in the late eighteenth century – when it was given extra-deep first-floor windows – retains large amounts of panelling and its original staircase; but it is relatively modest (the house is only two windows wide), making it clear that the original houses in the street varied significantly in their architectural aspirations. This is an interior well worth penetrating.

Number 44 Early-nineteenth-century façade, also only two windows wide.

Number 48 has a fine, large and boldly detailed façade of about 1750, perhaps with elements of the 1703 house surviving behind. Much mutilated, adapted and extended, this elevation must once have been noble because its surviving brickwork is of beautiful quality. The very finely rubbed and gauged first-floor window arches still offer a tantalising glimpse of what once was. Especially nice, and typical of the mid eighteenth century, is the stone-made block cornice, ultimately inspired by that on the Pantheon in Rome. The storey above the cornice – with its wide workshop windows – is a nineteenth-century addition marking this mansion's later industrial use.

Number 54 is one of the architecturally and historically most satisfying houses in the street. It was built in 1705 and its brick elevation, although now painted pink, appears to date from then, with only the ground floor significantly altered. Most noticeable are the half-windows on each storey, a detail that enjoyed a tremendous vogue in London from the late 1690s and well into the first decade of the eighteenth century. These half-, or demi-, windows are now blocked, but could once have been open to light small closets contrived in the space formed by the house's large and deeply projecting chimney-stacks. Inside, the good and original staircase survives. The house was first occupied, until about 1740, by a 'Captain Defour' – probably Paul Dufour, who developed nearby Dufour's Court (now Place) off Broadwick Street, and from 1788 by Elizabeth Billington, who is described in the *Dictionary of National Biography* as 'the greatest singer England has ever produced'. Due to 'her generous and amorous disposition',[77] Mrs Billington was known as the 'Poland Street Man Trap'. This was the period when Soho had become well established as a sedate and discreet centre of London's sex industry.[78]

Number 62 The Star and Garter public house. Its façade is now stuccoed and so hard to date. The *Survey of London* states that this was one of the earliest sites to be developed in Poland Street but that the existing

building must date from the early nineteenth century.[79]
Certainly the public-house ground-floor frontage – with
its elegant pilasters – looks early nineteenth century, but
with large-scale scrolls added later. The building has been
in use as a pub since at least 1825.

Nearly opposite the Star and Garter is an admirable
composition, numbered 1–5, that appears to be a terrace of six identical buildings, each with a single wide,
ground-floor arch. In fact, this was built as a showroom
and office for a motor car company. The subtle but
beautifully designed Art Nouveau details that enliven
the broad classicism of the composition include, as well
as flowing plant forms, the date 1902. This seems very
early for a car showroom. The architects were Bartlett
& Ross. Altogether delightful. The ornamentation also
includes the initials E.R., presumably the name of the
car company, Riley perhaps.

Dufour's Place

In 1719 and 1721 the Pulteney estate leased the central
portion of Pawlett's Garden, adjoining and south of a
recently created burial ground, to Paul Dufour (see p.
327). In the legal documents Dufour was described as
'esquire', so he was a gentleman dabbler in real estate.
He covenanted to build within two years substantial
brick houses on the ground and by 1721 had constructed
four houses in a court, Dufour's Place, leading north off
Broadwick Street. These houses have long been demolished. The following year a paviour named John Mist,
acting in part with Dufour but also in direct agreement
with the Pulteney estate, agreed to build six houses facing

onto Broadwick Street and backing onto Dufour's Place. These were completed by 1723 and survive as numbers 48–58 Broadwick Street (see p. 318).

The formation of Dufour's Place was completed in 1736 when six houses (numbers 1–6) were built on its west side, which was part of Pesthouse Close.

Dufour's Place is now an arid enclave, dominated by an eccentric six-storey brick-clad office tower, designed in the 1980s by Quinlan Terry in an idiosyncratic classical manner. I suppose the idea is that, if Georgians built high-rise office blocks, this is how they would look. Rather oddly, the main door and window above it employ Mannerist false perspective, which is surely more Jacobean than Georgian. Also Jacobean are the crowning Baroque pediment, scrolls and obelisks, which presumably represent an attempt to reinvigorate Georgian traditions by adding a little bit of something different.

Marshall Street

Marshall Street was laid out in the mid 1730s on Pesthouse Close by the land's owner, Lord Craven. It is the northward continuation of an earlier court off the north side of Beak Street (see p. 25).

Number 37, on the corner with uniform numbers 2–8 Ganton Street, is a fine house of c.1821–5, with wide windows, an arched door and a good fanlight.

Numbers 33–36 A uniform terrace of c.1825.

At the north end of the street, at the junction with what is the east portion of Foubert's Place, are the much-mutilated remains of the Craven Chapel of 1821 – essentially just the outer walls, with the original windows

extended vertically to light the floors inserted within.
But there are a few good details surviving, notably the
elegant stone-made consoled door on Foubert's Place.
The architect was probably Robert Abraham.

Beak Street

The street's western part is shown on a survey map of
1585 and formed an ancient highway from Piccadilly to
what is now Oxford Circus.[80] This highway was part
of the boundary between Mulghay Close (part of the
Pulteney estate in the late seventeenth century) on the
south and Six Acre Close on the north. In about 1680 the
ground on the north side of the street (between modern
Regent Street and Kingly Street) came into the possession
of Thomas Beake, who held a post at court as one of the
'Queen's Messengers'. The central and eastern portion of
the street was known as Silver Street, with only the short
section at the west end called Beak Street, but in 1883
all became Beak Street. Development started in the mid
1680s. It was very modest in its ambitions: John Strype in
his *Survey of the Cities of London and Westminster* of 1720
describes it as just 'another small street'.

Numbers 15–27, at the west end, form a good group.
Number 15, on the corner with Kingly Street, is a much-
altered eighteenth-century building, and in the 1950s was
home to the unlikely sounding Gestapo Club (see p. 120).

Numbers 17 and 19 are late-eighteenth- or early-
nineteenth-century, 17 with wide workshop windows.

Number 21 (incorporating an arch to Kingly Court)
probably dates from *c.*1730, but was much altered in
the 1840s. At the rear of the house the brickwork and

window arches look early, as does the position of the chimney-stacks to the rear rooms. These are set against the rear elevation in a most sculptural manner – an unusual arrangement, more common in the seventeenth century than the eighteenth, and seemingly confirming this building's early origin.

Number 23 A good and complete house and shop front of *c*.1820–30, with a handsome fanlight and first-floor cast-iron balconies with Grecian-style motifs. It also has a chimney-stack set against its rear wall, presumably also reflecting the house's 1730s – or earlier – origin.

Kingly Court is galleried and was, according to Richard Horwood's early-nineteenth-century London map, a 'Repository of carriages'. It has now been transformed into a roofed court for shops and restaurants and is connected via passages to Kingly Street and Carnaby Street. Today the court is a bright and breezy tourist destination, but when I first knew it and photographed it almost fifty years ago, it was a most atmospheric enclave, quietly decaying and seemingly lost in time. It was still gas-lit, with a large lantern placed on a wall just through the Beak Street arch and attached to a curious and derelict building, only two floors high, the façade of which was covered in wonderfully patinated early-nineteenth-century Roman cement, with scored joints as if it were made of stone blocks. The building's segmental windows suggested a construction date in the 1720s. Then, it seemed, nothing could save this modest structure – but it has endured, its façade painted and tidied up in an almost indecent manner and now housing offices.

Numbers 41–3, Canaletto House and Yard Leased in 1687 by Isaac Symball to John James, carpenter. A wider than average Beak Street house that incorporates a passage to an internal court. Antonio Canaletto lodged here from at least 1749 to 1751, a sojourn interrupted by a journey to Italy in the winter of 1750. On 26 July 1749 a newspaper advertisement states:

> Signor Canaleto hereby invites any Gentleman that will be pleased to come to his House, to see a Picture done by him, being A view of St. James's Park, which hopes may in some Measure deserve their Approbation. The said view may be seen from Nine in the Morning until Three in the Afternoon, and from Four until Seven in the Evening, for the Space of fifteen Days from the publication of this Advertisement. He lodges at Mr. Richard Wiggan's, Cabinet-Maker, in Silver-Street, Golden Square.[81]

An advertisement dated 30 July 1751 invited gentlemen to visit the same address to view a 'Representation of Chelsea College, Ranelagh House, and the River Thames'. [82]

Number 45 Built in the early eighteenth century but re-fronted.

Number 49 The Old Coffee House public house. The building dates from the mid eighteenth century and the pub is mostly late-nineteenth-century. It's currently one of Soho's more pleasant and traditional pubs – an increasing rarity in the area.

Opposite, on the corner with Great Pulteney Street, is the Sun and Thirteen Cantons public house, dated 1882. Again, a most decent pub for Soho.

Numbers 50–54 (with frontages also to Lexington Street and Great Pulteney Street) were built in 1904–5 by Alfred Grace, with a green-tiled 'self-washing' elevation.

Numbers 65–71 Built in 1718–19 by Richard Powell, carpenter – a pair, part re-fronted and rebuilt from the eighteenth to the early nineteenth century. There are remains of shop fronts of c.1840, with Corinthian capitals.

Number 73 (with 75–79) Built in 1718 by Caleb Waterfield and Thomas Cook, carpenters, and Nymphus Osborne (number 75), a Soho bricklayer. Number 73 has what appears to be an early-nineteenth-century façade, but the half-windows (blank) are a typical late-seventeenth- or very early eighteenth-century detail. Re-faced and retains remains of an early-nineteenth-century shop front.

Number 75 was the Three Compasses public house (and a Masonic lodge as early as 1728).[83] It was rebuilt in Jacobean style in 1847 but closed as a pub in 1886.

Numbers 77–79 date from the early eighteenth century but were re-fronted c.1800. On 79 is a shop front of 1850. On 77 and 79 the brick window arches and occasional horizontal courses of bricks have been stained red. Unusual and puzzling.

It was presumably a now lost building on one of the corners of Beak / Silver Street with Upper James Street that's mentioned by the alcoholic Newman Noggs in Charles Dickens's *Nicholas Nickleby*: 'if ever you want a shelter in London … they know where I live, at the sign of the Crown, in Silver Street, Golden Square … at the corner of Silver Street and James Street, with a bar-door both ways'.[84] The only slightly puzzling thing is that there is a pub of some age – also called the Crown – on the corner of Little James Street and Brewer Street. Were there two Crowns – one on each side of Golden Square? Or has Dickens misremembered and got his James Streets confused?

Excursions into Great Pulteney Street, Warwick Street, Golden Square, Lower John Street, Lower James Street

Great Pulteney Street

Laid out on the Pulteney estate in 1718, with thirty-six building leases granted by Sir William Pulteney from December 1718 to December 1720. It was one of the best streets of west Soho, comparable with the streets south of Soho Square, relatively wide, and with an intriguing if subtle shift of axis a third of the way along its length. It was residential rather than commercial in use through most of the eighteenth and nineteenth centuries, but now only a few of its early houses survive amidst replacement architecture devoid of interest (plates 1 and 2).

Number 23 Built *c*.1722/4, of *c*.1790 externally with a door surround with keystone and voussoirs. Thomas Sandy lived here 1751–3. Good original interior.

Number 35 Of 1720, three windows wide and four storeys above a basement, like all the houses in this group. Stucco-fronted, probably in the 1830s.

Number 36, also of 1720, appears to have been re-fronted – certainly colour-washed, but well done and some time ago. The ground floor was clad with stucco, presumably in the early nineteenth century when there was a fashion for this treatment.

Number 37, likewise of 1720, has a generally original brick façade, but sash boxes recessed in late-eighteenth-century manner. As with all the houses in this group, the windows have flat lintels made of rubbed brick, a slightly old-fashioned detail for 1719–20. This house has the only original doorcase in the group, with carved consoles supporting a cornice and a cushion-like pulvinated frieze.

Number 38 Of c.1719, with a handsome Doric pedimented doorcase of c.1780. Its brick façade is generally original, set above a stuccoed ground floor. It was occupied by John William Polidori, friend of Lord Byron, and author in 1819 of the pioneering Romanic movement novel *The Vampyre*.

Number 39, of 1719, has its original façade but is stucco-fronted.

Number 40 has a façade of 1719 and is well preserved. The red-brick dressings to the windows are usual for the date, but the flat brick lintels to the windows and the flat-faced string course above the first-floor window heads are slightly old-fashioned and typical artisan design of the period.

Numbers 38–40 were built by William Ludby, carpenter, but the entire group is loosely uniform. Impressive.

For me it remains impossible to walk along Great Pulteney Street and not mourn the loss of number 24. I didn't know the house personally because it was demolished in the early 1960s, having endured over two centuries of changing fortunes and wartime bombing (two of its neighbours – 25 and 26 – were burnt out by fire bombs during the Blitz). It had been built in 1720 and was one of the finest and best-preserved early Georgian houses in Soho. It had a particularly good brick façade and doorcase with carved consoles, and inside it retained virtually all its panelled rooms – of the highest quality – plus a spectacular staircase rising in a generous panelled well, and numerous early fire surrounds.

This was a Soho house of exceptional perfection and grandeur, and its destruction was an unforgivable act of barbarism.[85]

Warwick Street

Warwick Street was in existence by the sixteenth century (its line is shown on the 1585 estate plan of the area reproduced as plate 1a in the *Survey of London*, vol. XXXIV), as part of the lane connecting the road to Uxbridge, or Tyburn Road (now Oxford Street) to the east end of Piccadilly. The lane had its origin not only as a route between two major thoroughfares but also as a boundary between Gelding Close on its east and Mulghay Close on its west. In the mid seventeenth century the lane was known as Dog Row, and by the time it started to be lined with buildings, from the mid 1670s, it was called 'Marrowbone' Street because it led north to Marylebone. By the time of Ogilby and Morgan's London map of 1681–2 it had become Warwick Street; it is uncertain how or why this name was chosen.[86]

When control of Gelding Close was divided in 1675 (see p. 341), James Axtell took the land at the north end of the east side of Warwick Street, while Isaac Symball took the area forming the south end of the east side. The land parallel to the house plots on the west side of Golden Square was granted to speculators building houses facing onto the square. So the portion of Warwick Street west of Golden Square was generally used for the construction of coach-houses and stables serving houses on the square. From its origins, therefore, Warwick Street was not only subservient in its architectural ambition to Golden Square but also, to a degree, little more than its service road.

The ground forming the west side of Warwick Street, being part of Mulghay Close, was in different ownership and had a different building history. This land had, as we noted earlier, belonged to the Abbot and Convent of Abingdon until surrendered to the Crown in 1536 at the time of the Reformation. By 1590 Thomas Pultney (*sic*) had acquired a lease on these former monastic lands which by 1651 had been united into a five-acre parcel known as Mulghay Close or, occasionally, as Dog Field. The Pulteney family's interest in this Crown land was confirmed in 1661 by Henrietta Maria, who had received the land as part of the jointure settled on her by her husband Charles I when he was king, and in 1668 in a Crown lease that ran into the 1730s. After this Mulghay Close was laid out for building, including Swallow Street, the western boundary of Soho. The operations of the speculating builders to which the Pulteneys granted leases seem to have been so wayward, with houses started but not completed, that Sir Christopher Wren – in his capacity as Surveyor General of the King's Works – petitioned the king to intervene, which he duly did, issuing a proclamation in April 1671 to stop works. The speculators, severely chastened, promised to complete the existing houses in brick and stone, not to start new ones and not to let buildings to 'noisome' trades. Building restarted, and the west side of Warwick Lane was soon lined with houses.

These buildings were almost certainly not of the best sort and all were swept away when, in the early eighteenth century, the Pulteney family initiated its policy of rebuilding its Soho lands.[87] No doubt it was partly because Warwick Street was a service street for Golden Square, and partly because of the inferior quality of its Mulghay Close buildings, that in 1720 John Strype, in his *Survey of the Cities of London and Westminster*, rather dismissed it as 'a Place not over well built or inhabited'. However, he did note that there were, at its north end near the junction with Beak Street, 'some good Houses on both Sides'.[88]

The atmosphere of a subservient service road still lingers around Warwick Street, perhaps more so now than before. In large part this is due to the fact that its west side is formed mostly by the back sides of large retail and commercial buildings that face onto Regent Street, so many of the openings on Warwick Street are staff doors or lead to loading bays. And most buildings on the east side are large, unexceptional affairs in office use and include some of the rear elevations of the large early-twentieth-century commercial buildings on the west side of Golden Square. But among this generally undistinguished material there is one very rewarding gem.

The Roman Catholic Church of Our Lady of the Assumption is a building of tremendous historic importance – and not a little architectural significance – because, built in 1788, it marks the first phase of Roman Catholic emancipation in Britain. The Roman Catholic Relief Act of 1778 abolished onerous laws against Catholics and guaranteed their right to inherit land. The second Relief Act of 1782 permitted the establishment of Catholic schools, of dioceses under bishops, and the construction of churches, as long as they were discreet with no towers, spires or porticoes. With penal laws relaxed there was something of a modest boom in Catholic church-building, and this chapel is one of the best to survive. It was built here because a Catholic chapel, serving the Portuguese and then the Bavarian embassies housed in Golden Square, had stood near this site (see p. 346). The embassy chapel had been damaged in 1780 during the anti-Catholic Gordon Riots, repaired and put back into use, but when in 1788 the Bavarian embassy moved from Golden Square the future of this chapel was in doubt. Given the changes of law, a Catholic chapel no longer needed embassy protection to function; but who was to maintain it? A saviour appeared in the person of the Vicar Apostolic of the London region, James Talbot.

Upon the departure of the Bavarians, Talbot acquired long leases on the two former embassy buildings in the square and control of the chapel. The houses were useful for the diocese, but this was all about getting the chapel, or rather, getting a good site on which a bigger and better chapel – with a public face – could be built. Construction started in spring 1789 and the chapel was completed in 1791. Externally the chapel looks no different from other minor public buildings of the period, or indeed from chapels of other Christian beliefs. This of course was the intention. Catholics were safer in Britain than they had been for 250 years, but still they did not want to attract attention or provoke, and so were more than happy to follow the letter of the law and pursue discretion. The architect was Joseph Bonomi, a Roman Catholic and an Italian who had worked as an architect in Rome before moving to London in 1767, at the age of twenty-eight. In England he soon established himself as an able designer of country houses, in the then fashionable neoclassical manner of Robert Adam (for whom Bonomi had worked) and James Wyatt, so his appointment as architect for this West End Catholic chapel is no surprise.

Bonomi did a good job. The exterior of the chapel is restrained, built of brick, two storeys high and five windows wide, its only nod to monumentality being a three-window-wide central pediment rising from the building's cornice. The first-floor windows are arched and at ground level there are three doors serving the nave and aisles, each of which is furnished with minimal neo-classical details and a semicircular fanlight. The dark-red colour wash over the brickwork is the remains of a 1950s attempt to liven up this erudite and austere elevation. The gilded crosses and stars were also added at the same time.

The interior of the chapel has been significantly – but not catastrophically – altered and reordered and embellished, notably by the addition of a columned altarpiece in the 1850s that was in turn replaced in the 1870s by a Byzantine-style apse designed by J.F. Bentley. This was part of a plan to turn the chapel into a Byzantine-inspired fantasy. Money was not available and Bentley became distracted by the commission to design the vast Roman Catholic Cathedral in Victoria, Westminster, also neo-Byzantine. However, the beautification of the apse and altar continued gradually, with each additional veneer of marble and mosaic robbing the church of its admirably reticent Georgian character

Number 11, adjoining the chapel, has a plain brick front and must date from about the same time as the chapel. Its modesty of scale and ambition is a reminder of the original humble status of most of late-Stuart and Georgian Warwick Street.

Number 10, immediately to the south, is stucco-clad, with a projecting centre furnished with a wide – possibly workshop – window. This house dates from the early nineteenth century, again is humble, and confirms the street's relatively low status at the time Regent Street was being cut through the area, only a few hundred yards away.

Golden Square

Golden Square, created on a large field known as Gelding's Close (see p. 54), had a troubled early history. It lies in the parish of St James's, Westminster, and in 1670, when other land in the parish was being profitably transformed into smart new houses (notably St James's Square and its environs such as Jermyn Street), there was a move to build upon the close. But this was stymied initially because its leasehold tenure was contested. The primary claimants were John Emlyn and James Axtell, a carpenter or bricklayer. However, by the end of 1671 the dispute had been resolved by Emlyn and Axtell buying off competition. But that was not the end of their problems. During the 1670s there was a growing fear – on the part of court and government – that the expansion of London was too rapid, reckless and ungoverned, and that the consequences could be not just architecturally but also socially and politically disastrous. The construction of swathes of poor-quality houses on ill-drained sites was hardly calculated to create a handsome and habitable city and – perhaps worse still – would attract mobs of unruly settlers from the country. The rural economy would suffer, and if the majority of the settlers struggled to find work they could become riotous even rebellious.

Sir Christopher Wren, as Surveyor General of the

King's Works, reported to the Privy Council in March 1671 his concern about the excessive number of unlicensed buildings arising in 'Dog Fields, Windmill Fields and the Fields adjoining to So Hoe'.[89] This obviously rattled Emlyn and Axtell, who soon after petitioned the Privy Council (through a nominee named James Long) for a building licence. In the petition they explained their desire to erect on Gelding Close 'such houses as might accommodate Gentry, and not being the least Charge upon the Parish, but be an advancement to the Poor'. This petition was duly passed to Wren for his opinion.[90]

It failed. These were delicate times, in which the recent social and political upheaval of the Civil War still cast a long shadow. A second petition was submitted in 1673, but this time Axtell's name was omitted. The speculation is that Axtell dared not submit a second petition in his own name to the Privy Council because one of the men who in 1649 signed the death warrant for Charles I was Colonel Daniel Axtell, presumably a relative. Colonel Axtell had been hanged, drawn and quartered in 1660 for treason.[91] At the same time £200 was paid to a Mr Wright, a Chancery official, to obtain the required patent. Wren was again consulted and this time worried about the drainage of the land and that building upon the close might endanger the water supply to the royal palaces at Whitehall and St James's. But upon close inspection of the ground Wren withdrew his objections and in September 1673 Charles II granted a patent 'to frame, erect and build' such houses and buildings in the said close 'according to the modell and forme ... designe draught mapp or Chart' annexed to the patent. As the *Survey of London* explains, 'the new buildings were to be of brick or stone, and the petitioners were to maintain them in repair. There were to be "substantial pavements" and "sufficient sewers", and "noysome and offensive trades" were forbidden.'⁹²

The 'modell' of the plan of the square survives in the National Archives at Kew,⁹³ and is signed by Wren; but it is not clear whether this plan was made by Wren or merely approved by him. It is an interesting and subtle design. The square is almost a true square in shape, with all four corners kept closed, but in a most tentative manner. The re-entrant angles are formed by simply arranging that the street frontages of the houses in the streets entering the square are set slightly forward of the elevations of the houses in the square itself. The intention was to create a sense of enclosure in minimal manner and without compromising communication.

As for house elevations, the objective at Golden Square, as it had been at St James's Square, was to ensure that individual houses did not assert themselves but – through seemly uniformity and simplicity – gave the square a sense of relaxed harmony. There was no intention to pressure individual builders to create unified compositions such as palace fronts with central pediments, columns and pilasters.

Within a few months of the patent, construction of the square started when Emlyn and Axtell granted William Partridge, a local blacksmith, a building lease on a plot on which eventually rose numbers 17 and 19. Soon after work started, Emlyn's half-share in the close passed to Isaac Symball, to whom Emlyn was probably seriously in debt.

Axtell and Symball soon fell out and went to court over the division of their ownership of the close. This delayed progress and by the late 1670s both seem to have been

inclined to go it alone rather than attempt to collaborate.
By 1679 Axtell had divided his portion of the square into
building plots, but he died before work got under way.
Symball had made more progress, having leased several
plots by 1679. But Axtell's death, issues of inheritance
(Axtell's land went to two nieces who were minors and
legally unable to grant leases), and the uncertain nature
of the district for such a socially ambitious development
ensured that progress on the square was slow. It was not
until 1684, when the nieces' mother, Martha Axtell, made
a covenant with four local speculating tradesmen (including Partridge), that work resumed on the Axtell portion.
Martha Axtell appears to have been a shrewd businesswoman. She got better terms than Symball – higher rents
and shorter leases (which meant that buildings and land
would revert more quickly to her family) – and moved
faster. Much of her portion of the square was built by
the late 1680s. But then there was another setback. In
January 1695 Symball was playing cards in his Soho home
with a Mr Raneer when a quarrel broke out which ended
with Symball being stabbed to death.[94] So it was not until
the first decade of the eighteenth century that all four
sides of the square were complete. The disputes between
the Symball and the Axtell factions and the delays and
difficulties of letting buildings around the square had all
contributed to the compromise of the initial quest for
uniformity and architectural consistency of elevations. As
the *Survey of London* points out, 'of the first five houses to
be built in the square (Nos. 20–24, all on Symball's land)
only two (Nos. 20 and 21) had similar fronts, probably
because they were both built under the same lease. Nos.
22 and 23, although both leased to Andrew Laurence, had

differing heights, the latter having the same number of
storeys as its other neighbour, No. 24, which was one of
the first house to be built in Golden Square.'[95] Slightly
later buildings were more uniform, largely because
Martha Axtell and her four developer partners agreed
in 1683 to erect terraces of houses 'with heights of sto-
ryes, ornaments to the fronts, scantlings and goodness
of timber and substantialness in Brickwork answerable
to the buildings neere thereunto and of the second rate
of building'.[96] The 'rate' refers to the London Building
Act of 1667, which classed different scales and types of
building into various rates.

The consequence of this agreement was that the houses
built on Axtell's land achieved a reasonably high state of
uniformity, particularly those on the south side of the
square. Symball, probably noting the commercial as well
as artistic success of this approach, followed suit and the
leases he granted in 1685 contained covenants requiring
lessees to build houses 'uniform in front to the best of
the houses ... fronting the said Square ... with a height of
stories, ornaments to the front, scantlings and goodness
of timber and substantialness of brickwork answerable
to the said buildings designed for the pattern thereof'.[97]

These covenants governing the design and construction
of the houses around the square, and the circumstances
in which they evolved, are fascinating. They confirm
the desire to create architectural uniformity and reveal
the commercial and legal mechanism by which this was
achieved in late-Stuart London.

The intention to develop Golden Square as an aristocratic enclave, comparable to St James's Square, succeeded
at first. As the *Survey of London* notes:

By the time all thirty-nine houses had been completed
and occupied in 1707, there were living in the square a
duchess, six peers or future peers (including a future
duke), a bishop, six army officers and a number of other
residents of title. This was the heyday of Golden Square
as a political and social centre. Barbara Villiers, Duchess
of Cleveland, lived at No. 7. James Brydges, the future
Duke of Chandos ... lived at No. 20 and ... next to him
lived Henry St. John, later Viscount Bolingbroke, the
leading Tory politician of the day, whose house was
frequently the scene of the convivial assembly of his
political and literary associates.[98]

But Soho's gradual social decline, combined with the
development to the west and north of the aristocratic
Burlington, Cavendish-Harley and Grosvenor estates,
meant that the social prestige of Golden Square was
undermined and challenged. By 1740 only one peer still
lived there. Its gilded age as a place of fashion had passed.
Instead, as aristocrats moved west, the square gradually
became a favoured domain for foreign diplomats. The
first to arrive had been a Portuguese ambassador, who
lived at numbers 23 and 24 from 1724 until 1747; then a
Bavarian ambassador, who remained in the houses until
1788; the Brunswick ambassador lived at 19a from 1728
until 1734; the Russian Tsarina's ambassador at number 6
from 1732 to 1737, and the Genoese ambassador at number
30 from 1755 to 1759. The square also became the residence
of a number of more successful artists. One of the first
was Elizabeth Gamberini, a dancer, who lived at number
13 from 1753 to 1763, while Angelica Kauffman, the painter,

lived at number 16 from 1767 to 1781.

By 1839, according to Charles Dickens in *Nicholas Nickleby*, Golden Square had become 'a great resort of foreigners', and was then no more than a gloomy backwater; 'although a few members of the graver professions live about Golden square, it is not exactly in anybody's way to or from anywhere. It is one of the squares that have been: a quarter of the town that has gone down in the world, and taken to letting lodgings.'[99] In *Nicholas Nickleby* Dickens placed Ralph Nickleby in Golden Square (probably in number 7, demolished long ago, and once occupied by a friend of Dickens), and describes the square's community:

Two or three violins and a wind instrument from the Opera band reside within its precincts. Its boarding-houses are musical, and the notes of pianos and harps float in the evening time round the head of the mournful statue, the guardian genius of a little wilderness of shrubs, in the centre of the square. On a summer's night, windows are thrown open, and groups of swarthy mustachio'd men are seen by the passer-by lounging at the casements, and smoking fearfully. Sounds of gruff voices practising vocal music invade the evening's silence, and the fumes of choice tobacco scent the air. There, snuff and cigars, and German pipes and flutes, and violins, and violoncellos, divide the supremacy between them. It is the region of song and smoke. Street bands are on their mettle in Golden Square, and itinerant glee singers quaver involuntarily as they raise their voices within its boundaries.[100]

As well as a place of boarding houses and small hotels,

mid- and late-nineteenth-century Golden Square housed French Roman Catholic nuns (at 23 in the 1870s), a French Protestant school for descendants of seventeenth-century Huguenots and a fencing school – both at number 10. Also, doctors and other professionals such as solicitors and engineers and architects occupied offices in the square, almost invariably within its late-seventeenth- and early-eighteenth-century houses. But in the late nineteenth century came change, redevelopment and a regrettable surge in scale that broke the spell – indeed the backbone – of Dickens's long-forgotten square. During the last quarter of the nineteenth century it became the centre of London's woollen and worsted trade and, · as the *Survey of London* records, this new commercial character 'was reflected in the demolition before 1914 of nineteen of the thirty-nine domestic buildings in the square and in the subsequent erection of large new office and warehouse blocks'. The artistic consequence has been most unfortunate. The *Survey of London*, generally most measured in its appraisals of London's changing scene, is mildly but determinedly – and rightfully – damning about the fate that had befallen Golden Square. In 1963, when the *Survey* volume covering Golden Square was published, it observed that the square 'now presents a sorry contrast with its original appearance ... The central area, with its anaemic paved garden, seems much reduced in size by being enclosed by buildings that vary greatly in width, height and scale, and affect a wide range of styles and a medley of materials. With a few notable exceptions, they jostle and vie with each other, and the south end, in particular, presents a jagged skyline of ill-assorted gables, a nightmare *Grande Place* effect.'[101]

In 1963 there were, according to the *Survey of London*, four surviving domestic buildings of architectural or historic interest in the square – numbers 11, 21, 23 and 24 – and three 'later buildings which call for comment' – Holland and Sherry's warehouse in the south-west angle, numbers 25–29 by Mewes and Davis, and numbers 34–36 by Leonard Stokes. Fortunately these survive and still represent all that is important architecturally about Golden Square. During the last fifty years or so, nothing of any artistic significance has been added, despite the square being the self-proclaimed 'centre' of London's 'creative', film and media industries with advertising agencies and film production companies littering it and the streets around it. This, of course, is a most sorry reflection of the architectural poverty of our times.

Number 11 This site was leased for fifty-one years in 1684 by Martha Axtell and her associates to William Pye, a local carpenter. A covenant in the lease required Pye to build a house 'uniform in front and answerable in the building thereof to a messuage of Andrew Laurence fronting the square'. Laurence had built number 23 in the same year and this covenant adds extra information about the manner in which the main projectors of the square achieved architectural uniformity: they constructed 'model' houses and then bound subsequent speculating builders to emulate them.[102]

In 1778 the house was demolished and rebuilt with details of a fashionable, neoclassical form inspired by the contemporary work of Robert Adam. In 1954 the façade of the house was rebuilt in a reasonably faithful manner but with the bricks, pointing and mortar all being clearly modern and somewhat crude, particularly the window arches. At the same time the neoclassically detailed string course and cornice were also rebuilt using original material – made of Coade stone, a patent terracotta most popular at the time. The door surround, loaded with neoclassical details – including Doric pilasters with fluted necking and guilloche ornament on their shafts, urns, rams' heads, altars, garlands and a lyre – is most unusual and also of the original reused Coade stone. The interior of the house survives from the 1778 rebuilding, and includes a first-floor ceiling featuring Poseidon and a handsome timber-built staircase with a cast- and wrought-iron balustrade.

Numbers 19a and 20 were demolished in 1886 and replaced by the existing warehouse and office building for Holland and Sherry. This building portrays very accurately the way things were going to go in Golden Square, old houses being swept away and larger commercial buildings built instead. In fact, although this single building replaced two houses, it does not rise particularly high and is a handsome and fascinating example of classical design. The façade is formed by narrow brick piers, treated as pilasters, with windows set between them. The only odd thing is that this bold design looks as if it was produced in the 1840s, so it is certainly something of a throwback.

Number 21 This house appears to have been rebuilt – or at least very thoroughly remodelled – in the late eighteenth century (plate 31) With its widely spaced windows and austerity of elevation it possesses the air of sophisticated simplicity fashionable at the time. The only significant external ornament is the broad fanlight above the front door, but even this is becomingly reserved. The interior is equally simple, boasting little more than elegant plaster cornices in the main rooms. The occupants of the previous house on the site included the Jacobite states- man Viscount Bolingbroke from 1702 until 1714, when he fled to France to join the Old Pretender. The house and its contents were sequestered by the Commissioners for Forfeited Estates and then occupied by Lady Masham, formerly Bolingbroke's political ally.

Number 22 is a wonderfully insensitive interloper. It is the width of a single late-seventeenth-century house but rises, as a striking sliver of a building, seven storeys high and so looms over its aged neighbours in the manner of a mini-skyscraper. It is broadly classical, with a central crowning pediment and bay rising the full height of the building, but its large windows are spare in detail, giving the building an industrial utilitarian look.

It was built in 1915 as offices and showrooms for a Huddersfield woollen firm and designed by the architects Naylor and Sale. The audacity of this newcomer and its utter disregard for the scale and prevailing architectural character of the square says much about weak planning controls at the time and about the contempt with which historic sites like Golden Square were viewed. The very design of the building, with its brutal and blank party walls, was a provocation to neighbouring owners to follow suit and build high. Luckily the immediate neigh- bours showed decent restraint.

Number 23 Built in 1675 with the now lost 22. The sites had been granted by Isaac Symball to Cadogan Thomas of Lambeth, merchant, for a 1,000-year term. The façade of the house has been much altered but the first- and second-floor portion, with flat window lintels and string courses, is probably original. The top floor is almost certainly an early addition and the simple front door, with its semicircular fanlight, is a late-eighteenth-century alteration. Inside, the original late-seventeenth-century staircase survives, set within a fully panelled compartment.

The house was first occupied in 1684 by Lord Hunsdon, and in 1724 taken, as we have noted, by the Portuguese ambassador and then the Bavarian ambassador, Count Haslang, who remained in post until his death in 1783. When in 1780 anti-Catholic Gordon Rioters attacked the house and its chapel, to the rear on Warwick Street, it was assumed that the rioters were not so much after the chapel as the large store of spirits the ambassador – thought by many to have abused his diplomatic privilege to profiteer as a smuggler – was believed to have secreted within his embassy. Horace Walpole perhaps expressed the common opinion at the time when he wrote that Haslang was 'a prince of smugglers' and that 'great quantities of rum, tea and contraband goods were found in his house [by the rioters]. Thus one cannot lament.'[103]

Number 24, probably the first house to be built in the square, was begun in 1675 and is one of the oldest surviving domestic buildings in London. The building lease was granted by Isaac Symball to Andrew Laurence. It is now a curious house to contemplate. *The Survey of London* states that its 'much altered carcase [is] of about the same date as number 23',[104] but the floor levels and window heads are higher than those of number 23, confirming that the visual uniformity of the square was compromised from the beginning. But perhaps stranger is the design of its elevation. With its segmental window arches and red-brick window dressings it looks like typical work of the second decade of the eighteenth century. But the bond of the brick is continuous with that of number 23 and the colour matches, which is odd if the façade of 23 is late-seventeenth-century. If this is in fact the case, and the façade of 24 dates from the 1720s, there should be a straight joint between the two. But there is not. It's hard to reach a conclusion about this puzzle, other than that, despite their difference, both façades in fact date from the 1720s. But why was one rebuilt in the style of the time and another in the style of the 1670s? We know that from 1724 both houses were occupied by the Portuguese ambassador so a related treatment to their façades during the 1720s was easy to achieve. Number 24 has an arched front door of late-eighteenth-century design to match that of number 23. Both doors were, presumably, commissioned by the Roman Catholic Vicar Apostolic. The fanlight also matches that of 23, and the radiating bars are of unusual design. They appear to be made of cast metal (probably lead rather than iron, although the *Survey of London* suggests they are made of wood) and each bar is topped with a foliate design. Can they be intended to represent palm trees, and so carry a Christian message?

Numbers 25–29 A massive commercial block, built in 1923–4, which not only occupies the sites of five late-seventeenth-century houses on Golden Square but also extends to the west to occupy the sites of early houses on Warwick Street. The model offered by number 22 – heedless of the square's architectural history or existing character – was pursued with a vengeance. The huge block was built to house offices and warehousing for the woollen firm of Dormeuil Frères, who evidently aimed to rise to the status of its large West End site by employing

one of the grandest London architectural practices of
the time. Mewès and Davis, who in 1905 had designed
the Ritz Hotel, were brought in to – presumably – give
this block of offices and warehousing some architectural
panache. Mewès and Davis had developed a Franco-
American Beaux-Arts classical style – expressed with
vigour at the Rue de Rivoli-inspired Ritz – combined
with fast and efficient modern methods of construction.
The result in Golden Square is a long, high and rigidly
symmetrical palace front, clad in Portland stone over a
steel structural frame. The relationship between windows
and wall is pretty traditional – the steel frame makes wide
windows and narrow areas of wall possible – and the
central emphasis of the composition is rather timid (essentially only a pediment above an upper-level window),
with most thought, it seems, going into the problem of
how to build high while keeping broadly faithful to the
Renaissance conventions of classical composition.

As with sixteenth-century palazzi, there is a rusticated
ground floor (in fact double-storey in height because it
incorporates a tall basement), a two-storey piano nobile
(with upper windows crowned with cornices), an attic-like
third floor, then a main cornice and above it yet another
attic. Topping all is a tall roof, incorporating dormers and
another floor level, so seven useful floors were achieved,
and the conventions of traditional urban classical composition adhered to – just about. But, having said that, the
façade is a lacklustre affair, Parisian in flavour, with little to
do with Soho history, its main characteristic being monot-
ony rather than sublime restraint. The *Survey of London*
calls it 'unexciting', which I think is being generous.

Numbers 34–36 A large commercial building, erected

on the sites of three late-seventeenth-century houses, that dominates the north side of the square. It was erected for the wool merchants Gagniere in 1914, a year before the mini-skyscraper of number 22, and so is – just – the earliest surviving example of the wave of tall commercial buildings that were to transform the appearance and life of the square. As it happens, this first experiment in high-rise commercial architecture in the square is by far the most interesting and successful. The architect was Leonard Stokes, and he forged an idiosyncratic essay that blends the structural and artistic potential offered by modern steel-framed construction with the pedigree and delight afforded by the use of history and ornament to realise the functional requirements of the commercial brief.

So the windows are large – as steel-framed construction permitted – and the interior light. The historic pedigree comes from the use, albeit in a very personal and minimal manner, of the classical language of design. So, again, it has a symmetrical façade with an array of classical details, some most odd, such as the wreath-like cartouche capitals topping the rusticated pilasters. The delight comes from some luscious carved detail, mostly plant-inspired and a strange fusion of Art Nouveau, Baroque and Rococo – for example, the cavetto cornice with its acanthus leaf and shell carving in an amended late-seventeenth-century style and, incorporated within the ground-floor arcade, cartouches and keystones with swirling asymmetrical plant forms and lettering. Sykes was evidently attempting to create a modern, functionalist and commercial architecture that was still based – to a degree – on tradition and that incorporated history-inspired as well as more organic ornament. Nikolaus Pevsner, who always had an eye open for pioneers of functionalist 'Modern' design, was enthusiastic. He wrote that this 'fine façade' was in the 'modern spirit' and was particularly impressed that the 'large tripartite windows' had 'hardly any period details'.[105] This façade, once you get your eye in, is thought-provoking, which is quite an achievement for any twentieth-century commercial architecture.

Lower John Street

Numbers 1 and 2 Modest houses of c.1800

Number 4 Of c.1685, altered, stucco-clad but with half-windows to each storey, typical of the date. These are all blank, but if open could have lit small closets formed by the deep projection of the chimney breast into the volumes of the rooms.

Lower James Street

Number 7 Late-eighteenth-century.

Carnaby Street

Carnaby Street was laid out in 1685, within the Six Acre Close. It takes its name from Karnaby House, which stood on the east side of the street and – started in 1683 – seems to have been the structure around which the new street was orientated. The house had been constructed by the bricklayer Richard Tyler, who built much on Six Acre Close. Carnaby Street was lined by buildings by 1690, most of them small and occupied by Huguenots, and rebuilt during the 1720s when the land came under the control of William Lowndes (see p. 88). The street remained modest in its social aspirations and was again largely rebuilt from 1821 to 1825, along with the streets to its east, after the closure and demolition of Carnaby market (see p. 94). Consequently, between Carnaby and Newburgh Streets and up to Ganton and Marshall Streets there are substantial remains of an 1820s 'model' shopping and residential area, with uniform houses and shop fronts. The force behind this early-nineteenth-century redevelopment was Lord Craven, who from the late eighteenth century extended his interest from Pesthouse Close to the east to Six Acre Close, on which these streets mostly stand (see p. 54).

The buildings, built largely on the site of Carnaby market, are often individually handsome with simple but sophisticated detail. If nothing else, they reveal how the basic component of the late-Georgian city – terrace houses run up by artisans – can possess erudite beauty and simple dignity; how structures built for profit can be works of art by accident. Buildings like those in Newburgh Street, mostly intended as homes above shops, still offer lessons in urban design, and still present prototypes that can only be emulated and rarely bettered.

Numbers 22–30 (continuous) were built in the early to mid 1820s (but 22 and 23 were re-fronted) in a simple and uniform manner that relates to contemporary developments of houses with shops in adjoining Marshall Street (notably 33–37), Ganton Street (2–8) and Newburgh Street (1–10 and 11–12). These developments are connected to Carnaby Street by Lowndes Court and Marlborough Court, which also contain modest early-nineteenth-century commercial buildings.

Numbers 45, 46 and 47 are also of *c*.1820–25; all are four windows wide but, in number 45 the middle brick pier of the façade is slightly wider than the flanking piers. This suggests that this house was built as two, two-window-wide houses.

As well as these buildings in Carnaby Street and the adjoining streets and courts, all of which form a generally coherent development, particularly moving are the uniform shop fronts in Newburgh Street and Marshall Street with their elegant pilasters and occasional minimalist fanlights (for example, 37 Marshall Street).

Ganton Street

Numbers 2–8 form a uniform group of *c*.1821–5, related to adjoining terraces of similar scale and age in Marshall Street and Newburgh Street (plate 32). All are with shops, as was no doubt originally the case.

Numbers 10 and 12 with a corner house (number 17 Newburgh Street) date from *c*.1720, and are modest and much-altered survivals of the period when the Carnaby Street area was rebuilt by the Lowndes estate. They all have flat window heads, are all clad with later stucco and all have later shop fronts.

Of similar date is the stucco-clad house on the corner of Little Marlborough Street and Great Marlborough Street which closes the vista north along Carnaby Street, and which now forms part of the store Liberty. Until the 1980s this housed the Grapes public house – regarded as Carnaby Street's local – which had been at this location since at least the 1830s.

Numbers 24 and 26 A modest and plain pair of

c.1790, number 26 with particularly pleasing brickwork in authentic condition. Well-wrought brick window arches and much tuckpointing survive. Both have modern shop fronts.

Foubert's Place

The Shakespeare's Head public house, on the corner with Carnaby Street, is a full-blooded gabled and brick-built neo-Tudor building of *c*.1900 – and not without a touch of wit, because above the pub's main door is a bust of Shakespeare peering from a small casement. The hand is missing, having been blown off, it is claimed, during the war when a bomb dropped nearby – a fairly unlikely story since bombs are not generally so surgical. The pub claims to date from 1735, when it was owned by Thomas and John Shakespeare. Its site is intriguing because it roughly marks the boundary between ancient fields and estates including Six Acre Close and the Millfield.

The centre of the north side of the street is formed by a mixed group of modest early-nineteenth-century brick-built houses with later shops; **Number 13** is a good example.

Number 12 is a modest two-window-wide house of *c*.1800, perhaps with fragmentary remains of an early-nineteenth-century shop front.

Number 22 is two windows wide and four storeys high, with top windows square in proportion to read as an attic. The front is stucco-clad and has crude architraves to the windows, but the house probably dates from the Lowndes redevelopment of the early 1720s.

Kingly Street

Known until 1906 as King Street, this long, narrow street ran almost parallel to Swallow Street before it was mostly swept away in the early nineteenth century for the construction of Regent Street. Kingly Street evolved as a footpath from Marylebone and Piccadilly through Six Acre Close (see p. 54). The close was Crown land on leasehold to the Pulteney family. A short length of the north end of Kingly Street marked a boundary within the Millfield. Despite its narrowness, Kingly Street's location on the western edge of Soho, relatively near the aristocratic estates, around Hanover Square and Piccadilly, ensured that, at the beginning of the eighteenth century, it was well occupied. In 1720 John Strype noted, in his *Survey of the Cities of London and Westminster*, that it was 'a pretty good street, having divers very good houses fit for Gentry'. Things have changed. Kingly Street now forms much of the western edge of Soho and, as a boundary street living in the shadow of Regent Street, has a rather strange character. Its west side consists almost exclusively of the looming rear portions of large twentieth-century stores fronting onto Regent Street, but its east side is a lively mix of generally small-scale eighteenth-, nineteenth- and early-twentieth-century buildings in a wide variety of commercial uses – including three pubs, which is now a rarity in any London street.

The street numbering starts from the south end, on the corner with Beak Street. The east side, marking the edge of the Lowndes estate, was first built between 1688 and 1693, but generally rebuilt during the 1720s as part of the coherent redevelopment of the estate. William Lowndes, a politician and shrewd investor in real estate, had acquired the land in 1692–3 when Sir William Pulteney's trustees decided to sell the part of Six Acre Close in which he had an interest; this was to pay debts and legacies following Sir William's death in 1691. Initially Lowndes could make little money from his new property because the rents on the existing late-seventeenth-century buildings were reserved for the speculators who had built them. But the position changed in 1723, which prompted Lowndes to initiate a programme of rebuilding.

Numbers 1 and 2 stand on land forming the north edge of Gelding Close and so were initially developed, in the 1680s, under the control of James Axtell and Isaac Symball (see p. 366). Number 1 was probably rebuilt or re-fronted in the early nineteenth century and its front stuccoed in the mid nineteenth century. It is only two windows wide, but its elevation is framed by a pair of giant Doric fluted pilasters supporting a handsome entablature ornamented with consoles. The Doric capitals have neoclassical detail – all very sophisticated. Presumably the design echoes, in reduced manner, the architecture built along Regent Street, under John Nash's control, between 1817 and 1825. This building suggests the aspirations of early-nineteenth-century Kingly Street, recently ennobled by the construction nearby, on Crown land, of Regent Street, one of the most architecturally ambitious streets in Britain. Number 2 is a good brick house of c.1800 still with its original house door, which incorporates an arched opening with a plain but pretty fanlight.

Numbers 7 and 8 An intriguing pair. Stuccoed, with much nineteenth-century ornament and modern shops;

but the size, disposition and proportion of the windows reveal that they date from the Lowndes rebuilding of the east side of the street soon after 1720. Number 7 retains a panelled entrance hall (which can be glimpsed through the fanlight above the door), complete with cornice, and a dog-leg staircase with closed strings, turned balusters and column newels – all typical of the 1720s.[106]

Numbers 9, 10 and 11 form a curious group of three stuccoed four-storey houses, each framed by giant pilasters – a mix of Doric and Ionic – linked by wide arches, so it seems that the three two-window-wide houses (which date from the 1720s) are peering through a huge arcade. A most strange conceit, also perhaps inspired by nearby Regent Street, although the somewhat crude detailing on these houses suggests a later nineteenth-century date. The reason for this ornamental façade is, perhaps, that it stands nearly opposite the narrow Tenison Court and so would, more or less, have closed a vista from Regent Street. Number 9 once housed the Bag O'Nails public house, which became a music club in the 1960s and was where Jimi Hendrix gave one of his earliest London performances, in November 1968. It's now a private members' club.

Tenison Court itself was once of considerable interest. Its north side was occupied by a proprietary chapel built in 1702 by Dr Thomas Tenison, the Archbishop of Canterbury. The chapel was dedicated to St Thomas in memory of the English medieval saint who was killed in Canterbury Cathedral. The east end of the chapel played a visually dominant role in Kingly Street. The elevation was well composed, although with virtually no architectural detail. Obviously, money had been an issue. The centre was tall, contained a large arched east window, and was topped by a steep-sided pediment that was formed in a most curious manner: it followed the slope of the top portion of the wide pitched roof that covered the building's central nave. This was a charming attempt to give a simple vernacular structure classical pedigree and was in its way most successful. The lower portions of the pitched roof, set below the raking sides of the pediment, looked reminiscent of Andrea Palladio's seminal sixteenth-century Venetian churches – notably San Giorgio Maggiore – with their main façades displaying overlaid and intersecting pediments of different widths and heights (see p. 280).

This pediment-topped centre broke forward of lower wings containing the aisles. Each of these wings had, on the Kingly Street elevation, a door and an arched window, slightly smaller in scale than the central window. The simplicity of this elevation was made somewhat dour because it was covered with cement, patchy and unpainted, which had been applied in the 1950s as a solution, far cheaper than proper re-pointing, to the problem of water penetration through portions of the façade brickwork.

St Thomas's has a very elevated history. In the mid 1680s Tenison, when rector of St James's, Piccadilly, had erected a wood-built 'tabernacle' on the site that was a private church open to the public. It became a fashionable place in which to hear sermons in an age when sermons were regarded as – potentially at least – popular entertainment. This successful chapel was at least a part of Tenison's route to high office, being made archbishop in 1694. But Tenison's tabernacle soon became more than just a chapel offering him a preaching platform. It did attract large congregations from all parts of the city, but it also played an increasingly important role in local parish business because the population of the area was rising rapidly in the late seventeenth century, putting pressure on the new churches of St James's, Piccadilly, and St Anne's, Soho. Soon they were unable to cope, so the tabernacle became a chapel-of-ease for them – essentially a third parish church for Soho and for the east portion of the parish of St James's. By 1702 the timber tabernacle, although not old, was no longer up to the job and the trustees running it chose to rebuild.

The designer is unknown, but a carpenter named John Ludby was put in charge of construction and it is more than likely that the design was also his. The project was placed under the supervision of Sir Christopher Wren, who had been involved in the design of St Anne's, Soho, and had designed St James's, Piccadilly.[107] The broad similarity of the east elevations of St Thomas's and St Anne's suggests that Wren's role in the design of the latter might have been more than merely supervisory. Internally the church had a basilica plan, with a wide and high central nave with a shallow arched plaster ceiling. The nave was flanked by lower aisles containing galleries supported on columns, and was lit primarily by the arched windows in the east elevation. Again, much like St Anne's.

When I first saw the church in the very early 1970s it seemed unused but not derelict. The *Survey of London* volume on the area, published in 1963, observed that it had been put in good repair in recent years, had become a centre of 'liturgical research' but, somewhat ominously, also recorded that its future 'is at present uncertain'. This should have been warning enough, but I was young and trusting and assumed this remarkable survival was protected by its age and status – notably its connection with the Archbishop of Canterbury and with Wren, and by its recently enhanced rarity as an early-eighteenth-century church in the heart of the West End. After all, it had been spared during the Second World War whereas the body of St Anne's had been destroyed and St James's gutted. I photographed the church's admittedly somewhat gloomy exterior, and moved on in search of seemingly less high-profile and more vulnerable historic buildings to document. But I was naïve. When I next visited the church, not long after, it had been reduced to rubble, a mound of which was visible through its small east doors. This was a shocking eye-opener. Evidently no building was safe if it stood in the way of profitable rebuilding schemes, and any weaknesses – such as this building's gradual loss of its congregation, its poor maintenance and unsightly cement-rendered exterior – would be ruthlessly exploited. I remain staggered by this demolition, which was a particularly vicious act of barbarous desecration.[108]

Number 14 The Red Lion, a handsome little public house designed in neo-Tudor manner in the early twentieth century, with a tier of shallow bay windows. It possesses a pretty Tudor/early-seventeenth-century-style interior with much panelling and generous joinery. The pub's design dates from a time when brewers were attempting to make their pubs more family-friendly affairs, usually offering small dining rooms and snugs, to counter pubs' fearful reputation as desperate, male-dominated, heavy-drinking establishments that intimidated women and middle-class customers. History was a tool in this campaign, with neo-Tudor and neo-Georgian being the preferred styles for the newly comfy and friendly pubs.

Number 18 Another pub, the Blue Posts. Slightly earlier – indeed, more of a standard late-Victorian pub design – and, typically, a bit showy, with a large arch at second-floor level embracing a balustraded open gallery from which there could never have been much of view, other than the chimney-stacks of Regent Street.

Number 19 This appears to be a mid-nineteenth-century house.

Number 34 Yet another public house, the Clachan, dated 1898 and conceived as an ornate and escapist 'gin-palace' – typical of the time – with much flamboyant seventeenth-century-style ornament, including an oriel and a turret reflecting its Scottish theme. The interior would have been furnished with mirrors and etched and cut glass, magnifying the effect of the bright, flickering gas lamps with which the pub would originally have been fitted. The object of all this ostentation was to cast the pub in stark, enticing and attractive contrast to the cramped and drab homes which most of its local customers would have occupied and, no doubt, longed to escape. Although altered, the interior retains much, including the bar, ornamented ceiling, cast-iron columns with handsome capitals, and a glazed timber-made screen. The plan of the interior would have been a late-Victorian world in miniature that mirrored the social structure of the age, with a saloon bar for the local bosses, a public bar for the workers and snugs for those seeking a bit of privacy.

Great Marlborough Street

In the very early eighteenth century this was one of the great and stately streets of Soho, indeed of London. Initially its occupants were grand and it remained relatively well inhabited even in the late nineteenth century, when much of west Soho had descended into the twilight world of squalor, overcrowding and sweated labour suffered by immigrant communities. But little of the architectural quality or atmosphere of this once-fine street survives, and now there are less than half a dozen buildings of age and architectural distinction.

The street's origin and early ambitions lie in the confident vision of the speculating builder Joseph Collens, who in 1704 laid it out in high style on the portion of the Millfield then held leasehold by the gentleman investor John Steele. Together they were able to persuade other speculators to put money into a number of large houses and – more importantly – secure occupants of means and high status.

The east end of the street was laid out on Little Gelding's Close, the development of which also lay in Collens's sphere of influence. Buildings here seem to have been somewhat less ambitious.

The name of the street was intended to add a touch of patriotic class by commemorating the Duke of Marlborough's politically and strategically highly significant victory at Blenheim in 1704. In apparently the same patriotic spirit, the narrow street running north from the centre of Great Marlborough Street to Oxford Street is called **Ramillies Street**, commemorating a battle fought by Marlborough in 1706. Does this date the street? In fact it does not, because originally and until 1885 it was named Blenheim Street. Off Blenheim Street was a mews originally called 'Blenheim Mewse', serving the houses on the north side of Great Marlborough Street. This makes it clear that by 1704 the arrangement had been established – soon developed on a large scale on the Cavendish-Harley and then the Grosvenor estates – of creating urban blocks formed by houses facing main streets, with a yard or garden to the rear of the houses, and at the far end of that a coach house, stables and servants' lodgings served by a mews. This was a most convenient plan if the house was large and valuable enough to justify the space required, and became the standard form in London for spacious developments on green-field sites into the mid nineteenth century.

Blenheim Street was well known in the early nineteenth century as the location of Joshua Brookes's 'Vivarium', a large, stone-built grotto in which he kept live birds and animals, including an eagle, a fox, a racoon and a tortoise. This folly did not long outlive his death in 1833.

The only notable thing now about Ramillies Street is that it terminates with a flight of steps that rise several metres to connect with Oxford Street. Level changes do not seem to have been a major issue during the development of Soho. In other parts of London as it expanded in the late seventeenth and early eighteenth centuries, ground often had to be levelled, generally to deal with undulations made by earlier buildings, by ditches and field boundaries, or because of watercourses and ancient roads raised slightly on causeways. Often the levelling was achieved speedily and cheaply by the prodigious dumping of ash and garbage. But there is no record in Soho of large-scale levelling between different field closes and estates – the River Tyburn lay well to the west, and the Tyburn Brook further west still. The flight of steps at the end of Ramillies Street, marking the north edge of the Millfield, is the only evidence that there was an issue. Presumably the surface of Oxford Street, an ancient highway, had over the centuries been strengthened and raised so that it sits on something of a causeway, while Blenheim Street – not artificially terraced – sloped gradually down following the natural undulation of the land. This difference in levels had probably been accentuated in the seventeenth century when brick-earth was extracted from the location.

There are only scanty records of Great Marlborough Street's original appearance, many of its early houses having been lost before they were properly documented. But surviving evidence suggests that Collens and Steele managed to obtain a fair degree of uniformity of height and treatment of elevations and this, together with the quality of the detailing and finish of the individual houses, did much to give the street a sense of magnificence most rare in early-eighteenth-century Soho. This architectural grandeur, enhanced by the generous width of the street, was endorsed by its early occupants. In 1716 there were no fewer than five peers living there: the Earls of Sutherland, Bute, Yarmouth and Ilay (the eldest son of the Duke of Argyll, who also lived hard by) and Lord Onslow.

The *Survey of London* contains contemporary assessments of the new Soho street. They are most revealing.[109] E. Hatton, in his *A New View of London* of 1708, described it as 'pleasant', with 'good buildings',[110] and in 1714 John Macky, in *A Journey through England*, insisted the street was as fine as any of London's ornamental squares, because 'though Not a square it surpasses any Thing that is called a Street, in the Magnificence of its Buildings and Gardens, and inhabited by prime Quality'.[111] This description is fascinating.

The mention of gardens perhaps refers to the large
private gardens behind the houses on the north side of the
street (as shown on Richard Horwood's London map of
1819), but these would not have been visible to the public.
And many of the houses on the south side can have had
little more than large rear yards. So this is more likely a
reference to some sort of garden in the wide street, which
presumably means an avenue of trees rather than a narrow planted walk in the centre, and certainly not gardens
in front of individual houses. Rocque's 1746 London map
shows no evidence of gardens in Great Marlborough Street
but would not necessarily record trees if they existed, so is
not conclusive evidence. What is certain is that the street
must have felt more like a long, narrow square than it
does today, and even more so after 1737 when its west end
was closed by buildings. This was due to the initiative of
the Duke of Argyll when he developed his small portion
of the Millfield (see p. 54). Originally, as shown on John
Strype's map of 1720, the west end of Great Marlborough
Street was open to fields or wasteland at the western edge
of the Millfield. This seems a poor way to terminate such
an ambitious street, but this part of the Millfield was
outside Steele's control, having been leased to the Duke
of Argyll. In the late seventeenth and eighteenth centuries
in Soho land ownership was everything. Very rarely were
attempts made to unify developments on different estates
to achieve grand urban effects – Broadwick Street being
the notable exception (see p. 316). However, in this north-
west corner of Soho in the first decade of the eighteenth
century the Duke of Argyll was quietly hatching his own
building plans. He had leased this small portion of the
Millfield in about 1706 and soon built a large house for

himself, set behind a forecourt and tucked behind the west end of Great Marlborough Street, on the site of what is now the London Palladium.

In 1734, twenty years after Macky's unstinted praise, Great Marlborough Street faced a far less sympathetic critic. James Ralph was a committed supporter of the then well-established Palladian school of classical design, pioneered in the early seventeenth century in England by Inigo Jones and given renewed power and prestige in the early eighteenth century by the highly influential Lord Burlington and a small body of architects he supported or patronised, including Colen Campbell, William Kent and Roger Morris. They promoted a sober form of design, in stark contrast to the exuberance of the Baroque. In the second decade of the eighteenth century Burlington had started to develop his own small estate immediately to the west of Soho, and commissioned Campbell to design Burlington House, set in a courtyard off Piccadilly. The houses built on this estate did much to form the new fashion for the Palladian. So by 1734 Ralph, predictably intolerant of Baroque licence and invention, found fault with Great Marlborough Street and its no doubt individualistically and perhaps idiosyncratically detailed mansions. But it was not just inventive or 'licentious' Baroque classical detail or compositions that Ralph and his fellow doctrinaire Palladians did not like. For them, loose uniformity of scale and design was not enough: they also wanted groups of individual houses to be unified within a coherent and consistent single palatial design with details – such as pediments, columns and pilasters – placed logically to give terraces central emphasis, or used to impart satisfactory termination to important urban

vistas. The Grosvenor estate had attempted, and partly
succeeded in, this Palladian approach, with Campbell
producing a model design in 1725 for Grosvenor Square in
which houses are unified by the use of columns, are given
subtle central emphasis by the use of arched windows,
and pretty well succeed in looking like a single palatial
building. This was Ralph's ideal, and so he found Great
Marlborough Street disappointing. In his *Critical Review
of the Publick Buildings, Statues and Ornaments in and about
London and Westminster*, published in 1734, he wrote that
although 'Great Marlborough Street is esteemed one of
the finest in Europe ... I think it can have this character
on no other account but its length and breadth'. He
dismissed the varied buildings 'on each side' as 'trifling
and inconsiderable' – no doubt because they had not been
dragooned into a unified design – and complained that
the 'vista' along the street had not been considered or
controlled, and 'ended neither way in any thing great
or extraordinary', such as prospect-closing pediments or
colonnades of appropriate design and scale. Evidently
Ralph was particularly put out by the street's open and
unresolved west end. 'Nothing', he wrote, 'can possibly
give a greater advantage to the view, than something
beautiful or magnificent to terminate it' – something
clearly absent in Great Marlborough Street.[112]

Number 1 The Coach and Horses public house. The
building probably dates from the early eighteenth century
but has been considerably altered. Its façade is now rendered, with corners dressed with quoins. This treatment
probably dates from the mid nineteenth century. There
has been a public house of this name on this site since
at least 1739. It was constructed on the portion of the

street laid out on Little Gelding's Close which was not under the control of Steele, although it was land in which Collens had an interest (see p. 85). Architectural ambitions for this part of the street were lower than at its west end.

Numbers 19–21 A former purpose-built police station and magistrates court, designed in a sedate Baroque Revival manner in 1913 by J.D. Butler. It is stone-faced, finely detailed and composed in traditional manner with a rusticated ground-storey crowning cornice and a balustrade above its third storey. The building was evidently designed to match the fine and large early-eighteenth-century houses that in 1913 were its neighbours in Great Marlborough Street and in adjoining Argyll Place. Alas, the context has been brutally transformed, leaving this thoughtful and civilised building sadly marooned; the police station and court closed in 1998 and it now houses a smart hotel called, inevitably the Courthouse.

Number 47 is the only significant survivor of the street's original and no doubt magnificent buildings. It was clearly an ambitious house, presumably constructed in or soon after 1704, but now greatly altered. It is five windows wide, with the centre windows flanked by piers that are very slightly wider than those that flank other windows. This was a Baroque device to give an elevation a sense of movement and to emphasise its centre, where the windows might also be embellished with especially rich brick detailing. We do not know if this was the case here because all has long been obscured beneath rather heavy Victorian stucco with Grecian-style ornaments

The Survey of London records that in the mid eighteenth century this house was occupied by the Pollen family, to whom Sir Benjamin Maddox's Soho estates descended. So presumably this house was at that time regarded as one of the better ones in the street.[113]

Number 48 An early building, again much altered but with the brick façade still visible. The first house on the site was constructed in 1711 but largely rebuilt in 1774 (perhaps behind the retained façade) by Edmund Francis Calze (real name Cunningham) to serve as 'a large Place of entertainment for the Publicke … called the Cassino'.[114]

Cunningham, like many speculating builders in London, was more hopeful than skilful. He was a portrait painter turned property entrepreneur – and by July 1774 was bankrupt, his attempts to make money by holding musical masquerades in the house having proved a dismal failure. The business was taken over by a succession of other proprietors who also failed to make a go of musical entertainments and masquerades in Great Marlborough Street. Presumably they were hoping to imitate Mrs Cornelys's more successful efforts with her Carlisle House masquerades in Soho Square. But the real lesson she offered was that – despite initial success – with such enterprises there was always the fear of bankruptcy, to which in 1772 she succumbed (see p. 166). By 1781 the adventure of the 'New Rooms' in Great Marlborough Street was over and the house settled down to the respectable function of providing offices for lawyers and music publishers. It has been altered since the 1780s: the attic storey is an addition and inside there is a simple staircase of c.1800.

The remaining buildings of interest in the street are far from modest. There is **Ideal House (now Palladium House)**, a seven-storey-high block of 1927 faced with polished black granite and topped by a polychromatic Art

Deco frieze. It looks like a stunted New York Art Deco skyscraper, which is not surprising since it was designed for the New York National Radiator Company by architects including Raymond Hood, who had designed the company's New York building and went on to design the Rockefeller Center in New York City.

Then there is **Liberty**, surely the most architecturally extraordinary store in London. It was designed in 1923 by E.T. and E.S. Hall in an extravagant timber-framed and stone late-medieval or Tudor style to express, in idiosyncratic manner, some of the 'Old World' values of William Morris and of the Arts and Crafts movement to which Liberty aspired. This is a companion building to that on Regent Street, built in 1922–5 in overblown classical style to match the street's emerging character as it was rebuilt in the early twentieth century.

Argyll Street

In 1712 John Campbell, 2nd Duke of Argyll, extended the house he had built in 1706 at the west end of Great Marlborough Street and enlarged it yet further in 1720 by the addition of two wings. Argyll had served with distinction with Marlborough and it might well have been his suggestion to name the new street adjoining his house in honour of his former commander. In all probability the 1720 additions were designed by the 'carpenter' Roger Morris.[115] This was almost certainly the pioneering Palladian architect who had worked for Lord Burlington's protégé Colen Campbell, who in 1715 had dedicated a design for a house in the 'style of Inigo Jones' to Argyll.[116]

Morris also worked with the 'architect-earl' Lord

Pembroke, and in 1724 designed the seminal Palladian villa Marble Hill House in Twickenham for George II's former mistress, the Countess of Suffolk; in 1729 he designed (with Campbell) a most important London Palladian house, 12 Grosvenor Square; and in 1727 he was appointed, by the Crown, the Clerk of the Works at Richmond New Park Lodge. So in appointing Morris as architect Argyll was making a bold statement of support for the prevailing aristocratic and courtly taste for the Palladian. That the designer of the wings was Roger Morris was more or less confirmed in 1736 when Argyll signed articles of agreement with Morris and the leading architect James Gibbs to jointly lay out and 'build on the ground of the said Duke ... one New Street of dwelling Houses to be called Argyll Street'.[117] Gibbs was the architect of St Martin-in-the-Fields, had been building on the nearby Cavendish-Harley estate and in 1717 had designed Argyll's English country seat, Sudbrook House in Surrey. It was through Argyll's patronage as Master-General of the Ordnance that in 1727 Gibb secured the valuable sinecure 'Architect of the Office of Ordnance'. In gratitude Gibbs dedicated his 1728 *Book of Architecture* to Argyll for 'the early encouragement I received ... in my Profession'. In 1734 Argyll arranged for Morris to be appointed 'Master Carpenter to the Office of Ordnance'. This was obviously a close-knit team operating under an almost feudal hierarchy with Argyll at it head.

Between 1706 and 1732 Argyll had gradually been acquiring the leasehold of the open ground around his house, including two bowling greens, and planted part of it as a garden. But in 1733 he bought the freehold from Benjamin Pollen (the heir of the Maddox Soho estates), and three years later the duke vacated his own house so that it could be altered to allow the development of his small freehold estate to go ahead. As well as one principal new street – now Argyll Street – the development included the short Little Argyll Street and terraces at the junction of the south end of Argyll Street and Great Marlborough Street that became known as Argyll Place. This junction, which took the form of an L-shaped block of buildings closing the western vista along Great Marlborough Street, was started in 1737, and so a few years after James Ralph wrote his dismissive description (see p. 371).

But the enclave of Argyll Place was not to last. In 1913 and 1914 its handsome houses were demolished to allow Great Marlborough Street to connect with Regent Street and create plots for the construction of large Baroque Revival commercial blocks. Records made at the time of demolition, including photographs, reveal the incredibly rich interiors of these late-1730s houses. They were indeed urban palaces.

The builders of Georgian London were often ruthless individuals, but the duke's decision to essentially evict himself from his beautifully embellished and well-situated family home to make money from speculative house-building is surely an extreme example. However, in mitigation, he had handed the construction of the new streets that compromised the setting of his family home and garden to two of the most able architects then working in Britain. So, perhaps, the desire for profit was mixed with a concern for beauty.

Now Argyll Street and Little Argyll Street are forlorn places, backwaters between the commercial behemoths on Regent Street and Oxford Street, which retain only the most fragmentary remains of their initial dignity and are among the lost and generally forgotten architectural wonders of London. Argyll Street in particular must have been a Palladian paradise and, with its solemn and precisely proportioned uniform elevations, a statement about how the city ought to look. It must also have been something of a political statement. Like most Palladians, Argyll was a Whig, a Protestant and a supporter of the Hanoverian regime and parliamentary (as opposed to French absolute) monarchy. These convictions gave him a keen sense of British national pride and identity that the stately, restrained and ordered architecture of the street was no doubt intended to express. Its current architectural cacophony is, of course, a tragic but true indication of how much times have changed.

Number 8 is the best-preserved fragment and gives a hint of the street's original appearance. The façade has been rendered with what looks like Roman cement, but the proportion and disposition of windows are a Palladian design statement. This work was executed by the speculating bricklayers William Gray and Richard Fortnam, although presumably working under the control of Roger Morris. The ground floor has been entirely altered, but the high-ceilinged first-floor piano nobile with its double square windows, the first-floor windows of perhaps 3:4 proportion, and the square attic windows above a cornice form a quintessential Palladian composition that was most advanced when built in the mid to late 1730s. When constructed, this house flanked the forecourt of the already existing Argyll House.

This handsome house was home to Washington Irving, who lived here from 1830 to 1832 when Secretary to the

US Legation. As well as being a diplomat Irving was the first internationally acclaimed American writer, whose *Sketch Book of Geoffrey Crayon*, containing the tales of 'Rip Van Winkle' and 'The Legend of Sleepy Hollow', was serialised – to great popular acclaim – in New York in 1819–20 and soon appeared in London in a two-volume edition. The *Sketch Book* had been written soon after Irving's first London visit in 1815. The young Charles Dickens was a great admirer of this work and he later told Irving, perhaps when visiting him in this house, that the tales had become 'second nature' to him as a child.

Number 10 is now stucco-clad and embellished with late-nineteenth-century detail. But its proportions and window and floor dispositions are similar to those of number 8, suggesting it is of the same date and that the terraces framing the street were of uniform design, although of slightly different width. The first-floor shutters appear to date from the early nineteenth century, at which time the interior might well have been remodelled.

This was the home of Major-General William Roy, an eminent military figure and one of the key men behind the creation, from 1791, of the outstanding Ordnance Survey maps of Britain, although a posthumous triumph for Roy since he died in 1790. As their name suggests, these were military in purpose and intended to give British forces the edge, if the French invaded, by providing them with detailed information about the lie of the land and where to position ordnance to best advantage.

Number 18, the Argyll Arms, is thought-provoking. Its façade – now heavy with late-nineteenth-century cement ornament and heightened – could possibly be, at heart, a 1730s house: its window proportions and positions suggest so. Internally it retains a fine, if much reorganised, pub interior of 1895. There is a lot of glass and glitter, mahogany screens that create a series of snugs, mirror-clad walls, and a fine wrought-iron staircase in the rear serving the first floor.

The London Palladium In 1862 the entrepreneur George Haig purchased Argyll House and replaced it with a vast palace of entertainment and drinking named the Corinthian Bazaar and Exhibition Rooms, which opened in 1868. It did not thrive, passed through varied ownership, and in 1909, having been acquired by Walter Gibbons, was largely demolished to make way for what was essentially one of the largest and most opulent music halls in London – the Palladium. Haig's Corinthian portico to Argyll Street was retained (although its central columns were altered), but it fronted a new interior fitted out in French Rococo style and painted in white and gold with coloured marble. All was intended to evoke the glory of Roman public architecture. The architect was the seasoned theatre designer Frank Matcham. The music hall opened on Boxing Day 1910, with tea and drinks served during the interval in a 'Palm Court' – thought to be the epitome of sophistication and elegance. The performances staged at the Palladium naturally reflected changing popular tastes.

In the early days Sir Thomas Beecham's company offered truncated versions of grand opera, then there was ballet, pantomimes, farces and minstrel shows, and from the mid 1950s it became – under its new manager, Val Parnell – part of the world of glamorous popular entertainment and commercial television. Parnell paid high prices to get the stars of the day, mostly from America, to appear in great style, and until 1965 used it as a venue for his once vastly popular televised musical variety show, *Sunday Night at the London Palladium*. Now it's the regular home of big-scale musical productions – arguably going back to its origins, but offering 'populist' rather than 'grand' opera.

Oxford Street Underground station

The walk is over, but there is one more thing to see if you leave Soho by means of Oxford Street Underground station.

The Underground railway system presents a hidden and often overlooked history of London. The construction of this subterranean world, which started in 1863 with the section of the Metropolitan Railway between Paddington and Farringdon, naturally changed over time as technology evolved. But whatever technology was used, the Underground railway – the world's first – remained an engineering challenge. The cut-and-cover system used initially was succeeded by tunnels, which got progressively deeper as services increased in number and speed, and as means of locomotion evolved. And, of course, when the Underground arrived, an area rapidly changed, economically and socially.

The Central Line station at Oxford Circus was opened by the Prince of Wales in July 1900. It was part of the Central London Railway (CLR), from Cornhill in the City (now Bank station) to Shepherd's Bush, which had won parliamentary approval in August 1891. The engineers for the CLR included Sir John Fowler and Sir Benjamin Baker, who were the force behind the just-completed and stupendous Forth Bridge. The Bakerloo Line, also planned under the direction of Baker, arrived at Oxford Circus in 1906.

The above-ground entrance to the station is a good example of the house style developed for the Bakerloo Line by Leslie Green. It's a two-storey structure formed around a robust steel frame – which allowed open-span internal spaces and the possibility of commercial space being constructed above – clad with ox-blood-red glazed terracotta blocks with moulded classical details. At first-floor level, just below a dentilled cornice, are wide, semicircular arched windows set above ground-floor openings.

It's a very handsome piece of work which illustrates that, at ground level, the early Underground stations made a positive visual contribution to the urban setting within which they – quite literally – suddenly popped up. In their civilised language of design and modest scale these stations make a startling comparison with their cavernous new counterparts, set within large-scale commercial development, which you can see at Tottenham Court Road and at the Crossrail station at the junction of Dean Street and Oxford Street.

Bibliography

Adcock, Arthur St John (ed.), *Wonderful London: The World's Greatest City*, includes 'Round About Soho' by Alec Waugh (London Educational, Silver Jubilee Souvenir, London, 1927).

Amery, Colin and Dan Cruickshank, *The Rape of Britain* (Paul Elek, London, 1975).

von Archenholz, Johann Wilhelm, *A Picture of England: containing a description of the laws, customs, and manners of England* (London, 1789).

Bell, Anne Olivier (ed.), *The Diary of Virginia Woolf, Volume 1, 1915–1919* (Penguin, 1977).

Benjamin, Thelma Hilda, *A Shopping Guide to London* (R.M. McBride, New York, 1930).

Boswell, James, *Life of Johnson* (Oxford University Press, Oxford. 1953 edn).

Britton, J. (ed.), *The Original Picture of London* (1828).

Burford, E.J. and Wotton, Joy, *Private Vices – Public Virtues: Bawdry in London from Elizabethan Times to the Regency* (R. Hale, London, 1995).

Burke, Thomas, *Nights in Town: a London Autobiography* (Allen & Unwin, 1915).

Burney, Fanny, *Memoirs of Doctor Burney* (London, 1832).

Calder-Marshall, Arthur (ed.), *Prepare to Shed Them Now: The Ballads of George R. Sim* (London, 1968).

Cardwell, J.H., *Two Centuries of Soho: Its Institutions, Firms and Amusements* (Truslove & Hanson, 1898).

Cardwell, J.H. and Freeman H.B., *Men and Women of Soho: Famous and Infamous* (Truslove & Hansom, 1903).

Chancellor, E. Beresford, *The Romance of Soho* (Country Life, 1931).

Cole, Sophie, *The Lure of Old London* (Mills & Boon, 1921).

Collins, Norman, *Doctor in Soho* (Elek Books, 1956).

Cohen-Portheim, Paul, *The Spirit of London* (J.B. Lippincott and Company, Philadelphia, 1935).

Crisp, Quentin, *The Naked Civil Servant* (Jonathan Cape, 1968; republished Penguin Classics 1997).

Cruickshank, Dan, *The Secret History of Georgian London: How the Wages of Sin Shaped the Capital* (Random House, London, 2009).

Cruickshank, Dan, and Burton, Neil, *Life in the Georgian City* (Viking, London, 1990)

D'Arblay, Madame, *The Diary and Letters of Madame D'Arblay*, vol. III.

Davis, I.M., *The Harlot and Statesman: The Story of Elizabeth Armistead and Charles James Fox* (Kensal Press, Abbotsbrook, Buckinghamshire, 1986).

Defoe, Daniel, *A Tour Thro' the Whole Island of Great Britain. Divided into circuits and journies* (London, 1724–1727).

De Quincey, Thomas, *Confessions of an English Opium Eater* (London, 1821).

Dewes, Simon, *Soho* (Rich & Cowan, 1952).

Dexter, Walter, *The London of Dickens* (Cecil Palm, 1923).

Dickens Junior, Charles, Dickens's Dictionary of London: An Unconventional Handbook London, 1888; 1893 edn).

Farson, Daniel *Soho in the Fifties* (Michael Joseph, 1987).

Fothergill, Stephen, *The Last Lamplighter: a Soho Education* (London Magazine Editions, London, 2000).

Fryer, Jonathan, *Soho in the Fifties and Sixties* (National Portrait Gallery, London, 1998).

Glicco, Jack, *Madness After Midnight* (Elek Books, London, 1952).

Green, Matthew, *London: A Travel Guide Through Time* (Penguin Random House, London, 2015).

Guillery, Peter, *The Small House in Eighteenth-century London* (Yale University Press, London and New Haven, 2004).

Gwynn, Robin D., *Huguenot Heritage: The History and Contribution of the Huguenots in Britain* (Sussex Academic Press, 1984).

Gwynn, Robin D., 'The Number of Huguenot Immigrants', *Journal of Historical Geography*, vol. 9, no. 4 (1983),

Hare, Kenneth and St George, Dorothea, *London's Latin Quarter* (with illustrations, John Lane, London, 1926).

Haywood, A. (ed.), *Autobiography Letters and Literary Remains of*

Mrs Piozzi (Thrale) (Longman, Green, Longman & Roberts, London, 1861).

Hooker, Denise, *Nina Hamnett: Queen of Bohemia* (Constable, 1986).

Houlbrook, Matt, *Queer London: Perils and Pleasures of the Sexual Metropolis.* (University of Chicago Press, Chicago, 2005).

Hutton, Mike, *The Story of Soho: The Windmill Years 1932–1964* (Amberley, Stroud, 2013).

Inglis, Lucy, *Georgian London: Into the Streets* (Viking, London, 2013).

Luke, Michael, *David Tennant and the Gargoyle Years* (Trafalgar Square, London, 1991).

Lysons, Daniel, *Collectanea: An album containing a collection of advertisements and paragraphs from newspapers relating to … trades, professions etc, from 1660 to 1825* (British Library, London, vol. II, p. 161; BL Digital Store C.191.c.16).

Mayhew, Henry, *London Labour and the London Poor*, vol. 3 (Griffin, Bohn and Company, London, 1861).

Meyrick, Kate, *Secrets of the 43 Club* (London, 1933; Parkgate Publications for 1994 edn).

Nairn, Ian, *Nairn's London* (Penguin, Harmondsworth, 1966).

Nightingale, The Reverend Joseph, *London and Middlesex*, vol. III, part 2 (London, 1815).

Nocturnal Revels; or, The History of King's-place and Other Modern Nunneries, by a 'Monk' of the order of St Francis of Medmenham (M.Goadby, London, 1779).

O'Keefe, John, *Recollections of the Life of John O'Keeffe: written by himself* (London, 1826).

Parkin, Sophie, *The Colony Room Club, 1948-2008: A History of Bohemian Soho,* (Palmtree Publishers, Antwerp, 2012).

Pevsner, Nikolaus, and Cherry, Bridget, *Buildings of England: London 1; The Cities of London and Westminster* (Penguin, Harmondsworth, 1973).

Radclyffe Hall, Marguerite, *Adam's Breed* (Cassell & Co., 1928).

Ransome, Arthur, *Bohemia in London* (Chapman & Hall, 1907).

Rimbault, Edward Francis, *Soho and its Associations: Historical, Literary and Artistic,* ed. George Clinch (Dulau & Co., 37 Soho Square, 1895).

Smith, J.T., *Nollekens and his Times* (Century Hutchinson, London, 1986).

Speiser, Peter, *Soho: The Heart of Bohemian London* (British Library, London, 2017).

Sims, G.R., *Living London: Its Work and Its Play, Its Humour and Its Pathos, Its Sights and Its Scenes* (Cassell, 1901).

Sims, G.R., *How the Poor Live and Horrible London*, Chatto and Windus, London, 1889.

Summers, Judith, *Soho* (Bloomsbury, 1989).

Survey of London, vols XXIX and XXX, *The Parish of St James, Westminster (Part I South of Piccadilly)*, ed. F.H.W. Sheppard (London County Council, London, 1960) and vols XXXI and XXXII, *The Parish of St James, Westminster (Part II North of Piccadilly)*, ed. F.H.W. Sheppard (London County Council, London, 1963); vols XXXIII and XXXIV, *The Parish of St Anne Soho*, ed. F.H.W Sheppard (Athlone Press, University of London and Greater London Council, London, 1966).

Strype, John, *Surveys of the Cities of London and Westminster*, London, 1720).

Walkowitz, Judith R., *Nights Out: Life in Cosmopolitan London* (Yale University Press, London and New Haven, 2012).

Waterhouse, Keith, *Soho or Alex in Wonderland* (Hodder & Stoughton), 2001.

Wildeblood, Peter, *West End People* (Weidenfield & Nicolson, 1958).

Willetts, Paul, *Members Only: The Life and Times of Paul Raymond* (Serpent's Tail, 2010).

Willetts, Paul, *North Soho 999: A true story of gangs and gun-crime in 1940s London* (Dewi Lewis Publishing, London, 2007).

Wilson, Colin, *Adrift in Soho* (Victor Gollancz, Ltd, 1961).

Wilton, G. C., *The Story of Soho* (1925).

Wortley, Richard, *Skin Deep in Soho* (Jarrolds Publishing, 1969).

Wyndham, Horace, *Nights in London: Where Mayfair Makes Merry* (with illustrations, 1926).

Woolf, Leonard, Preface to *A Writer's Diary, Being Extracts from the Diary of Virginia Woolf* (Hogarth Press, London, 1953).

Woolf, Virginia, *Jacob's Room* (Harcourt Brace & Company, New York, 1923).

Notes

Introduction

1 Sophie Cole, *The Lure of Old London* (London, 1921), p. 131.

2 Colin Amery and Dan Cruickshank, *The Rape of Britain* (Paul Elek, London, 1975, pp. 135–6).

3 Thomas Burke, *Nights in Town: A London Autobiography* (London, 1915), p. 177.

4 'Measure of Change', Bahar Durmaz-Drinkwater and Stephen Platt (University of Nottingham). Published on-line June 2020, with Isin Can-Traunmuller, as 'Do Perceptions of Neighbourhood Change Match Objective Reality?'.

Soho: An Overview

1 *Survey of London*, ed. F.H.W. Sheppards, vols XXXIII and XXXIV, *St Anne Soho*, ed. F.H.W. Sheppard (London, 1966), p. 25.

2 See ibid., plate 1a.

3 Daniel Defoe, *A Tour Thro' the Whole Island of Great Britain*, vol. 1, ed. G.D.H. Cole (Frank Cass & Co., London, 1968, pp. 331–2).

4 *Survey of London*, vol. xxxiv., p. 516.

5 Ibid., p. 517.

6 Quoted by Peter Guillery, *The Small House in Eighteenth-century London* (London and New Haven, 2004), pp. 55–6.

7 http://www.vam.ac.uk/content/articles/s/paul-de-lamerie-objects/

8 Lucy Inglis, *Georgian London: Into the Streets* (London, 2013), p. 171.

9 Robin D. Gwynn, 'The Number of Huguenot Immigrants', *Journal of Historical Geography*, vol. 9, no. 4 (1983), pp. 384–98; Dan Cruickshank, *Spitalfields: The History of a Nation in a Handful of Streets* (London, 2015), p. 147.

10 See Cruickshank, *Spitalfields*, pp. 160–61.

11 John Strype, *A Survey of the Cities of London and Westminster* (London, 1720), bk IV, ch. II, p. 48.

12 See Dan Cruickshank, *The Secret History of Georgian London: How the Wages of Sin Shaped the Capital* (London, 2009).

13 *Nocturnal Revels; or, The History of King's-Place and Other Modern Nunneries, by a 'Monk' of the order of St Francis of Memenham*, 2 vols (M. Goadby,

London, 1779), p. 29.

14 Ibid.

15 Bloch, *Sexual Life in London* (London, 1958), pp. 26–30.

16 Ibid., pp. 124–6.

17 *Nocturnal Revels*, p. 29.

18 Ibid., p. 30.

19 E.J. Burford, *Private Vices – Public Virtues: Bawdry in London from Elizabethan Times to the Regency* (London, 1995), p. 150.

20 Daniel Turner, *Syphilis: A Practical Dissertation of the Venereal Disease* (London, 1717), p. 203.

21 Thanks to Martin Postle for information and insights and for bringing my attention to this quote in I.M. Davis, *The Harlot and the Statesman: The Story of Elizabeth Armistead and Charles James Fox* (London, 1986), p. 13.

22 See ibid.

23 See *Survey of London*, vols XXXIII and XXXIV, pp. 388–9.

24 Thomas de Quincey, *Confessions of an English Opium-Eater* (1821; Vintage Books, London, 2013), p. 30.

25 Dan Cruickshank and Neil Burton, *Life in the Georgian City* (London, 1990), p. 10; Johann Wilhelm von Archenholz, *A Picture of England: containing a description of the laws, customs, and manners of England* (London, 1789).

26 Cruickshank and Burton, *Life in the Georgian City*, p. 9; Jos. Hayling, 'Lighting Report', Westminster Central Library, A2279.

The Estates

1 *Survey of London*, vols XXXIII and XXXIV, plan on p. 21.

2 Ibid., p. 29.

3 Ibid., pp. 42–51.

4 J.T. Smith, *Nollekens and his Times* (London, 1986), pp. 21–2.

5 *Survey of London*, vol. xxxiii, p. 288.

6 Ibid., p. 289.

7 *Survey of London*, vol. xxiv, pp. 380–3.

8 John Strype, *A Survey of the Cities of London and Westminster*, bk VI, ch. VI, p. 86.

9 *Survey of London*, vols XXXIII and XXXIV, p. 425.

10 See Cruickshank, *The Secret History of Georgian London*, pp. 126–39.

11 *Survey of London*, vols XXXI and XXXII, *St James, Westminster*, part 2, ed. F.H.W. Sheppard (London, 1963), p. 27, fig. 2.

12 *Survey of London*, vols XXIX and XXX, *St James, Westminster*, part 1, ed. F.H.W. Sheppard (London, 1960), pp. 21–8.

13 *Survey of London*, vols XXXI and XXXII, pp. 219–29.

14 National Archives C66/3304, no. 14, quoted in ibid.

15 Strype, *A Survey of the Cities of London and Westminster*, bk VI, ch. VI, p. 84.

16 *Survey of London*, vols XXXI and XXXII, pp. 223, 243.

17 Ibid., pp. 219–29.

18 Ibid., pp. 250–67.

19 Ibid., pp. 243–9.

20 Ibid., pp. 209–18.

21 Ibid., pp. 41–56.

22 Ibid., pp. 116–37.

23 Ibid., pp. 27, 196–208.

24 Ibid., pp. 176–95.

25 Ibid., pp. 24–31; 176–95.

26 Ibid., pp. 196–208.

27 Ibid.

28 Strype, *A Survey of the Cities of London and Westminster*, bk VI, ch. VI, p. 87.

29 Ian Nairn, *Nairn's London* (Harmondsworth, 1966), p. 74.

Soho's Social Decline

1   Walter Dexter, *The London of Dickens* (1923; London, 1930 edn), pp. 151–2.

2   Enid Starkie, *Arthur Rimbaud* (London, 1947), p. 234.

3   Thelma Hilda Benjamin, *A Shopping Guide to London* (New York, 1930), p. 180, quoted in Peter Speiser, *Soho: The Heart of Bohemian London*, p. 17.

4   LSE Booth/B/354, bk XIII:I, Police Districts 2,3,4, p. 213.

5   Ibid., p. 207.

6   Ibid., p. 219.

7   Ibid.

8   Ibid.

9   Ibid., p. 221

10 Ibid.

11 Ibid., p. 223.

12 Ibid.

13 Ibid., p. 228.

14 Ibid., p. 231.

15 Ibid., p. 223.

16 Ibid., p. 239.

17 RG12, piece 88, f. 135, pp. 2–4.

18 *Illustrated London News*, 27 October 1906, quoted in Speiser, *Soho*, p. 44.

19 Judith R. Walkowitz, *Nights Out: Life in Cosmopolitan London* (London and New Haven, 2012), p. 23.

20 Ibid., p. 24

21 George R. Sims (ed.), *Living London* (London, 1915, 3 vols).

22 Burke, *Nights in Town*, p. 253, quoted in Speiser, *Soho*, p. 7.

23 Walkowitz, *Nights Out*, p. 34; Arthur Ransome, *Bohemia in London*
(London, 1907; OUP, 1984, ed. Rupert Hart-Davis . p. 122.

24 Cole, *The Lure of Old London*, pp. 136-7.

25 Virginia Woolf, *Jacob's Room* (Harcourt Brace & Company, New York,
1923), pp. 162-3; *The Diary of Virginia Woolf*, vol. 1, *1915–1919*, ed. Anne Olivier
Bell (Penguin, 1977), p. 135, quoted in Walkowitz, *Nights Out*,
p. 157, and in Speiser, *Soho*, p. 71.

26 Horace Wyndham, *Nights in London* (London, 1926, with illustrations
by Dorothea St John George).

27 Ibid., pp. 78–90.

28 Ibid., p. 86.

29 Ibid., p. 90.

30 Speiser, *Soho*, p. 102.

31 Tom Clayton and Phil Craig, *Finest Hour* (1993: London, 2000), p. 215.

32 Jack Glicco, *Madness After Midnight* (London, 1952), p. 132.

33 Ibid., p. 10.

34 Ibid., pp. 21–3.

35 Kate Meyrick, *Secrets of the 43 Club* (London, 1933), p. 22.

36 Ibid., pp. 139–57.

37 Ibid., pp. 280–81.

38 Glicco, *Madness After Midnight*, p. 54.

39 Speiser, *Soho*, p. 122.

40 See Matt Houlbrook, *Queer London: Perils and Pleasures in the Sexual
Metropolis, 1918–1957* (University of Chicago Press, 2005), pp. 80–2.

41 Kenneth Hare, *London's Latin Quarter* (London, 1926), pp. 87–8.

42 Michael Luke, *David Tennant and the Gargoyle Years* (London, 1991),
p. 36.

43 Ibid., p. 48

44 Ibid.

45 Ibid., p. 49.

46 Ibid., p. 50.

47 Ibid., p. 199.

48 Daniel Farson, *Soho in the Fifties* (London, 1987), p. xi.

49 Ibid., pp. 1, 7.

50 Ibid., p. 82.

51 Ibid., p. 51.

52 Ibid., p. 74.

53 Ibid., p. 97.

54 Ibid.

55   Ibid.

56   Ibid., p. 44.

57   Ibid.

58   John Wortley, *Skin Deep in Soho* (London, 1969), pp. 78–88.

59   Much of this information in coffee bars is thanks to Matthew Green, author of *London: A Travel Guide Through Time* (London, 2015).

The Walk

1   The Reverend Joseph Nightingale, *London and Middlesex*, vol. III, part 2 (London, 1815), p. 666; and Nightingale, *The Bazaar* (London, 1816); *Survey of London*, vols XXXIII and XXXIV, pp. 58–9.

2   *Survey of London*, vols XXXIII and XXXIV, p. 59.

3   *Dickens's Dictionary of London: An Unconventional Handbook* (1888; London, 1893 edn), p. 222.

4   *Survey of London*, vols XXXIII and XXXIV, p. 73.

5   Henry Mayhew, *London Labour and the London Poor*, vol I (London, 1861), p. 232–3. See also Simon During, *Modern Enchantments: the cultural power of of secular magic* (Harvard University Press, 2002), pp. 110–11. During characterizes 21 Soho Square as the 'White house . . . famous magic brothel . . . in which commercial sex was enhanced by dark, baroque special-effects and natural-magic devices.' E.F. Rimbault, in his *Soho and its associations* of 1895 (pp. 27–9) had noted, in a gentler but similar manner, that 'Hopper's Hotel' was from the late 1770s 'notorious in the annals of fashion' with 'an unsavoury notoriety for many years' as a place of attraction for 'a certain class', and which customers could enter and leave with almost magical secrecy.

6   Isaac Ware, *A Complete Body of Architecture* (1756; London, 1768 edn), vol. I, p. 347.

7   *Survey of London*, vols XXXIII and XXXIV, p. 90.

8   Ibid., p. 191.

9   Ibid., p. 174.

10   Ibid., p. 180.

11   Ibid., p. 393.

12   Ibid., p. 411, fig. 93.

13   Arthur Calder-Marshall (ed.), *Prepare to Shed Them Now: The Ballads of George R. Sims* (London, 1968), p. 43.

14   *Survey of London*, vols XXXIII and XXXIV, p. 472.

15   *Survey of London*, vols XXXI and XXXII, pp. 68–84.

16   Ibid., pp. 111–15.

17   Strype, *A Survey of the Cities of London and Westminster*, bk VI, ch. VI, p. 84.

18   Ibid.

19   *Survey of London*, vols XXXI and XXXII, pp. 41–56; *Recollections of the Life of John O'Keeffe: written by himself* (London, 1826), vol. I, pp. 79–80; PRO, SP44/138, *passim*.

20   Strype, *A Survey of the Cities of London and Westminster*, bk VI, ch. VI, p. 86.

21   *Survey of London*, vols XXXIII and XXXIV, p. 194, plate 9.

22   Ibid., p. 201.

23   Ibid., p. 151.

24   Ibid., pp. 164–5.

25   See Dexter, *The London of Dickens*, pp. 147–8.

26   Gustav Mayer, *Neue Beiträge zur Biographie von Karl Marx und Arbeiterbewegung, zehnter Jahrgang* (Leipzig, 1922), p. 58; and *Survey of London*, vols XXXIII and XXXIV, p. 134.

27   Ibid., p. 233.

28   *The Sphere*, 14 January 1914, p. 100.

29   *Survey of London*, vols XXXIII and XXXIV, p. 235.

30   Ibid., p. 246.

31   Ibid., pp. 221–2.

32   Ibid., pp. 228–9.

33   Ibid., p. 137.

34   Ibid., pp. 238–9.

35   *Autobiography, Letters and Literary Remains of Mrs Piazzi* (Thrale), ed. A. Hayward (Longman, Green, Longman & Roberts, London, 1862 edn), pp. 66–7. G. B. Hill (ed.), Boswell's *Life of Johnson* (Oxford University Press, Oxford, 1953 edition), p. 1144. (Here Boswell offers a slightly different version of Johnson's recollection of Bet's poem.)

36   Hill (ed.), *Boswell's Life of Johnson*, vol. IV, p. 103.

37   Old Bailey reference number: t17580913-33.

38   A. Hayward (ed.), *Autobiography*, (1861), pp. 66–7. Also mentioned in Boswell's *Life of Johnson*, roy. 8vo. edit, p. 688.

39   *Survey of London*, vols XXXIII and XXXIV, pp. 240–1.

40   George H. Duckworth notebook, LSE, Booth/B/354, Police District 3, 1898/9, p. 221.

41   RG 12, piece 88, f. 137, pp. 7–8

42   RG 12, piece 88, f. 138, p. 10.

43   RG 12, piece 88, f. 109, pp. 11 and 12.

44   RG 12, piece 87, f. 82, p. 32.

45   RG 12, piece 88, f. 142, p. 17.

46   RG 12, piece 88, f. 142, p. 18

47   RG 12, piece 88, f. 144, p. 12.

48   RG 13, piece 100, f. 110, p. 2.

49   RG 12, piece 100, f. 112, pp. 24–5.

50   RG 13, piece 100, f. 111, p. 27.

51 RG 13, piece 100, f. 113, pp. 28–9.

52 RG 13, piece 100, f. 110, p. 33.

53 RG 13, piece 100, ff. 117–19, pp. 35–9.

54 RG 13, piece 100, f. 114, p. 30.

55 *Survey of London*, vols XXXIII and XXXIV, p. 257.

56 'Upon the Building of National Churches', Christopher Wren and Stephen Wren, *Parentalia*, 1750, pp. 318–21.

57 *Survey of London*, vols XXXIII and XXXIV, p. 270.

58 *Survey of London*, vols XXXI and XXXII, p. 232.

59 Ibid., pp. 230–82

60 Ibid., pp. 230–42.

61 Ibid., pp. 230–42

62 RG 13, piece 98.

63 RG 12, piece 87, f. 82, p. 32.

64 See *Property Week*, 22 June 2012.

65 *Survey of London*, vols XXXI and XXXII, pp. 116–37.

66 Ibid., pp. 166–7.

67 Ibid., pp. 41–56.

68 Ibid., pp. 116–37.

69 Strype, *A Survey of the Cities of London and Westminster*, bk VI, ch. VI, p. 84.

70 *Survey of London*, vols XXXI and XXXII, pp. 116–37.

71 Ibid., p. 135.

72 Ibid., pp. 243–9.

73 Ibid., p. 214.

74 Ibid., pp. 243–9.

75 Fanny Burney, *Memoirs of Doctor Burney* (London, 1832), vol. I, p. 134.

76 *Survey of London*, vols XXXI and XXXII, pp. 243–9.

77 Ibid., p. 247.

78 *Memoirs of Mrs Billington* (London, 1792), p. 32.

79 *Survey of London*, vols XXXI and XXXII, p. 248.

80 Ibid., pp. 173–5.

81 See Daniel Lysons, *Collectanea: an album containing a collection of advertisements and paragraphs from newspapers relating to trades, professions etc. from 1660 to 1825, London*, at the British Library, vol. II, p. 161 (BL Digital Store C.191.c.16).

82 *Survey of London*, vols XXXI and XXXII, pp. 174–5.

83 Ibid., p. 135.

84 Dexter, *The London of Dickens*, pp. 150–51; Charles Dickens, *Nicholas Nickleby* (London, 1839), p. 64.

85 See *Survey of London*, vols XXXI and XXXII, pp. 116–37.

86 Ibid., pp. 167–73.

87 Ibid., pp. 339–41.

88 Strype, *A Survey of the Cities of London and Westminster*, bk VI, ch. VI, p. 84.

89 Wren Society transactions, vol. XVIII (1941), pp. 18–19, see *Survey of London*, vols XXXI and XXXII, pp. 138–45.

90 Wren Society, vol. XVIII (1941), p. 33; also, PC2/63, p. 108.

91 See *Survey of London*, vol. XXXI, p. 139.

92 *Survey of London*, vols XXXI and XXXII, pp. 138–45.

93 Dated 16 July 1673, National Archives MPA 69, *Survey of London*, vol. XXXI, p. 139.

94 Narcissus Luttrell, *A Brief Historical Relation of State of Affairs from September 1678 to April 1714*, vol. III (Oxford, 1857), p. 434.

95 *Survey of London*, vols XXXI and XXXII, pp. 138–45.

96 National Archives C8/299/102, *Survey of London*, vol. XXXI, p.142.

97 *Survey of London*, vols XXXI and XXXII, pp. 138–45; pp. 154–6.

98 *Survey of London*, vol. XXXI, p. 143.

99 Dexter, *The London of Dickens*, p. 152.

100 Dickens, *Nicholas Nickleby*, pp. 5–6.

101 *Survey of London*, vols XXXI, p. 145.

102 *Survey of London*, vols XXXI, p. 150.

103 Quoted in *Survey of London*, vol. XXXI, p. 158.

104 Ibid.

105 Pevsner and Cherry, *Buildings of England, London,* vol. I: *The Cities of London and Westminster* (Harmondsworth, 1973), p. 578.

106 *Survey of London*, vol. XXXI, p. 192.

107 Ibid., p.181.

108 Ibid.

109 *Survey of London*, vol. XXXI, p. 251.

110 E. Hatton, *A New View of London*, vol.II (London, 1798), p. 815.

111 John Macky *A Journey through England* (London, 1714), vol. I, p. 120.

112 *Survey of London*, vol. XXXI, p. 251, Ralph, *Critical Review*, p. 102.

113 *Survey of London*, vol. XXXI, p. 261.

114 Ibid.

115 Ibid., pp. 284–307.

116 *Vitruvius Britannicus*, vol. I (1715), plate 20.

117 *Survey of London*, vols XXXI and XXXII, pp. 284–307.

Acknowledgements

First and foremost, I must acknowledge my debt to the volumes of the *Survey of London*. These form the solid scholarship that must inevitably provide the foundation for any book about the growth and architecture of London. More particularly, I would like to thank the Soho Society and its chairman Tim Lord for help and information – including access to its library of Soho books; to David Bieda, a long-term resident of Dean Street, for decades of conversation and insights about Soho; to Clare Lynch and Leslie Hardcastle, both of whom have been most generous with their Soho expertise, and to Bahar Durmaz-Drinkwater for most kindly sharing her research into current patterns of occupation in Soho.

Finally, I would like to thank my publishers and my editor Lucinda McNeile for her untiring hard work and advice; and my family – Marenka, Bella, Alexander and Inigo – for their tolerance and support.

Index